Formulas of Repetition in Dante's Commedia
Signposted Journeys across Textual Space

In this first book-length study on recurrent linguistic patterns or "formulas" scattered across the textual space of Dante's *Commedia*, Lloyd Howard links the episodes in which they are found, guiding the reader to conclusions about what are often key points in the poem's meaning. He shows that such conclusions can be drawn only after a re-examination of the context that surrounds these linguistic signposts.

Formulas are usually understood as rhetorical devices that are found in close textual proximity and, because they are intended for emphasis, cannot possibly escape the notice of the reader. The formulas Howard traces in this study are far more difficult to find because they are hidden deep in the structure in the *Commedia* and at considerable distances from one another. For example, Howard demonstrates that when the reader notes that the formula "ne l'etterno essilio" – in eternal exile – re-occurs in *Purgatorio* 21 accompanied by the same rhyme words as when it first appears in *Inferno* 23, it is a sign that these two episodes can be linked for further interpretation, despite the 32 cantos of intervening textual space.

In the most general sense it is possible to define two principal ways of approaching the *Commedia*: one that examines specific episodes or cantos in isolation and one that follows the overt journey of Dante the pilgrim through the three realms of the afterlife. The approach offered in *Formulas of Repetition in Dante's* Commedia differs from both traditional ways of reading Dante, pursuing an alternate path outside the chronology set out in the *Commedia* – from the dark wood to the empyrean – and outside the canto order – first *Inferno*, then the *Purgatorio*, and lastly the *Paradiso*.

LLOYD H. HOWARD is associate professor in the Department of Hispanic and Italian Studies at the University of Victoria.

Formulas of Repetition in Dante's *Commedia*

Signposted Journeys across Textual Space

LLOYD HOWARD

McGill-Queen's University Press
Montreal & Kingston · London · Ithaca

Legal deposit second quarter 2001
Bibliothèque nationale du Québec

Printed in Canada on acid-free paper

This book has been published with the help of a grant from the
Humanities and Social Sciences Federation of Canada, using funds
provided by the Social Sciences and Humanities Research Council
of Canada.

McGill-Queen's University Press acknowledges the financial support of
the Government of Canada through the Book Publishing Industry
Development Program (BPIDP) for its activities. It also acknowledges the
support of the Canada Council for the Arts for its publishing program.

Chapter 1 reproduces, with some revisions, Lloyd Howard, "Linguistic
Configuration as a Clue to the Impossible Made Possible: *Inferno* I,
Purgatory XI, and *Purgatory* XII," *Italian Quarterly* 114 (Fall 1988): 5–9.
Chapter 3 reproduces, with some revisions, Lloyd Howard, "Decoding
the Parallelism of Three Descents into Dante's Hell," *Quaderni
d'italianistica* 14.1 (1993): 111–19.
Chapter 5, part 1, expands upon Lloyd Howard, "Linguistic Patterns and
Internal Structure in Five *canti* of the *Inferno*," *Quaderni d'italianistica* 11.1
(1990): 85–90; part 2 reproduces, with some revisions, Lloyd Howard and
Elena Rossi, "Textual Mapping of Dante's Journey Back to Political
Original Sin in Florence," *Modern Language Notes* 106 (1991): 184–8.

Canadian Cataloguing in Publication Data

Howard, Lloyd
    Formulas of repetition in Dante's Commedia: signposted journeys across
    textual space
    Includes bibliographical references and index.
    ISBN 0-7735-2192-5
    1. Dante Alighieri, 1265–1321. Divina commedia. 2. Dante Alighieri,
    1265–1321 – Technique. 3. Repetition in literature.
    I. Title.
    PQ4399.H69 2001   851'.1   C00-901426-8

This book was typeset by Typo Litho Composition Inc.
in 10/12 Palatino.

Contents

Acknowledgments

I would like to thank Marguerite Chiarenza, who first introduced me to Dante, and Charles Singleton, who helped guide me in my graduate work at Johns Hopkins. I am grateful to the University of Victoria for the study leaves they have granted me to develop my ideas further, to Elena Rossi for her helpful suggestions and her collaboration with me on an article which appears here in chapter 5, part 2, and to Catherine Harding for her advice on the Introduction. I am indebted to Elizabeth Chatfield for her careful reading of the manuscript, Tish Clayton for her ready assistance, and Cyril Hume for his constant support. I would like to express my appreciation to the editors of *Italian Quarterly*, *Quaderni d'italianistica*, and *Modern Language Notes* for granting me permission to include material previously published by them, and to the editor and staff of McGill-Queen's University Press for all they have done to make this publication possible.

Abbreviations

Bosco-Reggio Dante. *La Divina Commedia*. Ed. U. Bosco and G. Reggio. 3 vols. Firenze: Le Monnier, 1979.

Chivacci Leonardi Dante. *La Divina Commedia*. Ed. A.M. Chiavacci Leonardi. 3 vols. Firenze: Mondadori, 1991–7.

Conv. Dante. *Convivio*. In *Opere minori*, vol. 1: part 2, 3–885. Ed. C. Vasoli. Milano Napoli: Ricciardi, 1988.

Di Salvo Dante. *La Divina Commedia*. Ed. T. Di Salvo. 1 vol. Bologna: Zanichelli, 1987.

ED *Enciclopedia Dantesca*. Ed. U. Bosco et al. 6 vols. Roma: Istituto dell'Enciclopedia Italiana, 1970–8.

Mon. Dante. *Monarchia*. In *Opere minori*, vol. 2, 280–503. Ed. B. Nardi. Milano-Napoli: Ricciardi, 1979.

Porena Dante. *La Divina Commedia*. Ed. M. Porena. 3 vols. Bologna: Zanichelli, 1958–62.

Sapegno Dante. *La Divina Commedia*. Ed. N. Sapegno. 3 vols. Firenze: La Nuova Italia, 1955–7.

Singleton   Dante. *La Divina Commedia*. Ed. C.S. Singleton. 3 vols. Princeton: Princeton University Press, 1970–5.

Villani   Giovanni Villani. *Nuova Cronica*. Ed. G. Porta. 3 vols. Parma: Ugo Guanda, 1990.

VN   Dante. *Vita Nuova*. In *Opere minori*, vol. 1: part 1, 3–246. Ed. D. De Robertis. Milano-Napoli: Ricciardi, 1984.

Note on Text and Translations

Quotations of the *Commedia* are from *La commedia secondo l'antica vulgata*, ed. Giorgio Petrocchi (Milano: Mondadori, 1966–7).

All translations of the *Commedia* and some of Villani's *Cronica* are taken from Singleton, with some modifications of my own particularly in relation to the linguistic patterns of repetition. Translations of the *Vita Nuova* are those of Barbara Reynolds (Harmondsworth: Penguin Books, 1969); and translations of the *Convivio* are those of Christopher Ryan (Saratoga, Calif.: Amma Libri, 1989). All other translations from Italian are my own.

Formulas of Repetition in Dante's Commedia

Introduction

This study will follow recurrent linguistic patterns, or formulas, embedded in the *Commedia*, devised by the poet to guide the reader along an alternate interpretive journey across textual space. The term "formula" was defined in the 1930s by the noted scholar of orally transmitted texts, Milman Parry, as "a group of words which is regularly employed under the same metrical conditions to express a given essential idea."[1] Parry's definition has since undergone considerable adaptation. Those analysing orally transmitted Old English texts, for example, have moulded Parry's definition to fit their tradition and their language, whereby "a group of words" could be reduced to one word, the formula need not be "regularly employed," and there need not be any "metrical conditions."[2] With regard to the written text that is the *Commedia*, "formula," simply put, will be used to signify a group of words and rarely one word, which are repeated but not regularly employed.

Such formulas, as defined above, are not commonplace in the *Commedia*. Where they do occur, in close textual proximity, they form an obvious signal or cue to the reader that the poet wishes to underscore his point. These signals are obvious because they tax the memory little if at all. For example, as Dante and Virgil enter the gate of Hell in *Inferno* 3, the anaphora of the inscribed words is impossible to miss:

"*Per me si va* ne la città dolente,
per me si va ne l'etterno dolore,
per me si va tra la perduta gente.*"

["Through me you enter the woeful city,
through me you enter eternal grief,
through me you enter among the lost."]

(1.3.1–3)

Had "per me si va" appeared only once, these four monosyllabic words spoken by Hell's gate to the newly arrived condemned souls would not draw the necessary attention to the presence of the nine-verse inscription. The incremental repetition of this formula allows for the focus to shift from the "woeful city" to the "eternal pain" that the "lost people" will now endure, and prepares the way ultimately to the climax of this inscription two tercets later: "Lasciate ogne speranza, voi ch'intrate" ["Abandon every hope, you who enter"] (1.3.9). Another example occurs at the top of the mountain of Purgatory when Beatrice reveals herself to Dante from the other side of the Lethe with the words "Guardaci ben! Ben son, ben son Beatrice" ["Look at me well: well I am, well I am Beatrice"] (2.30.73). The thrice-repeated "ben" and the twice-repeated "ben son" signal this first appearance of the unveiled Beatrice,[3] a pivotal moment in Dante's journey to personal salvation, after his ten-year thirst of not having seen her face since her death in 1290. The fact that "ben" is repeated three times, here where Dante's personal Christ unveils herself before him, attaches further significance to the moment. Had Beatrice identified herself in the simplest way possible and said without repetition "Guardaci, ben son Beatrice," the anger, the irony, and the number symbolism of the three of the Trinity contained in the repetition would be lost. The repetition in this instance drives home the point that the teary-eyed Dante had better abandon his futile search for Virgil and concentrate instead on Beatrice and salvation. The address has its desired effect: Beatrice has Dante's undivided attention, and like a truant child before a stern mother he looks down in shame.[4]

What is not so obvious in the *Commedia* is that linguistic patterns of recurrence or formulas exist which are neither in close textual proximity nor regularly employed. For example, the thematically unimportant formula "guardommi un poco e poi" ["he looked at me for a moment and then"] is repeated in *Inferno* 10 after first appearing in *Inferno* 6. Despite the four cantos of textual space that lie between the two episodes, there is a connection between them. In *Inferno* 6 this formula describes Ciacco's last "look" at Dante, just after his final words which have revealed that Dante's political heroes, including Farinata, are all lower down in Hell. In *Inferno* 10 the formula relates to Farinata alone, since it is Farinata who "looked at Dante a moment and then" spoke his first words to him. The simple words "he looked at me a moment and then" never again appear in the *Commedia*.

The more thematically relevant formula "ne l'etterno essilio" ["in eternal exile"] appears only twice: in *Inferno* 23 and *Purgatorio* 21. The formula is relevant in that it defines the place to which Caiaphas in the first instance and Virgil in the second are condemned: Hell. The repetition of the formula is also an invitation to the reader to consider what else Caiaphas and Virgil share. If they seem dissimilar, do the people they represent share something in common, especially around the time of Christ? Would this question have been formulated at these junctures if not for the repetition of the formula? Suddenly an avenue of interpretation based on a specific point of departure is now open to the reader.

Formulas such as "guardommi un poco e poi" or "ne l'etterno essilio" reveal far more than the "ben son" precisely because they serve as signposts, guiding the reader on an alternate journey across the cantos of the text. The alternate journey is one which takes the reader back and forth through textual space, as for example with "ne l'etterno essilio": the reader who recognizes the repetition of the "ne l'etterno essilio" signpost in *Purgatorio* 21 takes the backward glance to *Inferno* 23, before returning to *Purgatorio* 21 to interpret the significance of the two highlighted episodes. The back and forth of such a signposted journey offers the opportunity to interpret a message which may not be otherwise evident.

If the reader would go forth on this alternate journey, the memory must retain each signpost in order to spot and recognize the next, as a trail is blazed through the forest of textual space. To put it another way, the task for the reader is to make that mental stretch, to have the keen memory required to overcome the obstacle that is the intervening space. The idea of one who depends entirely on memory to find the way is already familiar to the reader of the *Commedia*. Following the fiction that Dante is setting down in words his already completed journey in the flesh through Hell, Purgatory, and Paradise, this book, the *Commedia* in all its incredible complexity, owes its existence to Dante's power of memory: "Veramente quant'io del regno santo / ne la mia mente potei far tesoro, / sarà ora matera del mio canto." ["Nevertheless, so much of the holy kingdom as I could treasure up in my mind shall now be the matter of my song."] (3.1.10–12).

Today with the aid of concordances and computers, less demand is placed on the human memory to overcome the obstacle of textual space. But in Dante's time, when individuals were still trained to rely on their own power of recall, was such a signposted alternate journey as this one an option for the reader?

Without embarking on a discussion of memory in general or its role in the oral tradition of the ancient world and the Middle Ages, it is obvious that the creation, retention, and transmission of those narratives depended entirely upon individuals' ability to remember. We who live in an information age that began with the invention of the printing press should suspend any scepticism we might have regarding the ability people once had to recall words in such texts.[5]

While in the later Middle Ages memory may not appear central to the creation and transmission of written texts, Mary Carruthers maintains that that period remained a "memorial culture," with memory still central to human learning.[6] As proof, she points out that reliable evidence suggests that the *Summa theologica* was composed and dictated by Thomas Aquinas from memory.[7]

With regard to texts written in the vernacular, authors were more likely to address an audience of listeners not readers, and in the twelfth and thirteenth centuries reading was still perceived as something "heard" and not "seen."[8] Recent scholars of the history of readership generally agree that a shift took place in the fourteenth century from an oral orientation to a visual one, from ear to eye.[9] Current debate centres on whether the shift happened over a relatively brief period of time, or gradually, not completed ultimately until the arrival of the printing press.

Regardless of whether the shift was swift or gradual, Dante's readers lived right in the middle of it. Learned members of his audience with both the oral and the visual orientation were trained not just to listen or read a text but to commit it to memory as well. Carruthers maintains that "*Memoria* unites written with oral transmission, eye with ear, and helps to account for the highly 'mixed' oral-literate nature of medieval cultures."[10]

John Ahern ably demonstrates that cantos from the *Commedia* were commonly sung before and after Dante's death by both literates and illiterates,[11] and draws the following conclusion: "the very spontaneity with which literates and illiterates alike memorized and performed the *Comedy* suggests that Dante composed this poem, like his canzoni, for reading, singing, and memorizing."[12] Based on the response of literates such as Dante the pilgrim and Virgil in *Purgatorio* 2 to Casella's musical rendering of Dante's *Amor che ne la mente mi ragiona*, one could further conclude "that Dante envisioned a twofold reception of his canzoni: critical detached decoding of the words on the page; and rapt listening to the same words as an acoustic or musical event." Dante may have also idealized such an audience for the *Commedia*: "Thus it could be argued that Dante intended twofold reception solely for skilled readers."[13]

Evidence in two particular passages in the *Commedia* shows that Dante recognized that skilled readers with a keen intellect would gain an understanding of his work not possible for those less blessed. In *Inferno* 9 Dante interrupts the narrative to address one small segment of readers, those with a healthy intellect capable of understanding what lies beneath the "veil of strange verses": "O voi ch'avete li 'ntelletti sani, / mirate la dottrina che s'asconde / sotto 'l velame de li versi strani." ["O you who have sound understanding, mark the doctrine that is hidden under the veil of the strange verses."] (1.9.61–3).[14] He again addresses these same readers in *Purgatorio* 8 when he declares: "Aguzza qui, lettor, ben li occhi al vero, / ché 'l velo è ora ben tanto sottile, / certo, che 'l trapassar dentro è leggero." ["Reader, here sharpen well your eyes to the truth, for the veil is now indeed so thin that certainly to pass within is easy."] (2.8.19–21).[15]

Along with the healthy intellect comes the concomitant memory. Dante points out in the *Convivio*: "Conviensi adunque essere prudente, cioè savio: e a ciò essere si richiede buona memoria de le vedute cose, buona conoscenza de le presenti e buona provedenza de le future. E, sì come dice lo Filosofo nel sesto de l' Etica, 'impossibile è essere savio chi non è buono' " ["A person ought, then, to be prudent, or wise. To be so he must have good memory of things seen, good knowledge of the present and good foresight regarding the future. Furthermore, as the Philosopher says in the *Ethics*: 'It is impossible for a person to be wise if he is not good'"] (IV xxvii 5). The "buona memoria de le cose vedute" ["good memory of things seen"] is required both of Dante the poet ("se la memoria mia in ciò non erra ..." ["if my memory err not in this ..."] 2.20.147) and of the reader who pursues the alternate signposted journey.[16] Among Dante's audience of skilled readers, who by any standard had extraordinary powers to learn and recall a storehouse of literary texts, there would be some whose memories could well seize upon a familiar linguistic pattern and recall to mind the previous instance of that same pattern and perhaps also the text that surrounded it.

The purpose of my study is to pursue this alternative path and follow a journey outside of the chronology set out in the *Commedia* from the dark wood to the Empyrean, outside of the canto order, outside of necessarily reading first the *Inferno*, next the *Purgatorio*, and last the *Paradiso*. This alternate or hidden journey, with repeated linguistic patterns as signposts, guides the reader towards a particular destination, probably not *Paradiso* 33, but a goal all the same where new conclusions can be drawn, though only after a re-examination of the context which surrounds the signposts that point the way.

The first itinerary of this alternate journey, examined in chapter 1, begins in *Purgatorio* 11 with the formula "persona viva" ["living person"]. The reader who is unaware that "persona viva" acts as a signpost would only see the literal meaning in Omberto Aldobrandesco's reply to Virgil's query indicating the way to the "passo" ["pass"] by which Dante as a "persona viva" can ascend to the second terrace. But the reader whose memory triggers and recalls that "persona viva" appeared once before in the text will follow this signpost back to *Inferno* 1 and more closely examine the tercets surrounding it. What will be noted by such a reader is that "passo" appears in the rhyme position one line above "persona viva" and "basso" ["low"] three lines below it:

... passo
... persona viva
...
...
... basso

The reason why "passo" and "basso" stand out for such a reader is that "passo" and "basso" appear in exactly the same position surrounding "persona viva" in *Purgatorio* 11. Such a reader will be able to juxtapose the "passo" of the prologue scene in the dark wood through which no one had ever been able to proceed alive ("... che non lasciò già mai persona viva" ["... which never left anyone alive"] 1.1.27), a "passo" that leads inevitably to the death of the soul and eternal damnation, with the "passo" between the first and second terrace of Purgatory through which Dante will climb on his way to eternal life and salvation.

As the reader then follows the return journey from *Inferno* 1 back to *Purgatorio* 11, the significance of "persona viva" also changes from death to life, from "no one alive" to "a living person." Dante's successful climb in *Purgatorio* 11 is now underlined, right alongside his unsuccessful climb. By means of this signposted itinerary, the reader can bridge the textual space contained in the forty-four cantos fixed between them, space that could otherwise obscure the simple message that they bear.

Similarly, as chapter 2 will show, there is embedded in the text a formula, "l'infernale ambascia" ["the anguish of Hell"], which appears only twice in the *Commedia*. When Adam responds in *Paradiso* 26 to Dante's question regarding the language he first spoke, Adam refers to his own descent into "the anguish of Hell" ("l'infernale ambascia"), condemned to Limbo until he is rescued by Christ, when

Christ harrows Hell. Upon encountering the formula "l'infernale ambascia," the reader may recall its previous occurrence back in *Purgatorio* 16. On Purgatory's third terrace, that of the wrathful, Dante finds himself blinded by the smoke; encouraged by Virgil, similarly blinded, he asks Marco Lombardo to lead them through the smoke, explaining that in exchange he will tell Marco the "maraviglia" of his own journey in the flesh. Dante outlines for Marco the circuitous route he has just taken, coming up into Purgatory through "the anguish of Hell" ("l'infernale ambascia"). Upon re-examination of the tercets surrounding the formula in *Purgatorio* 16, the reader guided back from *Paradiso* 26 will notice that two words look familiar: "lascia" ["leaves"] and "fascia" ["swathes"]. In both instances "lascia" and "fascia," along with "ambascia," make up Dante's *terza rima*.

By taking the signposted journey from Paradise, where Adam explains to Dante how he is now "swathed" ("fascia") in joy, back to *Purgatorio* 16 and examining the context of "fascia," the reader sees the relationship between them disclosing itself. In Purgatory it is Dante journeying still "swathed" in the flesh, the same flesh referred to in *Purgatorio* 9.10 as "quel d'Adamo" ["somewhat of Adam"] (v. 10). In *Paradiso* 26 when Adam proclaims that he is "swathed" in joy, there is no reference to original sin and the fact that Adam himself is no longer swathed in his flesh. Adam is now a soul like all the others, even though Christ, who had taken on human flesh, the flesh of Adam, delivered him to Paradise after harrowing Hell. By taking the retrospective journey back to *Purgatorio* 16, we find a juxtaposition, not to mention the irony, between Dante swathed within the flesh of Adam, and Adam swathed in joy, but not his own flesh. Implicit in this juxtaposition between the two episodes, some forty-two cantos apart, is the tragedy of Adam's loss of his flesh, a loss not otherwise featured in the *Commedia*, neither in Earthly Paradise nor for that matter in Adam's sphere of the fixed stars.

The formula "vo' che sappi" ["I want you to know"], highlighted in chapter 3, appears twice in *Inferno* 4, with the second occurrence set a mere twenty-nine lines after the first. As the formulas appear in close textual proximity, there is little change in context. Virgil and Dante are just now descending into the blind world of Hell ("Or discendiam qua giù nel cieco mondo ..." ["Let us descend now into the blind world ..."] 1.4.13) with Virgil first and Dante second. As they enter the first circle, Limbo, Virgil explains that he is pale not from fear as Dante believes but from observing the piteous plight of his fellow sufferers in Limbo. When Virgil pronounces the words "vo' che sappi" to Dante in the first instance, he is stressing the lack of sin on the part of his fellow souls, and by extension his own lack of sin.

When Virgil repeats the formula he underscores that before Christ descended into Hell, an event he personally witnessed, no souls were ever saved. The repetition here is an overt rhetorical device which drives home Virgil's urgent need for Dante to appreciate and empathize with Virgil's personal plight and that of his fellows in Limbo.

The challenge for the reader is to recall in *Inferno* 12, where the formula emerges for the third and last time, that "vo' che sappi" appeared twice in close succession some eight cantos earlier.[17] Once the sign is recognized, from the vantage point of the seventh circle the itinerary unfolds of an alternate journey back to the first circle. And with the relevant text of *Inferno* 4 in mind, obvious parallels reveal themselves. For the third time it is again Virgil who speaks the words "Vo' che sappi" to Dante, and again Virgil refers both to his own state in Limbo and to Christ's descent into Hell. However, now Virgil adds something that was previously mentioned in *Inferno* 9: namely that there had been another descent into lower Hell, his own ("Or vo' che sappi che l'altra fiata / ch'i' discesi qua giù nel basso inferno ..." ["Now I want you to know that the other time I came down here into nether Hell ..."] 1.12.34–5). Within the context of this signposted journey, the links are therefore both overt and concealed. The context that surrounds "vo' che sappi" in all three cases remains Virgil both as a soul in Limbo and as a first-hand witness to Christ's descent and its effects on Limbo and Hell in general. But added information that emerges in the text of *Inferno* 12 begs to be examined within the context of *Inferno* 4, signalled by the repetition of the formula "vo' che sappi." This concealed link juxtaposes the descent of Virgil, who journeyed down to the ninth circle to save one soul ("... per trarne un spirto del cerchio di Giuda" ["... to draw forth a spirit from the circle of Judas"] 1.9.27), with that of Dante commencing his own descent into Hell, led by Virgil ("Io sarò primo, e tu sarai secondo" ["I will be first, and you second"] 1.4.15). Without journeying from *Inferno* 12 back to *Inferno* 4 and bypassing the textual space that lies like a barrier between the two episodes, we would miss this parallel between Virgil's prior descent to the ninth circle and Dante's initial descent to the first circle. Virgil first descended into lower Hell before Dante followed second. Now as guide Virgil is again journeying down to lower Hell, again to save someone's soul, Dante's, with salvation also possible for those who read the book that Dante will write. Those who learn from this book will be among the last to enter Paradise, just as those whom Christ saved were the first.

From Virgil's vulnerability, accentuated by the initial appearance of the formula "vo' che sappi" in the first circle of Hell, the focus shifts in chapter 4 to Dante's vulnerability now in the second circle, that of the lustful. After Francesca's eloquent story of love turned to woe, Virgil asks Dante what he is thinking, in words so simple that they would not give the reader pause for second thought: "disse: 'Che pense?'" ["he said: 'What are you thinking?'"]. What would also elude the interest of the reader in *Inferno* 5 is that "disse: 'Che pense?'" is fixed within a particular configuration of rhyme words as follows:

... spense

...

... offense

...

... disse: "Che pense?"

What is Dante thinking? He replies that he is seeking to reconcile the sweetness of a courtly love between a pair so noble as Paolo and Francesca with the tragic story she recited so seductively, which recounted how their love ended in death at the hands of her husband and resulted in their damnation to the second circle of Hell.

For some sixty cantos the linguistic pattern "disse: 'Che pense?'" does not again surface. But in *Purgatorio* 31 the same pattern re-emerges here for the second and last time in the *Commedia*. Furthermore, it is fixed in the same linguistic configuration:

... spense

...

... disse: "Che pense?"

...

... offense

The repetition of the formula raises the question: is there a relationship between Dante's encounter with the courtly lady Francesca down in Hell and his encounter with his former courtly lady Beatrice here in Earthly Paradise? Was the vulnerability exhibited by Dante before Francesca a foreshadowing of his vulnerability before Beatrice, now that he has to explain his behaviour during the ten wasted years since Beatrice's death in 1290?

The reader whose memory is triggered by the repetition of the formula "disse: 'Che pense?'" in the text of *Purgatorio* 31 will recall *Inferno* 5 and the text that surrounds its first appearance. When Virgil asks Dante what he is thinking, Dante replies that he is thinking about "dolci pensier" ["sweet thoughts"]. In *Purgatorio* 31 when Beatrice asks him the same question, Dante's response, that "Le presenti cose /

col falso lor piacer volser miei passi ..." ["The present things, with their false pleasure, turned my steps aside ..."] (vv. 34–5), comes into clearer focus to those readers who have reconsidered *Inferno* 5. Dante's thoughts in *Inferno* 5 almost lead to his undoing (indeed, he faints as a dead weight falls when Francesca speaks her last words at the end of the canto). Now before Beatrice, Dante thinks over his behaviour of the previous ten years and recognizes that Francesca's attractions are false. A journey back to *Inferno* 5 at precisely this juncture brings closure to Dante's encounter with Francesca in a way not possible earlier, where Dante the pilgrim, fresh from his time in the dark wood, is still all too vulnerable to the attraction of superficial beauty.

In the wasted years after Beatrice's death, Dante was not solely preoccupied with courtly ladies. He also had another fixation at this time: to be a good politician in Florence. In chapter 5, Dante's curiosity concerning his political role models comes to the fore. In *Inferno* 6, the canto immediately following his encounter with Francesca, he is obsessed by a great desire to learn from Ciacco the fate of the "worthy" politicians of thirteenth-century Florence: Farinata, Tegghiaio, Iacopo Rusticucci, Arrigo, and Mosca. Ciacco's response could not be more clear. They are among the darkest souls ("Ei son tra l'anime più nere" v. 85). Thus it is no surprise when Dante later encounters these souls (save Arrigo), precisely in the order in which he names them in *Inferno* 6. The reader is put on notice that a number of individuals, here five named souls, will be encountered later on if, as Ciacco points out, Dante's journey takes him down that far. While it is simple enough for the reader to link Dante's encounter with Farinata in *Inferno* 10, Tegghiaio and Iacopo in *Inferno* 16, and Mosca in *Inferno* 28 with the Ciacco episode in *Inferno* 6 where their fate is disclosed to Dante, what has hitherto gone unnoticed by Dante scholars is that a surprisingly large number of recurrent linguistic patterns connect these cantos, but are woven through the Catalano and Loderingo episode in *Inferno* 23 (Catalano and Loderingo, unworthy politicians, also played a role in the governance of Florence in the late 1260s). The linguistic patterns listed below are unique to these episodes in the *Commedia*, with the exception of "de la gola" ["of gluttony" 1.6.53; "of the throat 1.23.88"], which does not reoccur in the *Inferno*, and "aspetta" ["wait"], which as an imperative addressed to Dante by one of his guides does not reoccur in the *Commedia*:

"dimmi chi tu se'" ["tell me who are you"] (Ciacco: 1.6.46)
"dirne chi tu se'" ["to tell us who you are"] (Tegghiaio, Iacopo: 1.16.32)
"dir chi tu se'" ["to tell who you are"] (Catalano, Loderingo: 1.23.93)
"de la gola" ["of gluttony"] (Ciacco: 1.6.53)

"de la gola" ["of the throat"] (Catalano, Loderingo: 1. 23.88)
"nel dolce mondo" ["in the sweet world"] (Ciacco: 1.6.88)
"nel dolce mondo" (Farinata: 1.10.82)
"guardommi un poco e poi" ["he looked at me for a moment and then"]
(Ciacco: 1.6.92)
"guardòmmi un poco e poi" (Farinata: 1.10.41)
"O Tosco" ["O Tuscan"] (Farinata: 1.10.22)
"O Tosco" (Catalano, Loderingo: 1.23.91)
"aspetta" ["wait"] (Tegghiaio, Iacopo: 1.16.14)
"aspetta" (Catalano, Loderingo: 1.23.80)
"quando … fuor giunti" ["when they had reached"]
(Tegghiaio, Iacopo: 1.16.20)
"Quando fuor giunti" (Catalano, Loderingo: 1.23.85)
"tosca" ["tuscan"] (Catalano, Loderingo: 1.23.76)
"tosca" (Mosca: 1.28.108)
"per l'aura fosca" ["through the dusky air"] (Catalano, Loderingo: 1.23.78)
"per l'aura fosca" (Mosca: 1.28.104)

These recurrent linguistic patterns guide the reader on an alternate journey down into Hell, back through the 1200s from the present time in 1300 (when Dante as member of the Priorate of Florence helps restore calm to the neighbourhoods of Florence after fresh outbreaks of factional violence). The signposts guide, by way of a detour to the *bolgia* of the hypocrites where Catalano and Loderingo are condemned, ultimately down to Mosca. Catalano and Loderingo's destructive politics are the direct result of Mosca's words of some fifty years earlier, "Capo ha cosa fatta" ["A thing done has an end"] (1.28.107), which led to the murder of Buondelmonte. Mosca's utterance in 1216, which ushered in factional division and coloured Florentine politics for the balance of the century, is the destination of Dante's alternate journey, the source of political original sin in Florence.

Within the context of this signposted itinerary back in time, Dante politician is gaining first-hand knowledge of the pitiful fate of his role models, politicians who like him had to deal with factional strife in the years after the fall of their city in 1216. The placement of these political worthies among the blackest souls raises the question: had they not devoted so much of their time to grappling with political turmoil in Florence, might they have paused to look within and consider the perilous state of their immortal souls? This alternate journey is not to end looking up to God, but on the contrary looking down towards the pit of Hell and the "gente tosca" ["Tuscan people"] where the name of Florence is heard far and wide: "Godi, Fiorenza … per lo 'nferno tuo nome si spande!" ["Rejoice, O Florence … your name is spread through Hell!"] (1.26.1–3). These citizens of Florence remain so immersed in their petty politics that they cannot fathom what is really at stake, not just for their city, but ultimately for themselves as Christians.

Dante's encounter with two of his political heroes named in the Ciacco episode in *Inferno* 6, Iacopo and Tegghiaio, comes at the crossroads of another signposted journey, which is highlighted in chapter 6. In *Inferno* 16 when Dante is with Virgil on the elevated path and realizes that the three souls baking on the burning sand below are Iacopo, Tegghiaio, and Guido, his initial urge is to quit the safety of this path in order to embrace those souls who are suffering eternal fire as condemned sodomites. Indeed such was Dante's enthusiasm that he would have thrown himself down to join them, apparently with Virgil's approval, had he only been granted some protection from their fiery torment. The verbal expression used, "gittato mi sarei" ["I would have thrown myself"], is a locution that is repeated only once in the *Commedia*.

"Gittato mi sarei" resurfaces in *Purgatorio* 27, when Dante must walk through a wall of fire before he can leave behind the last terrace of Purgatory, the seventh terrace where the lustful are purified of their sin, and move on to Beatrice. While down in Hell Dante was able to avoid the fire, of the sodomites, but here in Purgatory, a pilgrim like the other souls, he must like them be prepared to pass through the purifying fire. As in *Inferno* 16, once again Dante's initial urge is to depart from his designated path, but on this occasion his intention is to avoid the fire not to climb down into it. This time, however, Dante will not have Virgil's approval to stray from this path. Virgil goes to considerable lengths to coax Dante into the fire, suggesting that he can prove for himself that this fire will not burn him materially by testing it on the "lembo," the edge of his clothes. The only other instance in the *Commedia* when "lembo" appears is back in *Inferno* 15, when Dante is traversing the desert plain along the raised pathway, with Dante's teacher, Brunetto Latini, another political hero and another unrepentant sodomite, striding below, along the "lembo" or bottom edge of Dante's clothes. After Dante has stepped into the fire the pain he feels is intense, even though he is not actually on fire. The intensity is so great that Dante, repeating "gittato mi sarei," would have thrown himself out of the fire into molten glass, which would have been cool by comparison. This fire is an extension of the fire which burned the penitent lustful in the previous canto, among whom was Guido Guinizzelli, Dante's poetic "father."

The single repetition of "gittato mi sarei" and the single repetition of "lembo" (in reference to clothing) serve as signposts which permit the reader to move forthwith from *Inferno* 16 to *Purgatorio* 27. They beckon the reader to examine the part Dante's political and poetic role models played in influencing the path he took in the 1290s, a detour away from Beatrice which landed him deep in the dark wood of sin. Now that Dante is on his way back to Beatrice he must avoid taking any more unnecessary detours. He must not throw himself into the fire and embrace his condemned political heroes in *Inferno* 16, nor must he shrink from the purging fire of the penitent lustful through which he must pass in *Purgatorio* 27 if he hopes to return to Beatrice. In the end Dante perseveres and passes through the wall of fire, keeping the one foremost in his thoughts, from whom he had detoured back in 1290.

Chapter 7 draws a link between Dante's life as a politician in Florence and his backsliding after the death of Beatrice. When Dante inveighs against the unjust rulers of "his Florence" in *Purgatorio* 6 he turns to an archery image to drive home his point: Florentines, as opposed to the bowmen of other lands, shoot recklessly and without justice in their heart. The rhyme words of the *terza rima* are "tocca" ["touch"], "scocca" ["it shoots"], and "de la bocca" ["on its lips"], within a wider *terza rima* configuration as follows:

tocca
...
scocca
l'arco
de la bocca
(In) carco
...
-arco

The formula "de la bocca" is repeated only once more in the *Commedia*, later in the *Purgatorio*. The accompanying rhyme words are also repeated, and are further interwoven within a wider configuration which is remarkably similar:

de la bocca
...
scocca
l'arco
tocca
carco
...
-arco

In *Purgatorio* 31 Dante's feeble "sì" to the accusing Beatrice is so low as to be inaudible. The weak response of the broken Dante is compared to the weak arrow shot from the apparatus of an archer which has been stretched so taut that it breaks. The arrow, like Dante's response, barely reaches its target.

The configuration which illuminates Dante's diatribe against Florentine politicians in the first instance, and Dante's own recent failings in the second, invites the reader who has reached *Purgatorio* 31 to glance back at *Purgatorio* 6, and explore the relationship between Dante's backsliding after Beatrice's death and the unjust Florentine rulers. On the face of it, both Dante and the current rulers of Florence make for poor bowmen. Is their common incompetence with the bow indicative of a shared weakness? The link highlighted by the formula of repetition adds further substance to the discussion that is raised in chapters 5 and 6: so involved is Dante in Florentine politics during the second half of the 1290s that he is blind to the state of his immortal soul, until inevitably in the spring of 1300, full of sleep, he falls into the dark wood. Beatrice points out in *Purgatorio* 30 that Dante had fallen so low by the spring of 1300 that nothing short of showing him the "perdute genti" could save him. Among the "lost people" are the worthy but damned politicians, named by Dante the pilgrim in *Inferno* 6, who might have repented of their sin if they had taken pause from their all-consuming political lives to reflect on the state of their immortal souls. Whether just or unjust, politicians will all the same end up in Hell if they remain mired in Florentine politics to the exclusion of all else. But such will not be Dante's fate. In contrast to the Florentine rulers of *Purgatorio* 6, Dante's arrow does in fact reach its designated target, even though his is an extremely weak shot. Beatrice can read Dante's lips and understand the "sì." He will make his confession and he will return to Beatrice.

Chapter 8 analyses the most complex repeated linguistic configuration in this study. In *Inferno* 23, when Dante is about to condemn the hypocritical actions of Catalano for fanning the flames of factional hatred in Florence, he is distracted by something which causes him to stop in mid-sentence. For Dante to be distracted from inveighing against one such as Catalano, the sight must be a momentous one. What he sees is the high priest of the Pharisees, Caiaphas, prostrate and crucified. In describing the scene, Dante refers to Caiaphas as one "ne l'etterno essilio" ["in eternal exile"]. The *terza rima* which contains "essilio," along with the rhyme words "Virgilio" and "concilio" ["council"], fits into a greater configuration as follows:

convenia
[2 lines later]

via
[2 lines later]
pria
[2 lines later]
concilio
[2 lines later]
Virgilio
[2 lines later]
ne l'etterno essilio
[8 lines later]
terza rima of words ending in "-chia"

The linguistic pattern "ne l'etterno essilio" reappears only once in the *Commedia*, in *Purgatorio* 21, not only with the same rhyme words, but again situated six lines below "pria" ["before"] and eight lines above the "-chia" rhyme:

via
[2 lines later]
venía
[2 lines later]
pria
[2 lines later]
Virgilio
[2 lines later]
concilio
[2 lines later]
ne l'etterno essilio
[8 lines later]
terza rima of words ending in "-chia"

The wonderfully complex linguistic configuration, repeated in *Purgatorio* 21, is a powerful signal that the reader should look back over thirty-one cantos of textual space to revisit *Inferno* 23 for further examination. How does "Virgil" relate to "eternal exile" and "council"? Within the context of *Inferno* 23, it would appear that there is no relationship. The "etterno essilio" is in reference to Caiaphas's eternal damnation, not Virgil's, with the "concilio" being the Council of the Pharisees. But, moving forward to *Purgatorio* 21, it is Virgil who begins to respond to the newly freed Statius and here refers to the "etterno essilio" as his own exile, with the "concilio" shifting from the Council of the Pharisees to the Heavenly Council which Virgil will never see, since he is condemned to the same eternal exile as Caiaphas by the "verace corte" ["true court"]. Both Caiaphas and

Virgil have been condemned to eternal exile by this court. The reader must now ask: What do Caiaphas and Virgil share in common? Could Virgil, the representative in *Purgatorio* 21 of that pagan Rome which rebelled against God ("... i' fu' ribellante a la sua legge ..." ["... I was rebellious to His law ..."] 1.1.125), somehow be deemed the counterpart to Caiaphas, a representative of the Jewish nation which rejected Christ? The question only arises if the reader notes the signpost in *Purgatorio* 21 and takes the backward glance to *Inferno* 23.

In *Paradiso* 26 when Adam describes the reason for his exile to Limbo where Beatrice urged Virgil to hasten to Dante's aid, the rhyme scheme "essilio"/"Virgilio"/"concilio" reappears. Here the "concilio" is again the Council of the Blessed, which Adam desired while he languished in Limbo for all those many years before Christ came. However, in this instance "essilio" is not modified by "etterno." There is no apparent reason for Adam to refer to Virgil by name, the last time Virgil's name appears in the *Commedia*. Why did he? If the reader takes a backward glance to *Purgatorio* 21, and recalls that there "essilio" is still modified by "etterno," the reason for the reference to Virgil in *Paradiso* 26 comes into sharper focus. In the mouth of Adam we hear the final words relating to "Virgilio." Adam juxtaposes the tragedy that is Virgil's eternal exile in Limbo with his own non-eternal exile, he who had been delivered from Limbo by Christ shortly after Virgil's arrival.

There is one final rhyme scheme which must be taken into the equation. In *Paradiso* 23 "essilio" and "concilio" are found again together in the *terza rima* scheme, with "essilio" referring to the Babylonian Captivity of the Jewish nation. But in this case "Filio" ["Son"] takes the place of "Virgilio." Again, if the reader glances back from *Paradiso* 26 with the missing modifier "etterno," this time to *Paradiso* 23 with the missing "Virgilio," all comes full circle. By leaping back and forth across great swaths of textual space, guided by the linguistic signposts, we see Dante's basic message slowly unfold: Had Virgil, the representative of that pagan Rome which can here be seen as the counterpart to the Jewish nation, believed in the "Filio" yet to come, Virgil would have been saved by Christ as Adam was saved, and consequently his exile would not have been an eternal one.[18]

In chapter 9, the unfolding message that is revealed by following the signposted journey, highlighted by the repeated linguistic pattern "fissi e attenti" ["fixed and attentive"], ends by a scrambling of that pattern.[19] The discourse centres once more on the detour Dante took in his life's journey in the first instance between 1290 and 1300, between the death of Beatrice and Dante's successful effort to leave behind his life of sin and follow Virgil out of the dark wood. When

Dante encounters his old friend Casella at the shore of Purgatory, he falls back into a pattern of behaviour which he should have left behind in the dark wood. His conversation with Casella focuses almost entirely on himself. Dante wants Casella, who used to sing his own courtly compositions, to sing him a song so that his soul can be consoled, just as Casella used to quiet his pains, pains which perhaps should not have been quieted. Casella gladly complies by singing one of Dante's own compositions, a love song in praise of Lady Philosophy of the *Convivio*, one to whom Dante turned after Beatrice's death. Dante, Virgil, and all the other penitent souls stop in their tracks, entranced by the sweetness of the song, "fissi e attenti" to the notes of Dante's song sung by Casella. Forgotten is the hard road to salvation that they should be taking, mirroring Dante's departure from the straight and narrow after Beatrice's death. The gravity of this uncalled for and unnecessary lingering on the shore of Purgatory is emphasized by Cato's angry rebuke.

The next stop in the text, signalled by the linguistic pattern "fissi e attenti," occurs in Earthly Paradise, just after Beatrice has unveiled her mouth, allowing Dante's eyes to see her face for the first time in ten years. Dante's eyes are "fissi e attenti" upon Beatrice's visage to the exclusion of all else. The saga of Dante's eyes, his "occhi miei," begins in chapter xxxv of the *Vita Nuova*, when upon the death of Beatrice he raised his eyes ("levai li occhi") to see whether others witnessed his grief ("videro li occhi miei quanta pietate ..."). His eyes meet those of the Donna Gentile (the Lady Philosophy of the *Convivio*), and by chapter xxxvii are taking too much delight in the sight of her. Now Dante turns his "occhi miei" back to Beatrice, this time admiring her beauty for its own sake. This is reminiscent of chapters xxxv to xxxvii of the *Vita Nuova*, before Dante's love took a nobler form at the end of the work. Again he is taken to task, in this case by the three theological virtues.

The destination of this signposted itinerary is also the goal of Dante's *in carnem* overt journey: the Empyrean. With the repetition of the formula "levai li occhi" Dante raises his eyes until at the end of their journey up the Celestial Rose they are "fissi e attenti" on the Virgin Mary seated on high. In juxtaposition with the earlier two instances, here Dante's eyes are fixed and attentive on a worthy aspiration. The reader guided by the repeated formula "fissi e attenti," who can look beyond the intervening textual space, can focus on the sublime moment in the final portion of *Paradiso* 33, keenly aware of the barriers that impeded Dante's way, that side-tracked Dante for years before he regained the true path of life's journey. In this final canto Bernard requests of the Virgin Mary that Dante be allowed to raise his eyes to God. And the Virgin Mary, with eyes fixed on Bernard, acknowledges his prayer. It is in this final episode of the *Commedia* where a form of "fisso" and a form of "attento" are last encountered, reflecting Dante's mind, "fixed, immobile and attentive" on the goal of his life's journey. The destination of this signposted journey and the pilgrim's overt journey is now one and the same. But the last signpost which points the way is more obscure. It is hidden by a scrambling of the linguistic pattern, though still identifiable to those able to see through the opaque glass, just as Dante the pilgrim strives to see God's image despite the veil before all mortals' eyes here at the end of the *Commedia*.

While the destination of this last signposted journey is in fact found at the end of the *Commedia*, as with the others the route taken is not a linear one. Progress on these journeys entails much going back and forth over already traversed textual space, before their full significance can be understood.

In a similar fashion, Umberto Bosco in "La 'Follia' di Dante" traces sixteen repetitions of the pair of words "folle" ["foolish"] – "follia" ["folly"] across textual space, focusing on the context in which they are found throughout the *Commedia*. By collapsing the text between the repetitions of the words he draws new conclusions, with the thematic relevance of the words always at the core of his argument.[20] Ultimately it is a lesson about Dante's "follia," not that of other souls (who exist as examples of those who have transgressed the limits imposed by God), which is the destination of Bosco's "linguistic journey" (my words). By following this journey the reader can better understand that Dante must know when to stop in his quest for knowledge and recognize his duties as a Christian, "... vincere con consapevole umiltà la propria 'follia'" ["... to overcome with conscious humility his own 'folly'"].[21]

In "Autoesegesi dantesca: la tecnica dell' 'episodio parallelo' (*Inferno* xv–*Purgatorio* xi)," Amilcare Iannucci looks at repetition in the *Commedia* as a way of commenting in the second instance on a prior parallel episode. It is Dante's way of glossing the text of the *Commedia* more subtly than he did in the *Vita Nuova*. Iannucci points out that the key second episode is almost always the briefer of the two.[22] In the example that he raises, Oderisi's observations on fleeting fame in *Purgatorio* 11 are brief in comparison to the lengthy Brunetto episode of *Inferno* 15, and yet sufficient as Dante's gloss to negate what Brunetto still holds most dear: "come l'uom s'etterna" ["how man makes himself eternal"] (v. 85). Iannucci's view that the briefer second episode is the key to explaining the first is borne out by what the signposted journeys in this study reveal. Dante clearly adopted many different strategies to achieve the same end: giving a later gloss to an earlier episode, across the often considerable textual space that lies between the two passages.

In more recent studies, Iannucci has looked at the question of parallel cantos in terms of what he calls "structurally determining" or "textually privileged" episodes, such as the prologue, Limbo, Paolo and Francesca, and Ulysses, the meaning of which extends far beyond the immediate context. Further, he identifies another kind of structurally determining episode: one which gathers in meaning instead of producing it. The episodes that gather in meaning occur in the *Purgatorio* and the *Paradiso*, usually in the middle of the *cantica* or at the end.[23] Of Iannucci's four "structurally determining" episodes which produce meaning in the *Inferno*, three are the point of departure for alternate journeys in my study – prologue (chapter 1), Limbo (chapter 3), and Paolo and Francesca (chapter 4) – while seven of the nine alternate journeys have their destination in those of his "structurally determining" episodes which gather in meaning, at either the middle or the end of the *Purgatorio* or the *Paradiso*. Iannucci refers to "intratextual strategies" employed by Dante where, for example, the Statius cantos can only be understood "if we see them and the whole episode in terms of its intratextual dependence on Limbo and Virgil's story," with the earthquake signalling not just Statius's salvation but also Virgil's damnation, thus concluding the Limbo theme.[24]

Zygmunt Baranski, in "Structural Retrospection in Dante's *Comedy*: The Case of *Purgatorio* XXVII," examines repeated elements from the perspective of *Purgatorio* 27, asserting that there are "pivotal cantos" that act as "echoing points" in the *Commedia*: "The inter-canto reminiscences offer a clue to how he is able to retain mastery over his hugely complex poem ... The poet continually, and not just in *Purgatorio* XXVII, demands and encourages reflection in the reader about what his poem has revealed and is revealing, so that the full impact of this might be appreciated and intellectually retained."[25] In a later study, "The 'Marvellous' and the 'Comic': Toward a Reading of *Inferno* XVI," Baranski identifies *Inferno* 16 as the first canto the reader encounters in the *Commedia* which is to be "read as part of a broader ideological and formal framework. Dante scatters textual markers to this effect. From inside the canto, he draws attention to the opening of the poem."[26] Both cantos highlighted by Baranski form the context for two signposted journeys in this study. Indeed, *Inferno* 16 and *Purgatorio* 27 are linked to each other in chapter 6, by means of the formula "gittato mi sarei," while *Inferno* 16 in chapter 5 is at the crossroads of three formulas: "dirne chi tu se'," "aspetta," and "quando ... fuor giunti." While Baranski focuses more upon repeated elements than linguistic repetition *per se*, the poet's expectation for the careful reader is the same: "the poet forces the reader's memory to return over what it already knows, so that he or she can appreciate, from a position of epistemological privilege, the condition of the pilgrim."[27]

Dante's use of linguistic repetition to signal the reader to look back was amplified by Singleton in "The Vistas in Retrospect." There Singleton highlights the repetition of "ruina" in *Inferno* 12 and the further signal that is "qui e altrove" ["Here and elsewhere"]:

Qui e *altrove*. The reminder is pointed, and the careful reader will not fail to catch the signal in the *altrove* and recall the *ruina* of Canto v: recall it, to let all that we learn from Virgil about this second *ruina* cast light upon that first. For we are indeed told important things now about the second ... What, I will ask, should those who gloss this poem for us, verse by verse, tell us, the reader, when we come to the first *ruina* in Canto v? That it comes as the merest word there and stands in darkest mystery, we have noted ... The *ruina* in Canto v is the first word of a "sentence" which proves to be made up of three "words" when it completes itself in Canto xxiii.[28]

For Singleton the repetition of "ruina" is a key signal embedded in the text, pregnant with meaning for an appreciation of the *Commedia* as a whole, and it must not escape the careful reader. Only now with deeper understanding gained from reading further in the text can the reader take that retrospective journey and re-examine the context in which "ruina" first occurs.

The thrice-repeated "ruina," or, as Singleton calls it, the three "words" which make up the "sentence," forms one of many alternate journeys available to the careful reader. Nine "sentences" or journeys are followed in this study, which demand an ever more careful reader, since they are not prompted by "here and elsewhere" ("qui e altrove"). In place of such a directional prompt, a repeated group of words, or one word alone, constitutes the formulas of repetition. Oftentimes they are fixed within complex linguistic configurations that surround the highlighted formula, again prompting the reader to look back because the given linguistic configuration found "here" was also encountered "elsewhere."[29]

By going back and forth on nine signposted journeys, the careful reader is afforded an interpretive opportunity which takes shape only if, as in a puzzle, the pieces scattered through textual space are placed side by side and fitted together to form new pictures, new perspectives on the *Commedia*.

1 Linguistic Configuration as a Clue to the Impossible Made Possible: *Inferno* 1, *Purgatorio* 11, and *Purgatorio* 12

In the prologue scene in *Inferno* 1, Dante's first attempt to find a way out from the dark wood, his difficult climb up the "dilettoso monte" ["delectable mountain"], fails from his fear of the she-wolf who causes him to despair of ever reaching that summit.[1] There is another summit, Earthly Paradise, which Dante has every hope of attaining once he has turned his back on the temptations of Antepurgatory and is allowed entry into Purgatory proper and the first terrace of the proud in *Purgatorio* 11 and 12. From here Dante, the "persona viva" ["living person"], will be shown the way to a "passo" ["pass"] through to the second terrace, an easy climb for him which does not fail. The reader will recall that "persona viva" and "passo," along with "basso" ["low"], also revealed themselves in *Inferno* 1. The contrast between the two climbs, signalled by the formula, "persona viva," within a configuration of the other repeated rhyme words, "passo" and "basso," will be the subject matter of this chapter.[2]

When Singleton discusses Exodus imagery in *Inferno* 1 and in Purgatory, he notes that it is only when Dante reaches the first terrace inside the gate of Purgatory that he is finally beyond the temptations, beyond the three beasts of *Inferno* 1 which had prevented his initial ascent.[3] Singleton has therefore already noticed a link between *Inferno* 1 and the first terrace of Purgatory.[4] In analysing the Pater Noster in *Purgatorio* 11 for Exodus imagery, he further points out that when the penitent souls pray, "Dà oggi a noi la cotidiana manna" ["Give us this day our daily manna"] (2.11.13), one key word has changed: the poet has substituted "manna" for "bread" ("Panem nostrum quotidianum da nobis hodie" Luke 11: 3). Singleton has interpreted the "manna" in the *Commedia* as divine assistance, precisely that assistance which could have aided the pilgrim within the Exodus imagery of *Inferno* 1.22–7. By contrast, in *Purgatorio* 11 the "manna" is given daily and allows the pilgrims inside the gate of Purgatory to persevere through "questo aspro diserto" ["this harsh desert"] (2.11.14).[5]

The first simile of the *Commedia*, which is also the introduction to Exodus imagery, compares Dante to the Israelites fleeing Egypt by way of the Red Sea:

> E come quei che con lena affannata,
> uscito fuor del pelago a la riva,
> si volge a l'acqua perigliosa e guata,
>   così l'animo mio, ch'ancor fuggiva,
> si volse a retro a rimirar lo *passo*
> che non lasciò già mai *persona viva*.
>   Poi ch'èi posato un poco il corpo lasso,
> ripresi via per la piaggia diserta,
> sì che 'l piè fermo sempre era 'l più *basso*.

[And as he who with laboring breath has escaped from the deep to the shore turns to look back on the dangerous waters, so my mind which was still fleeing turned back to gaze upon the pass that never left anyone alive. After I had rested my tired body a little, I again took up my way across the desert strand, so that the firm foot was always the lower.]

(1.1.22–30)

The linguistic formula, "persona viva," quoted above in final position in verse 27, is repeated in only one other instance in the *Commedia*, in *Purgatorio* 11.51. This single repetition of "persona viva" therefore shifts the focus forward to within the gate of Purgatory to a moment just after the Pater Noster.

When the penitent souls' prayer ends, Virgil beseeches them to point out the shortest way to the stair leading up to the next terrace, and also an easier access for his charge, who is still weighed down by mortal flesh. One of the proud, Omberto Aldobrandesco, responds:

> "... A man destra per la riva
> con noi venite, e troverete il *passo*
> possibile a salir *persona viva*.
>   E s'io non fossi impedito dal sasso
> che la cervice mia superba doma,
> onde portar convienmi il viso *basso* ..."

["... Come with us to the right along this bank and you will find the opening where it is possible for a living man to climb. And were I not hindered by the stone that subdues my proud neck, so that I must hold my face down ..."]

(2.11.49–54)

In both *Inferno* 1 and *Purgatorio* 11, the thematically salient "passo" appears one line before "persona viva," and "basso" comes three lines after it; all three are in final position.[6] The repeated configuration in these *terzine*, interlinked by the "persona viva" in *Inferno* 1 and *Purgatorio* 11, is as follows:

... passo
... persona viva
...
...
... basso

"La riva" also reappears, again in final position, one line before "passo," while in *Inferno* 1 "la riva" appears three lines before "passo."

This repeated configuration is a subtle signal by which the reader is induced to look back, as was the Pater Noster a few lines earlier when the proud souls of the first terrace pray "per color che dietro a noi restaro" ["for those who remain behind us"] (2.11.24). This moment in *Purgatorio* 11, coming after the Pater Noster but before Dante addresses those of the first terrace, is thus both an ending and a new beginning. Dante has completed his journey beyond the three beasts. He has entered the gate of Purgatory and, like the souls of the first terrace, can look back at those who are still on their way. With the repeated configuration ("passo," "persona viva," and "basso"), the reader is led to recall the Dante of *Inferno* 1 who was then unable to ascend to salvation.

The recurrence of "riva," "passo," "persona viva," and "basso" in *Inferno* 1 and *Purgatorio* 11 reinforces their continued meanings in these passages. Freccero refers to the "riva" in *Inferno* 1 as a "shore of a middle ground," a "dead end for any man left on his own."[7] The "riva" in *Purgatorio* 11, on the contrary, is the slope, indicated by Omberto, which Dante and Virgil can follow until they reach an opening which leads upward.[8]

The "passo" is the dark wood in *Inferno* 1 or, in the Exodus simile, the "pelago" or the "perilous seas."[9] It is a passageway which in *Inferno* 1 leads only to the death of the soul.[10] In *Purgatorio* 11 Omberto urges Dante and Virgil to walk with him and the others: "con noi venite, e troverete il passo" ["Come with us and you will find the passageway"] (2.11.50). In *Purgatorio* 12 when Dante and Virgil are before the actual "passo," the passageway to the second terrace, the reader is reminded of Omberto's "venite" when the angel, echoing Omberto's invitation, repeats: "Venite: qui son presso i gradi" (2.12.92). Dante's repetition of "passo" in *Purgatorio* 11 reminds the reader that this passageway is an opening, not a "dead end," a way for Dante to ascend to the next terrace on his journey.

Pagliaro defines the "persona viva" in *Inferno* 1 "nel senso più proprio di uomo che sia in vita, anima e corpo" ["in the truest sense of a man who is alive, soul and body"].[11] Within the negative context of "lo passo / che non lasciò già mai persona viva" ["the pass that never left anyone alive"], "persona viva" is a person who is neither alive nor saved. In *Purgatorio* 11 the text which surrounds "persona viva" must be understood in a wider context. When Virgil addresses the souls of the first terrace,

"Deh, se giustizia e pietà vi disgrievi
tosto, sì che possiate muover l'ala,
che secondo il disio vostro vi lievi,
    mostrate da qual mano inver' la scala
si va più corto; e se c'è più d'un varco,
quel ne 'segnate che men erto cala;
    ché questi che vien meco, per lo 'ncarco
de la carne d'Adamo onde si veste,
al montar sù, contra sua voglia, è parco,"

["Ah, so may justice and pity soon disburden you, that you may spread your wing which may uplift you according to your desire, show us on which hand we may go most quickly to the stair; and if there is more than one passage, show us that which is least steep, for he who comes with me here, for the burden of Adam's flesh wherewith he is clothed, against his will is slow at climbing up,"]

(2.11.37–45)

he presents Dante to these souls as a man of flesh, a "living person" weighed down by the flesh of Adam, and it is in this context that Omberto responds: "A man destra per la riva / con noi venite, e troverete il passo / possibile a salir persona viva" ["Come with us to the right along this bank, and you will find the opening where it is possible for a living man to climb"] (2.11.49–51). Omberto is inviting Dante and Virgil to join with the multitude of penitent souls moving towards an easier access to the passageway so that even one weighed down by the flesh as Dante is can make the climb. So "persona viva" here signifies simply a living man, that is a man still not divested of the flesh of Adam, now on his way to salvation, as opposed to a man neither alive nor saved in *Inferno* 1.

The "passo" in *Inferno* 1 allowed for no living man to cross through, but in *Purgatorio* 11 the words immediately preceding the "persona viva," "possibile a salir" ["possible to climb"], reveal that Dante's previously impossible ascent is now feasible, "possibile."

Freccero interprets the "lower" foot, "basso" being the last term in the configuration, as the wounded left foot that humankind inherited from Adam and which symbolizes his fall, leaving Everyman limping as "homo claudus."[12] In *Inferno* 1 the left foot "sempre era 'l più basso" ["was always the lower"], with "sempre" in the context of the prologue meaning that Dante's foot will never heal. In *Purgatorio* 11 the boulder on Omberto's back, the punishment of the proud, constrains him to keep his "viso basso" ["face down"].[13] In both instances, for Dante there, for Omberto here, walking is made awkward. However, while in the context of *Inferno* 1 the pilgrim's lower foot will always drag behind, in *Purgatorio* 11 there is no mention of "sempre": Omberto's awkward walking will cease one day when, healed of his sin, he will walk erect.

When the first "passo," "persona viva," and "basso" configuration appeared in *Inferno* 1, Dante had not yet reached the three beasts, the third of which frightened him back towards the dark wood. On the second appearance of this linguistic configuration, Dante has passed beyond the temptations, represented by the beasts in the prologue. Singleton maintains that Ante-Purgatory is imbued with Exodus imagery of temptation, such as Casella's song and the serpent in the valley of the princes.[14] With divine assistance in the form of Lucia, Dante has managed to turn his back on these temptations and need no longer fear "l'antico avversaro" ["the old adversary"] (2.11.20). That is for those "che dietro a noi restaro" ["who remain behind us"] (2.11.24), those who are still struggling against the temptations, against the beasts.[15]

The configuration "passo," "persona viva," and "basso" alerts the reader to the practical consequence of Dante's liberation from the "antico avversaro." The ascent, impossible for Dante in the prologue, now becomes possible in *Purgatorio* 12, in that passage signalled by the repetition of the imperative "venite":[16]

A noi venìa la creatura bella,
biancovestito e ne la faccia quale
par tremolando mattutina stella.

> Le braccia aperse, e indi aperse l'ale;
> disse: "Venite: qui son presso i gradi
> e agevolemente omai si sale."

[The fair creature came towards us, clothed in white and such in his face as seems the tremulous morning star. He opened his arms and then spread his wings and said, "Come: the steps are at hand here, and henceforth the climb is easy."

(2.12.88–93)

Not only is the ascent now possible, but the poet stresses how easy it will be. The she-wolf who had blocked Dante's way in *Inferno* 1 is here replaced by an angel, "la creatura bella." The pleasant, welcoming atmosphere in which Dante is here encouraged to ascend is in marked contrast to the desperate gloom of the prologue.[17]

The configuration of "passo," "persona viva," and "basso" compels the reader to look back and contrast the "passo" in *Inferno* 1, which left no man alive, with the subsequent "passo" in *Purgatorio* 11, which will lead, by means of an easy climb up the "gradi" in *Purgatorio* 12, to the second terrace. The Pater Noster made plain that Dante was beyond the "antico avversaro," but the repetition of the "passo," "persona viva," and "basso" configuration inevitably determines the comparison of Dante's now-easy climb with the previously impossible one back in the prologue.

2 The Descent into "l'infernale ambascia": The Journey and Adam's Flesh

On the third terrace of Purgatory both "blinded" guide and "blinded" pilgrim seek a way out of the dense smoke surrounding the penitent wrathful souls at prayer. At Virgil's behest, Dante addresses one of the souls and invites it to follow him and hear the marvel of his extraordinary journey. The soul, who will identify himself as Marco Lombardo, agrees to follow Dante as far as he is able:

> "Io ti seguiterò quanto mi lece,"
> rispuose; "e se veder fummo non *lascia*,
> l'udir ci terrà giunti in quella vece."
>   Allora incominciai: "Con quella *fascia*
> che la morte dissolve men vo suso,
> e venni qui per *l'infernale ambascia*."

["I will follow you as far as is allowed me," it replied, "and if the smoke does not let us see, hearing will keep us together instead." Then I began, "With those swaddling-bands which death unbinds I am journeying upwards, and I came here through the anguish of Hell."]

(2.16.34–9)

In *Paradiso* 26, Adam responds to Dante's unspoken curiosity concerning the language he spoke, because Adam can see what is on Dante's mind in that true mirror, God, who envelopes him in joy. Adam points out that his language was dead before the building of the Tower of Babel, and adds:

"Opera naturale è ch'uom favella;
ma così o così, natura *lascia*
poi fare a voi secondo che v'abbella.
    Pria ch'i' scendessi a *l'infernale ambascia*
I s'appellava in terra il sommo bene
onde vien la letizia che mi *fascia*."

["That man should speak is nature's doing, but whether thus or thus, nature
then leaves you to follow your own pleasure. Before I descended to the anguish of Hell the Supreme Good from whom comes the joy that swathes me
was named *I* on earth."]

(3.26.130–5)

The formula "l'infernale ambascia," is unique to these two cantos,
both times appearing in a configuration with "lascia" ["leaves"] and
"fascia" ["swaddling bands," "swathes"], which make up the other
two rhyme words of the *terza rima*.[1] It is the thesis of this chapter that
the repetition of the formula within its configuration compels the
reader to review Dante the pilgrim's reference to Marco Lombardo in
Purgatorio 16, that he has journeyed while still a living man ("con
quella fascia" ["with those swaddling-bands"]) through the "anguish
of Hell" and now beyond, in the context of Adam's reference to
Dante in *Paradiso* 26, that after death Adam sojourned long but not
eternally in the "anguish of Hell."

Although the prepositions which precede the formula differ in the
two instances, highlighting the fact that Dante only passed "through"
Hell ("*per* l'infernale ambascia") for the space of one full day,[2] while
Adam descended "to" Hell ("*a* l'infernale ambascia") to languish
there for 4302 years,[3] they inevitably draw the reader to juxtapose
Dante's journey into Hell and beyond with Adam's stay in Hell and
his ultimate salvation by Christ when he harrowed Hell. The repetition of the formula "l'infernale ambascia," in a configuration with
"lascia" and "fascia," is the clue for the reader to ask what Dante and
Adam have in common. A careful examination of these shared
features will help confirm the findings of such Dante scholars as
Singleton and Freccero who have focused on Dante's *in carnem* journey in the prologue scene and into Earthly Paradise, and related it to
Adam's life journey and the consequences of original sin.[4]

With the opening words "buio d'inferno" ["gloom of Hell"] in
verse 1 of *Purgatorio* 16, the poet draws on his ordeal when he journeyed through Hell ("per l'infernale ambascia") as pilgrim, to dem-
onstrate that on this third terrace the thick smoke blinding both
pilgrim and guide leaves them in greater darkness than anything

Dante had previously experienced, even in that infernal darkness. This cloud of smoke, which envelopes the penitent wrathful souls of the third terrace, clouds their vision, just as anger clouded their judgment during their lifetime.

As blinded pilgrim takes care not to be separated from blinded guide, they hear the voices of the penitent wrathful beseeching Christ, the Lamb of God, to grant them peace and release from their sins. It is that gentle Lamb, who with his life of humility not only came to atone for the sin of the proud Adam, thereby saving him and some of his descendants, but who can also save those wrathful souls who recognize that they were the very antithesis of Christ, and repent of their sins.[5]

The narrative is based on things heard not seen, because all are blinded by the thick smoke.[6] Just as Dante and Virgil were attracted to the voices of the penitents they heard praying for peace, so too is one particular penitent drawn to the voices of Dante and Virgil. This soul, Marco Lombardo, recognizes Dante as one who seems still in the flesh, not because he can see Dante's body, even though it dents the air, but rather from hearing Dante ask Virgil whether those praying aloud are spirits or not. When Marco challenges Dante to identify himself, Virgil prompts him to answer that they are going "sùe" ["up"], something that Virgil himself could have said. Why does Virgil not respond to that question if he has the ready answer? Perhaps the reason is to lay the groundwork for the dialogue between Marco and Dante on political ethics which will dominate the canto.[7] It is also possible that as Virgil and Dante move ever closer to their parting of the ways just outside Earthly Paradise, it is for Dante, not Virgil, to describe the journey up ("sùe") to the top of this mountain, a point Virgil will not reach, not even temporarily as guide.

Dante's initial address to Marco in the vocative may not appear particularly noteworthy. However, in light of the linguistic configuration which it anticipates, Dante's choice of words must be more carefully scrutinized:

> Ed io: "O creatura che ti mondi
> per tornar bella a colui che ti fece,
> maraviglia udirai, se mi secondi."

[And I, "O creature that are cleansing yourself to return fair to Him who made you, you shall hear a marvel if you follow me."]

(2.16.31–3)

In this invocation Dante describes Marco as one in the process of purifying himself so that he may return to God as a new man, cleansed of all sin. Here in the first two lines of the tercet is a depiction of one of Adam's seed returning cleansed to the original state enjoyed by Adam in Earthly Paradise before original sin, and to God who created him ("ti fece"), except that he is disembodied, like all spirits.[8]

The curious Marco is not sure what to make of the stranger who, unlike everyone else, seems not to be a spirit, and is eager to hear the "maraviglia" Dante promises to recount if Marco will accompany him, presumably through the smoke.[9] Marco is prepared to do so, but mindful of the limitations placed on the penitent wrathful by God, he can only go part way along the terrace:[10] "Io ti seguiterò quanto mi lece" ["I will follow you as far as is allowed me"] (v. 34). Marco, one of Adam's seed, in the act of cleansing himself of his sin, respects the limits placed upon him by God, limits not respected by the first father when he sinned.

The initial rhyme word of the linguistic configuration, "lascia," appears in the continuation of Marco's response to Dante's request that he accompany him. In essence, because the smoke prevents the shade of Marco from seeing the body of Dante, he must rely on his hearing only, just as Virgil and Dante have done on this terrace. Marco will never see this new presence, Dante himself, who is the "maraviglia" about whom he will learn. Marco's hearing will have to reveal what his eyes could otherwise have shown him: Dante still covered in his flesh. Both Marco's reference to the smoke which will not allow ("non lascia") the one to see the other, and the beginning of Dante's explanation of the "maraviglia," are contained within the two tercets making up the linguistic configuration, which I quote:

> "Io ti seguiterò quanto mi lece,"
> rispuose; "e se veder fummo non *lascia*
> l'udir ci terrà giunti in quella vece."
> Allora incominciai: "Con quella *fascia*
> che la morte dissolve men vo suso,
> e venni qui per *l'infernale ambascia*."

["I will follow you as far as is allowed me," it replied "and if the smoke does not let us see, hearing will keep us together instead." Then it began, "With those swaddling-bands which death unbinds I am journeying upwards, and I came here through the anguish of Hell."]

(2.16.34–9)

Dante's first words of explanation to Marco refer to his own body, his "fascia" which will be undone by death, "fascia" which makes up the second rhyme word of the linguistic configuration.

Just as in Dante's invocation to Marco in the tercet preceding the configuration Marco was described as in the process of returning ("tornar bella") to God, so here the attention shifts to Dante's journey, to his "return." Of course Dante is a "maraviglia" because death has not yet driven his body from his soul. Dante is on his way up to the top of Purgatory, to Earthly Paradise, and beyond, having already passed through "the anguish of Hell" ("l'infernale ambascia"). Dante passed through Hell before entering Earthly Paradise, and while his soul was still bound to his body, unlike Adam who dwelt in Hell after his death, a shade like all the others.[11]

During Dante's time in Hell, what is to be made of the noun "ambascia," or "anguish," through which he passed? Did he share the sinners' anguish? Dante's reference here to "l'infernale ambascia" appears to suggest that he did in some way suffer the torments of Hell,[12] much as all Adam's seed must suffer for his sin.

Dante now tells Marco of the heights to which he aspires, explaining his earlier reference about "going upward" ("vo suso"); however, he makes it clear that his journey upward is also bound within the limits set by God:

"E se Dio m'ha in sua grazia rinchiuso,
tanto che vuol ch'i' veggia la sua corte
per modo tutto fuor del moderno uso ..."

["And since God has received me so far into His grace that He wills that I see His court in a manner wholly outside modern usage ..."]

(2.16.40–2)

Dante, like Marco, and unlike Adam originally, is mindful of the limitations placed on him by God, and will move no further upward than God decrees. He hopes, however, that God will allow him to journey beyond Purgatory, beyond Earthly Paradise to his court, a "tornar bella" for Dante to the One who made him, once he, the seed of Adam, has cleansed himself of sin.

But Dante's journey differs from Marco's because Dante is still in the flesh. For this reason he is a "maraviglia" and describes his journey as "tutto fuor del moderno uso." We learn in *Inferno* 2 that the last one to take such a journey was St Paul, and before him was Aeneas ("Io non Enëa, io non Paulo sono" ["I am not Aeneas, I am not Paul"] 1.2.32).[13] Therefore one could interpret Dante's reference to his journey as not a part of modern use, since the last such journey took place some 1250 years before. However, in the sense that Dante's journey is one of cleansing himself of sin, it is also necessary to look back much further in time to the father of all sin, to Adam himself, who is the most "fuor del moderno uso" of all. If Dante's journey *in carnem* is outside of modern use, then so too are the gifts that were bestowed upon Adam when God created him, not the least of which was his remaining eternally *in carnem*. The body was not destined to die.[14] Death of the body is an outcome of original sin.

Dante closes his speech by asking this soul to identify himself and guide them to the "varco" ["passage"]: the way out of the dense smoke to the next terrace. Since Dante cannot see the shade of Marco, the latter no longer possessing even that reflection of the body, he calls on Marco to lead by his words: "e tue parole fier le nostre scorte" ["and your words shall be our escort"] (2.16.45).

God does indeed will that Dante see his court, and it is here that Dante encounters the shade of Adam. Dante, seed of Adam, addresses the first father with the vocative "O pomo che maturo / solo prodotto fosti ..." ["O fruit that were alone produced mature ..."] (3.26.91–2), Adam, who set the seed for all humankind without himself descending, having been created a mature man, like fruit (more precisely an apple) already ripe.

Of the four questions Dante puts to Adam, Adam answers the most important one first: the true cause of God's great wrath ("la propria cagion del gran disdegno" 3.26.113). Adam explains that the original sin was not one of gluttony, but pride. Adam and all his future descendants were not punished because Adam had tasted the fruit of the tree *per se*, but because Adam did what Marco Lombardo took great care not to do in *Purgatorio* 16, when he would not venture beyond the bounds of the dense smoke. Adam rejected the limits placed on his world by God, when in his pride he tasted of the forbidden tree:[15]

> "Or, figliuol mio, non il gustar del legno
> fu per sé la cagion di tanto essilio,
> ma solamente il trapassar del segno."[16]

["Now know, my son, that the tasting of the tree was not in itself the cause of so long an exile, but solely the overpassing of the bound."]

(3.26.115–17)

Adam's discourse shifts from the sin he committed in Earthly Paradise to its consequence for him personally after his death. He had to dwell in Limbo for 4302 years. Here the poet overtly links Adam's sojourn in Limbo with Dante's pilgrim journey:

> "Quindi onde mosse tua donna Virgilio,
> quattromila trecento e due volumi
> di sol desiderai questo concilio."

["In the place whence your lady dispatched Virgil, I longed for this assembly during four thousand three hundred and two revolutions of the sun."]

(3.26.118–20)

Why is it that Adam does not refer to Limbo by name, but as the place which Beatrice urged Virgil (who dwelled there with Adam for some fifty years) to quit and aid the misguided pilgrim? By referring to it as "onde mosse tua donna Virgilio," Adam is linking his own exile in Limbo, long since over, to Dante's journey when it was about to begin, guided first by "Virgilio" and from Earthly Paradise by Beatrice, "tua donna."

While overt, the link is a tenuous one until *Paradiso* 26, when Adam, in response to Dante's query regarding the language he spoke, repeats the formula of repetition within its configuration of rhyme words, which first appeared in *Purgatorio* 16:

"Opera naturale è ch'uom favella;
ma così o così, natura *lascia*
poi fare a voi secondo che v'abbella.
    Pria ch'i' scendessi a *l'infernale ambascia*,
I s'appellava in terra il sommo bene
ode vien la letizia che mi *fascia*."

["That man should speak is nature's doing, but whether thus or thus, nature then leaves you to follow your own pleasure. Before I descended to the anguish of Hell the Supreme Good from whom comes the joy that swathes me was named *I* on earth."]

(3.26.130–5)

Since "l'infernale ambascia" only appears on these two occasions in the *Commedia*, once with reference to Dante the pilgrim's journey through the "anguish of Hell" (in present time), and once with reference to Adam's descent to the "anguish of Hell" (back near the beginning of time), Dante's journey through Hell, briefly described in *Purgatorio* 16, is again highlighted here in *Paradiso* 26 in juxtaposition with Adam's lengthy stay in Hell. Dante's journey through the "anguish of Hell," his descent into humility, is of course necessary because as the seed of Adam he too must atone for Adam's pride, for which Adam himself endured 4302 years in the "anguish of Hell."

If one reviews the rhyme words of the linguistic configuration within the context of their first appearance, a number of important parallels are revealed.

On the surface the "lascia" in *Purgatorio* 16 does not appear to have anything in common with the "lascia" in *Paradiso* 26, since in the former instance it is the smoke which does not "allow" Dante and Marco to see each other, while in the latter instance it is nature which "allows" humans to choose the language they will speak. However, it is precisely this facility of speech which becomes the necessary substitute for the failed sense of vision, when Dante cannot see the shade of Marco nor Marco the body of Dante. It is speech which binds Dante to Marco Lombardo in *Purgatorio* 16, his presence perceived only through his voice, seemingly disembodied like the others. Indeed had Marco not possessed the ability to speak, Dante and Virgil would have been unable to sense his presence and request his aid and they might have lost their way. So as *Paradiso* 26 highlights, it is the facility to speak a particular language, which nature "allows" humans (seed of Adam) to choose for themselves, which was the lifeline for Dante and Virgil through the dense smoke of the third terrace in *Purgatorio* 16.

The "fascia" to which Dante refers in *Purgatorio* 16 is his body, in which he, as a living being, is going up the mountain, the unique *in carnem* journey, allowed by God, that is completely outside modern use ("tutto fuor del moderno uso" 2.16.42). This is the body Marco would have been able to see had it not been for the dense smoke. In *Paradiso* 26 the disembodied Adam cites "fascia" to point out that he is "swathed" by God in joy, now that he dwells among the blessed in Paradise. It is, however, through the repeated linguistic configuration, when recalling the first appearance of "fascia," within that configuration, that one realizes something important is missing in Adam's reference to his present "joy" (3.26.135). The living Dante being the seed of Adam is "swathed" in a mortal body which Adam can see, because here there is no dense smoke. Adam, however, lacks the body he lost for himself and his seed upon death, because he sinned in not accepting the limitations imposed upon him by God.

Dante makes two overt references to Adam, when describing his *in carnem* journey, both times pointing out that the fatigue he endures while climbing the mountain of Purgatory comes from bearing the weight of Adam's flesh.

In *Purgatorio* 9, when Dante beds down for the night in the valley of the princes with the souls of Virgil, Sordello, Nino Visconti, and Corrado Malaspina, his body, Adam's body, is so heavy a weight that after the long day's climb sleep quickly engulfs him:

> quand'io, che meco avea di quel d'Adamo,
> vinto dal sonno, in su l'erba inchinai
> là 've già tutti e cinque sedavamo.

[... when I, who had somewhat of Adam with me, being overcome with sleep, lay me down on the grass there where all five of us were already seated.]

(2.9.10–12)

Were it not for Adam's sin, the body Dante inherited from him would not have wearied, and Dante, like the other four disembodied souls beside him, would have had no need for sleep, that bodily limitation. More specific to this episode, Dante would not have missed out on the amazing way he was borne from the valley of the princes to the gate of Purgatory.

Awakening from that sleep, Dante finds himself inside the gate of Purgatory on the first terrace, among the penitent proud who, like him, each bear a heavy burden. Their burden is not their bodies, but the boulders which they must carry on their backs while purging themselves of their sin. Virgil addresses these souls and draws a parallel between the *contrapasso* which their pride has earned them and Dante's condition. Just as Virgil hopes that they will soon be freed from their burden, he also hopes that they might indicate to him an easier path up to the next terrace, because Dante too is weighed down, in his case by the flesh of Adam:

"... mostrate da qual mano inver' la scala
si va più corto; e se c'è più d'un varco,
quel ne 'nsegnate che men erto cala;
    ché questi che vien meco, per lo 'ncarco
de la carne d'Adamo onde si veste,
al montar sù, contra sua voglia, è parco."

["... show us on which hand we may go most quickly to the stair; and if there is more than one passage, show us that which is least steep, for he who comes with me here, for the burden of Adam's flesh wherewith he is clothed, against his will is slow at climbing up."]

(2.11.40–5)

One of the penitent proud, Omberto Aldobrandesco, invites Virgil and Dante to accompany himself and the other toiling souls to an easier way, through which Dante, who is weighed down by Adam's flesh, will be able to pass.

Omberto's pride and that of the other penitent proud on the first terrace is but a pale reflection of Adam's original sin of pride in that their sin was not against God, but against their fellow men. Omberto and the other penitent proud recognize the limitations placed upon them by God on this terrace, even if when living they did not recognize how limited were their endeavours compared to those of their fellows. Adam, however, refused to recognize the limitations imposed on him by God higher up on this mountain in Earthly Paradise, and that was nothing less than rebellion against God.[17]

The penitent proud will escort Virgil and Dante to the right, along the first terrace to a passageway where Dante will easily be able to climb to the second terrace despite being weighed down by the body of Adam:

> ... "A man destra per la riva
> con noi venite, e troverete il passo
> possibile a salir persona viva."

[... "Come with us to the right along this bank, and you will find the opening where it is possible for a living man to climb."]

(2.11.49–51)

On the first terrace the penitent proud are fully aware of how far they can accompany Virgil and Dante, unlike Adam when he sinned, just as Marco Lombardo on the third terrace of the wrathful is aware that he cannot accompany Dante beyond the dense smoke.

In the previous chapter, within the configuration of rhyme words "passo" and "basso," the link has already been established between Dante, the "persona viva" here and the "persona viva" in *Inferno* 1 who is neither alive nor saved. A parallel was drawn between Omberto Aldobrandesco, who is forced to keep his "viso *basso*" (2.11.54), and Dante, whose left foot "sempre era 'l più *basso*" ["was always the lower"].[18] For both Omberto here in *Purgatorio* 11 and Dante back in *Inferno* 1, walking is laborious. In Omberto's case it is due to his sin of pride, Adam's sin albeit of a milder kind, which he is purging by bearing a boulder on his back. In Dante's case, as Freccero indicates, the awkward stride is caused by the wounded left foot which he inherited from his forefather Adam, symbolizing Adam's fall through his sin of pride, leaving his seed forever "homo claudus," limping man.[19]

The two overt references to Dante journeying in the flesh of Adam in *Purgatorio* 9 and 11 strengthen the link between the Marco Lombardo episode in *Purgatorio* 16, where Dante explains to Marco that he is journeying in the flesh, and Dante's encounter with Adam in *Paradiso* 26. In *Purgatorio* 16 Dante describes his journey through the anguish of Hell ("per l'infernale ambascia" 2.16.39) and into Purgatory as completely outside of modern use ("tutto fuor del moderno uso"

2.16.42), because he is still a living man ("persona viva" 2.11.51), with those swaddling clothes, which death dissolves ("con quella *fascia* / che la morte dissolve" 2.16.37–8), which is the flesh of Adam ("quel d'Adamo" 2.9.10; "la carne d'Adamo" 2.11.44). When Dante actually meets the first father in *Paradiso* 26, Adam refers to his own journey, after his death and not in "the flesh of Adam," into the anguish of Hell ("a *l'infernale ambascia*" 3.26.133). Earlier he refers to his 4302 years in Limbo, the place where Dante's journey in Adam's flesh was set into motion by Beatrice ("onde mosse tua donna Virgilio" 3.26.118). Although Adam is no longer swathed in his flesh, here in Paradise, he is content with the joy with which God swathes him ("la letizia che mi *fascia*" 3.26.135).

Nonetheless, were it not for original sin, Adam and all his seed would be swathed in both Adam's flesh and the joy bestowed by God. But as Beatrice points out to Dante in *Paradiso* 7, Adam challenged the limits placed by God on his will:

"Per non soffrire a la virtù che vole
freno a suo prode, quell'uomo che non nacque,
dannando sé, dannò tutta sua prole."

["By not enduring for his own good a curb upon the power that wills, that man who never was born, in damning himself damned all his progeny."]

(3.7.25–7)

Adam's rejection of the limitations imposed by God (limitations now recognized by Adam's descendants in Purgatory) condemned him and all future descendants (that is the entire human race) to Hell.

After Adam had spent over four thousand years in the company of the other damned, his seed, in Hell, Christ came down to earth and took on human nature, uniting himself with that tainted flesh, the same flesh which encumbers Dante the pilgrim and which Adam lost for himself and his seed through death:

"onde l'umana specie inferma giacque
giù per secoli molti in grande errore,
fin ch'al Verbo di Dio discender piacque
u' la natura, che dal suo fattore
s'era allungata, unì a sé in persona
con l'atto sol del suo etterno amore."

["wherefore the human race lay sick down there for many centuries in great error, until it pleased the word of God to descend where He, the sole act of

His eternal love, united with Himself in person the nature which had estranged itself from its Maker."]

(3.7.28–33)

Following his death Christ harrowed Hell and delivered Adam to Paradise; but still without his body. Even the intercession of Christ himself could not wash out the stain, inflicted by Adam, on the human race. Death was now the lot of humankind. The soul would remain immortal, but not the body.

When the living Dante in Adam's flesh toils up the mountain of Purgatory and encounters Marco Lombardo, he seeks a "varco" to take him from the third to the fourth terrace, on his way "suso"[20] to the summit, to Earthly Paradise. But Adam and his seed no longer dwell in Earthly Paradise. He lost it for himself and his seed when he sinned.

However, the other loss, the loss of Adam's flesh, is not stressed in Eden, or when Dante encounters him in the seventh sphere of the fixed stars of Paradise. It is only by following the signposted journey from *Purgatorio* 16, where Dante's *in carnem* journey, wholly outside of modern usage, is highlighted, to *Paradiso* 26, where Dante meets Adam, that the reader can juxtapose the "fascia" reference in *Purgatorio* 16 with that in *Paradiso* 26 and recognize that in the latter, the reference to a body, to Adam's body, is missing. Indeed Adam has not been swathed in his body since before he was sent to the "infernale ambascia" over five thousand years earlier. Adam's flesh, the "fascia" borne by Dante through the "infernale ambascia," up the mountain of Purgatory, past Earthly Paradise and up through the heavens of Paradise, returns to Adam, but in the body of Dante. It does not, nor could it, stay with Adam. What was wrought by original sin cannot be undone. At the close of *Paradiso* 26 Dante, in Adam's flesh, turns from the first father, who has just spoken his last words regarding his readiness to sin ("Nel monte che si leva più dall'onda, / fu' io, con vita pura e disonesta ..." ["On the mountain which rises highest from the sea I lived pure, then guilty ..."] 3.26.139–40), and a new canto begins by hailing the true Father: "Al Padre, al Figlio, a lo Spirito Santo," / cominciò, "gloria!" tutto 'l paradiso ..." ["Glory be to the Father, to the Son, and to the Holy Spirit!" all Paradise began ..."] (3.27.1–2).

3 Decoding the Parallelism of Three Descents into Dante's Hell

When Dante declares in *Inferno* 2.32: "Io non Enëa, io non Paulo sono" ["I am not Aeneas, I am not Paul"], he is overtly establishing a link between his descent and the journey of Aeneas and Paul. The other inevitable link, that between Dante's descent and those of Christ and Virgil, is not stated in the text. It is the thesis of this chapter that there exists a linguistic code that links openly together the descents of Christ, Virgil, and Dante, and affirms the commonality of their purpose.

The code consists of the repetition of the noun "color" ["colour"] and the linguistic formula "vo' che sappi" ["I want you to know"]. In only two cases in the *Commedia* is "color" chosen with the lexical connotation of pallor: *Inferno* 4.16 ("E io, che del color mi fui accorto ..." ["And I, noting his pallor ..."]) and *Inferno* 9.1 ("Quel color che viltà di fuor mi pinse ..." ["That pallor which cowardice painted outwardly on me ..."]). In three instances in the *Commedia*, all in the first half of the *Inferno*, Virgil prefaces his explanations to Dante with the words "vo' che sappi." These occur in *Inferno* 4.33 ("Or vo' che sappi, innanzi che più andi ..." ["Now I want you to know before you go further ..."), *Inferno* 4.62 ("E vo' che sappi che, dinanzi ad essi ..." ["And I want you to know that before these ..."]), and *Inferno* 12.34 ("Or vo' che sappi che l'altra fiata ..." ["Now I want you to know that the other time ..."]).

The first component of this linguistic code, "color," guides us as far as *Inferno* 9 and the second one, "vo' che sappi," leads us ultimately to *Inferno* 12. *Inferno* 9 and *Inferno* 12 are linked because in them there occur the two key instances where Virgil refers to his prior descent (and both times he repeats "l'altra fïata" ["the other time"] to allude to when it took place). The linguistic formula "vo' che sappi" is a signal which leads the reader from *Inferno* 4, with its reference to the *descensus Christi*, to *Inferno* 12 where Christ's descent is once again recalled by Virgil along with his own descent to the ninth circle. The reference to Virgil's "color" and to the *descensus Christi ad inferos* in *Inferno* 4 reappears in *Inferno* 9, where for the first time there is mention of Virgil's earlier descent.[1] In all cases these words are employed when there is discussion of either the *descensus Christi* or Virgil's descent to Giudecca.

The first "vo' che sappi" occurs early in *Inferno* 4, as guide and pilgrim, now on the other side of the Acheron, are at the edge of the first circle: Limbo. A clap of thunder has just awakened Dante. Finding himself in strange, new surroundings, he is unable to see much of the "valle d'abisso dolorosa" ["the chasm of pain"] (v. 8) into which he is about to descend with Virgil. This valley or chasm is the "luogo etterno" ["eternal place"] (1.1.114) through which Virgil urged Dante to follow him, back in the prologue, and yet Dante's first sight of Virgil's face here before the seemingly bottomless pit is one of pallor:

> E io, che del *color* mi fui accorto,
> dissi: "Come verrò, se tu paventi
> che suoli al mio dubbiare esser conforto?"

[And I, noting his pallor, said, "How shall I come, if you are afraid, who are wont to encourage me when I hesitate?"]

(1.4.16–18)

In Limbo, the place of "sospiri" ["sighs"] (v. 26) and "duol" ["sadness"] (v. 28), Virgil's "color" causes Dante to fear that Virgil is ill equipped to lead him (vv. 17–18) and he questions his guide's qualifications. Indeed, if Virgil himself is fearful, how can he possibly quell Dante's own doubts here at the very start of such an audacious journey? Virgil explains that his "color" has nothing to do with fear, but compassion for his fellow dwellers in Limbo:

> Ed elli a me: "L'angoscia de le genti
> che son qua giù, nel viso mi dipigne
> quella pietà che tu per tema senti."

[And he to me, "The anguish of the people here below paints my face with the pity that you take for fear."]

(1.4.19–21)

Virgil assumes that Dante would have been curious about these "genti" ["people"] who stirred that anguish in him which Dante had taken for fear. Thus when Dante shows no interest in the "genti" Virgil mildly takes him to task and prompts the information himself:

> Lo buon maestro a me: "Tu non dimandi
> che spiriti son questi che tu vedi?
> *Or vo' che sappi*, innanzi che più andi,
>   ch'ei non peccaro; e s'elli hanno mercedi,
> non basta, perché non ebber battesmo,
> ch'è porta de la fede che tu credi;
>   e s'e' furon dinanzi al cristianesmo,
> non adorar debitamente a Dio:
> e di questi cotai son io medesmo
>   Per tai difetti, non per altro rio,
> semo perduti, e sol di tanto offesi
> che sanza speme vivemo in disio."

[The good master said to me, "Do you not ask what spirits are these that you see? Now, before you go farther, I want you to know that they did not sin; but if they have merit, that does not suffice, for they did not have baptism, which is the portal of the faith you hold; and if they were before Christianity, they did not worship God aright, and I myself am one of these. Because of these shortcomings, and for no other fault, we are lost, and only so far afflicted that without hope we live in longing."]

(1.4.31–42)

Virgil prefaces his description of the "genti," who had been the cause of his "color," with the words "vo' che sappi." Virgil "wants" Dante "to know," before going any further, why these "genti" deserve pity: their only sin was in not having been baptized and yet they remain in Hell.[2] The "or,"[3] followed by the formula (verb of volition "vo'" + "che" + the subjunctive "sappi"), followed by "before going further," compels Dante and the reader to pause and consider the magnitude of what is being said and the poignancy of Virgil being one of those souls ("e di questi cotai son io medesmo" ["and I myself am one of these"] v. 39). The context of the first occurrence of the formula serves to define the human dimension of Virgil's figure: the great poet is vulnerable, and it is precisely this vulnerability which makes him human.

The second occurrence of the formula "vo' che sappi" comes soon after the first, also in *Inferno* 4. Dante, reacting to what Virgil "had wanted" him "to know," asks his guide:

"Dimmi, maestro mio, dimmi, segnore,"
comincia' io per volere esser certo
di quella fede che vince ogne errore:
　"uscicci mai alcuno, o per suo merto
o per altrui, che poi fosse beato?"

["Tell me, master, tell me sir," I began, wishing to be assured of the faith that conquers every error, "did ever anyone go forth from here, either by his own or by another's merit, who afterwards was blessed?"]

(1.4.46–50)

Dante wants to ascertain that what he has learned by faith is correct: that Christ descended to Limbo and redeemed the worthy pre-Christians. Virgil responds:

　... "Io era nuovo in questo stato,
quando ci vidi venire un possente,
con segno di vittoria coronato.
　Trasseci l'ombra del primo parente,
d'Abèl suo figlio e quella di Noè,
di Moïsè legista e ubidente;
　Abraàm patriarca e Davìd re,
Israèl con lo padre e co' suoi nati
e con Rachele, per cui tanto fé,
　e altri molti, e feceli beati.
E *vo' che sappi* che, dinanzi ad essi,
spiriti umani non eran salvati."

[... "I was new in this condition when I saw a Mighty One come here, crowned with the sign of victory. He took hence the shade of our first parent, Abel his son, and Noah, and Moses, obedient giver of laws, Abraham the patriarch and David the king, Israel with his father and his children and with Rachel, for whom He did so much, and many others; and He made them blessed. And I want you to know that before these no human souls were saved."]

(1.4.52–63)

Indeed it is true, declares Virgil who witnessed the event, that "un possente" ["a Mighty One"] descended into Hell. A soul-resident wishing to describe Dante's own descent 1266 years later might provide an account comparable to Virgil's even though Dante is not really a "possente."[4] For a second time Virgil repeats the formula "vo' che sappi" and shifts the pilgrim's attention from the souls who left with the "possente" to an even earlier time. He "wants" Dante "to know" that such an event had never happened before. Virgil, with his partial knowledge of things Christian, has perceived the importance of this "possente" not only for those who ascended with him, but also for those like Virgil himself who witnessed Christ's descent yet were left behind in Limbo. Virgil had arrived in Limbo just in time to bear witness to this one-time liberation of select pre-Christians. But for Virgil Christ's descent has a greater significance than simply a unique event he witnessed. He is one who is left behind, not taken out of Limbo in the company of Abel, Noah, and all the others. On this occasion when pre-Christians were judged, when half of the Celestial Rose would be instantly filled by this throng now freed from Limbo, Virgil too was judged. And it was a negative judgment, for otherwise he would not have remained just a witness, a bystander looking on, an outsider for all eternity.

Generally Virgil's role as guide is distinct from his role as soul-resident, but in Limbo, the two roles are blurred. Virgil is both Dante's guide and a soul in Limbo who was there 1266 years before to witness the crucial event of the *descensus Christi* of which until now Dante the pilgrim had only abstract knowledge. When Virgil and Dante leave Limbo for the second circle, Virgil is once again simply the guide, almost as if Virgil the soul-resident had been left behind like Marcia, Homer, Ovid, Lucan, and the others.[5]

The third and last repetition of the formula "vo' che sappi" occurs as Virgil and Dante proceed towards the seventh circle. Here Virgil is master of the situation despite the menacing Minotaur who guards this circle of the violent. The repetition of the formula begs a comparison between Virgil's guiding competence at the approach to the seventh circle and his performance as guide in Limbo, the context of the first two occurrences of the formula. In this place, unlike Limbo, Virgil need not identify with the condemned, nor need he be defensive about those around him. After Virgil succeeds in verbally bludgeoning the Minotaur on the ruined slope, the two poets descend:

> Così prendemmo via giù per lo scarco
> di quelle pietre, che spesso moviensi
> sotto i miei piedi per lo novo carco.
>   Io gia pensando; e quei disse: "Tu pensi
> forse a questa ruina, ch'è guardata
> da quell'ira bestial ch'i' ora spensi."

[So we took our way down over that rocky debris, which often moved under my feet with the new weight. I was going along thinking and he said, "Perhaps you are thinking on this ruin, guarded by that bestial wrath which I quelled just now."]

(1.12.28–33)

With the third and last repetition of the formula below, Virgil recalls
the other time he left Limbo just after his death and further recalls, as
he did in *Inferno* 4, that very important event, the *descensus Christi*:

> *"Or vo' che sappi* che l'altra fiata
> ch'i' discesi qua giù nel basso inferno,
> questa roccia non era ancor cascata.
>   Ma certo poco pria, se ben discerno,
> che venisse colui che la gran preda
> levò a Dite del cerchio superno,
>   da tutte parti l'alta valle feda
> tremò sì, ch'i' pensai che l'universo
> sentisse amor, per lo qual è chi creda
>   più volte il mondo in caòsso converso;
> e in quel punto questa vecchia roccia,
> qui e altrove, tal fece riverso."

["Now I want you to know that the other time I came down here into the
nether Hell this rock had not yet fallen. But certainly, if I reckon rightly, it was
a little before He came who took from Dis the great spoil of the uppermost
circle, that the deep foul valley trembled so on all sides that I thought the universe felt love, whereby, as some believe, the world has many times been
turned to chaos; and at that moment this ancient rock, here and elsewhere,
made such downfall."]

(1.12.34–45)

Just as the poet subtly makes the link between *Inferno* 4 and
Inferno 12 by repeating "vo' che sappi," Virgil overtly links the
cantos by repeating his description of what he experienced when
Christ descended to Hell. He remembers here in *Inferno* 12 what he
thought in the "alta valle" (Limbo), when "un possente" crowned
with the symbol of victory had made blessed ("feceli beati") some
Old Testament figures and "altri molti" ["many others"], something
he has already described to Dante in *Inferno* 4. Now, he is confirm-
ing what the formula has already disclosed to us: there is a relationship between the earthquake that was described up there ("l'alta
valle") in *Inferno* 4 and the result of it described here in *Inferno* 12,
namely "la ruina."[6]

If one compares Virgil's account of Christ's descent after the second repetition of the formula back in the "alta valle" in *Inferno* 4 with
the third repetition of the formula in *Inferno* 12, this later description
is now less detailed. Here, for example, the great biblical figures are
not actually named. One presumes that this is because it has all been

said before. But if so, then why is Virgil repeating his account of the *descensus Christi*? Because here he is adding an important element that was omitted from *Inferno* 4, although he had prepared the reader for it there in verse 15:

"Or discendiam qua giù nel cieco mondo,"
cominciò il poeta tutto smorto.
"Io sarò primo, e tu sarai secondo."

["Let us descend now into the blind world here below," the poet began, all pale. "I will be first, and you second."]

(1.4.13–15)

The verse "Io sarò primo, e tu sarai secondo" describes the relation of guide to pilgrim and at the same time anticipates the reference to Virgil's own descent that will be explicit in *Inferno* 12, immediately following the third and last repetition of the formula "vo' che sappi." This is that he was the "first" outsider to venture into the depths of this "cieco mondo" ["blind world"], shortly before Christ's descent into Limbo, and now Dante is the "second."[7]

Virgil's prior descent is first described in *Inferno* 9, and just before that at the end of *Inferno* 8 he refers to the *descensus Christi*.[8] When Virgil's negotiations with the devils to gain entry into the city of Dis seem to have broken down, despite the sign of defeat which appears on Virgil's brow he nonetheless assures his charge that he will win in the end, because once before the devils tried and failed to thwart God's will, when Christ descended into Hell:

"Questa lor tracotanza non è nova;
ché già l'usaro a men segreta porta,
la qual sanza serrame ancor si trova.
    Sovr' essa vedestù la scritta morta."

["This insolence of theirs is nothing new, for they showed it once at a less secret gate, which still stands without a bolt. Over it you saw the dead inscription."]

(1.8.124–7)

With this allusion to the *descensus Christi* the reader is taken back to *Inferno* 4 and the detailed description by Virgil of this event. Preceding that description was the allusion to Virgil's pallor, his "color" (1.4.16), which had caused Dante to fear the folly of his barely commenced journey. Reference to "color" reappears on the first line of *Inferno* 9, just four lines after the above quotation:

Quel *color* che viltà di fuor mi pinse
veggendo il duca mio tornare in volta,
più tosto dentro il suo novo ristrinse.

[That color which cowardice painted outwardly on me when I saw my leader
turn back, repressed more speedily his own new color.]

(1.9.1–3)

As in *Inferno* 4 the pilgrim is now very fearful and for the same reason: the pallor in Virgil's face suggests that he may not be up to the
task of guiding. Thus a few lines later the nervous pilgrim asks his
guide for, and obtains, reassurance:

"In questo fondo de la trista conca
discende mai alcun del primo grado,
che sol per pena ha la speranza cionca?"
    Questa question fec'io; e quei "Di rado
incontra," mi rispuose, "che di noi
faccia il cammino alcun per qual io vado.
    Ver è ch'altra fïata qua giù fui,
congiurato da quella Eritón cruda
che richiamava l'ombre a' corpi sui.
    Di poco era di me la carne nuda,
ch'ella mi fece intrar dentr' a quel muro,
per trarne un spirto del cerchio di Giuda.
    Quell' è 'l più basso loco e 'l più oscuro,
e 'l più lontan dal ciel che tutto gira:
ben so 'l cammin; però ti fa sicuro."

["Into this depth of the dismal hollow does any ever descend from the first
circle where the sole punishment is hope cut off?" I asked; and he answered,
"It seldom happens that any of us makes the journey on which I go. It is true
that once before I was down here, conjured by that cruel Erichtho who was
wont to call back shades into their bodies. My flesh had been but short while
divested of me, when she made me enter within that wall to draw forth a
spirit from the circle of Judas. That is the lowest place, and the darkest, and
farthest from the heaven that encircles all. Well do I know the way, so reas-
sure yourself."]

(1.9.16–30)

As Christ, the incarnate God, left his body and made his way down
into Limbo past those who would have blocked his way, so too does
Dante, incarnate, led by Virgil, make his way down by God's will. And

Virgil soon after he lost his flesh ("Di poco era di me la carne nuda ..."
["My flesh had been but short while divested of me ..."] v. 25), like
Christ, descended.[9] Although Virgil descended much further down
than Christ, inside the city of Dis to Giudecca, the reason for the descent is similar. Christ descended to Limbo to take ("trasseci" *Inferno* 4.
55) the worthy pre-Christians so that they might be saved from Hell,
and Virgil descended to take ("per trarne" 1.9.27) "un spirto" and save
it from deepest Hell.

Virgil descended "l'altra fïata" as the "primo" into deepest Hell
and now accompanies Dante, the "secondo," once more into deepest
Hell.[10] Again in *Inferno* 12 Virgil refers to his prior journey by repeating "l'altra fïata," just after the formula, "vo' che sappi."

There is also a link in Dante's use of the verb "discendere" when
describing the three journeys or descents into Hell, first Virgil's,
then Christ's, then his own with Virgil (all linked by the linguistic
code). Before the first occurrence of the formula "vo' che sappi" in
Inferno 4, just before Virgil and Dante reach Limbo, Virgil declares:
"Or discendiam qua giù nel cieco mondo" ["Let us now descend
into the blind world here below"] (v. 13). The use of the verb
"discendere," plus the "cieco mondo," has particular significance
when one juxtaposes the present journey of Virgil and Dante with
Christ's one then. I repeat the question Dante asks Virgil in *Inferno* 9
which allows Virgil to tell of his prior journey down into deepest
Hell:

> "In questo fondo de la trista conca
> *discende* mai alcun del primo grado,
> che sol per pena ha la speranza cionca?"

["Into this depth of the dismal hollow does any ever descend from the first
circle where the sole punishment is hope cut off?"]

(1.9.16–18)

This question, with "discende," coming as it does just after the allusion to the *descensus Christi* at the end of *Inferno* 8, invites the reader to
connect Virgil's descent with Christ's. And finally Virgil's second reference to his prior descent, again in close textual proximity to the reference to the *descensus Christi*, is preceded by the third and last
occurrence of the formula:

> "*Or vo' che sappi* che l'altra fiata
> ch'i' *discesi* qua giù *nel basso inferno*,
> questa roccia non era ancor cascata."

["Now I want you to know that the other time I came down here into the nether Hell this rock had not yet fallen."]

(*Inferno* 12.34–6)

Virgil descended before Christ, by journeying from Limbo to the very bottom of Hell. Essentially this was so that one individual, Dante, could descend and then ascend, just as Christ descended and ascended to show the way for all humankind to descend and then ascend towards salvation: "descendit ad inferos ... ascendit ad caelos" (Apostle's Creed). The formula "vo' che sappi" in *Inferno* 12 focuses on Virgil, who descended to the ninth circle and then ascended back to Limbo. Virgil's descent is important for the pilgrim and also for the reader: Virgil, having been the "primo" to descend, will be able to lead Dante, the "secondo," some thirteen hundred years later, when he is again sent down again to guide Dante and make possible the journey, with all that that journey will determine, namely the writing of the book.[11]

The three repetitions of "vo' che sappi" plus the two repetitions of "color," when viewed together, constitute a linguistic code which leads the reader to examine the significance of the parallelism between Virgil's descent and those of Christ and of Dante into Hell.[12] Virgil, not saved by Christ, descended and ascended so that one soul might be saved the pain of the ninth circle ("... per trarne un spirto del cerchio di Giuda" ["... to draw forth a spirit from the circle of Judas"] 1.9.27). Christ descended and took ("trasseci l'ombra del primo parente ..." ["He took hence the shade of our first parent ..."] *Inferno* 4.55) a host of souls so they might be saved from the pains of Hell. The linguistic code, then, highlights the fact that the extraordinary descents of Virgil, Christ, and now Dante share one significant aspect: they all have to do with saving souls. It is precisely this highlighting of the common purpose of three descents which provides us with an insight that anticipates the culminating moment of Dante's meeting with Cacciaguida in Paradise: the Christian readers of Dante's book who will have descended and ascended with Virgil, with Christ, with Dante the pilgrim, may also be counted among those who will be spared the pains of Hell and will fill some of the few remaining places in the Celestial Rose.

4 Dante's Wasted Years: What Is He Thinking in *Inferno* 5 and *Purgatorio* 31?

In *Inferno* 5 in the second circle of the lustful, after two tercets which are introduced by "Amor," the condemned soul Francesca again repeats "Amor" after explaining how love was her undoing, leaving a temporarily stilled Dante the pilgrim:

> "Amor condusse noi ad una morte.
> Caina attende chi a vita ci *spense*."
> Queste parole da lor ci fuor porte.
>   Quand'io intesi quell'anime *offense*,
> china' il viso, e tanto il tenni basso,
> fin che 'l poeta mi *disse*: "*Che pense?*"

["Love brought us to one death. Caina awaits him who quenched our life." These words were borne to us from them. And when finally I heard those afflicted souls I bowed my head and held it bowed until the poet said to me, "What are you thinking of?"]

(1.5.106–11)

At the beginning of *Purgatorio* 31, as Beatrice continues to reprimand Dante for his backsliding during the ten-year period since her death, she demands that he speak to his error and confess it. Dante cannot bring the words forth from his mouth:

> Era la mia virtù tanto confusa,
> che la voce si mosse, e pria si *spense*
> che da li organi suoi fosse dischiusa.

Poco sofferse; poi *disse*: "*Che pense?*
Rispondi a me; ché le memorie triste
in te non sono ancor da l'acqua *offense.*"

[My power was so confounded that my voice moved and became extinct before it was set free from its organs. She forebore but little, then said, "What are you thinking? Answer me, for the sad memories in you are not yet destroyed by the water."]

(2.31.7–12)

The formula "disse: 'Che pense?' " ["he/she said: 'What are you thinking?' "] is unique to these two cantos in the *Commedia*. Further, in both instances of the formula, the rhyme word "pense" is in a configuration with "spense" ["quenched/made extinct"] and "offense" ["afflicted/destroyed"], which appear in the other two rhyme positions of the *terza rima*.[1] It is the thesis of this chapter that the repetition of the formula "disse: 'Che pense?' " within its wider configuration is a signal in *Purgatorio* 31 directing the reader's attention back to its first appearance in *Inferno* 5, so that Dante's answer to that same question can be compared and contrasted, across some sixty cantos of textual space, at two very different junctures in Dante's journey to salvation.[2]

The key question is asked in the formula, when first Virgil and then Beatrice "said: 'What are you thinking?' " What is Dante thinking? In *Inferno* 5 Dante responds immediately:

Quando rispuosi, cominciai: "Oh lasso,
quanti dolci pensier, quanto disio
menò costoro al doloroso passo!"

[When I answered, I began, "Alas! How many sweet thoughts, what great desire, brought them to the woeful pass!"

(1.5.112–14)

Dante the pilgrim's reference to the "sweet thoughts," the "dolci pensier" of the lovers, suggests his empathy towards the adulterous relationship which is developing between Paolo and his sister-in-law, Francesca. Within the context of courtly love, Dante, the poet of the "dolce stil novo," could not better convey the sense that this is a love which he understands full well and has experienced. And what of *Purgatorio* 31? Here Beatrice does not allow Dante to reply immediately, and when finally the fearful and confused pilgrim is able to utter more than "sì," his response comes some twenty-four lines after the original question "che pense?":

Piangendo dissi: "Le presenti cose
col falso lor piacer volser miei passi,
tosto che 'l vostro viso si nascose."

[Weeping I said, "The present things, with their false pleasure, turned my steps aside, as soon as your countenance was hidden."]

(2.31.34–6)

In contrast with *Inferno* 5, where he is tantalized through his own experiences of courtly love by the "dolci pensier" between Paolo and Francesca, here in *Purgatorio* 31 Dante at long last rejects such present things that bring immediate but false pleasure, "presenti cose" which so attracted Dante that they obscured Beatrice these ten years following her death. The repetition of the formula "disse: 'che pense?' " and the response it ultimately elicits from Dante heralds the return of his "pensare" from all that is false back to Beatrice.

Just before Dante crosses the Lethe, with Beatrice still some distance away from him on the other bank of the stream, he lifts his "beard" as she has requested, and focuses more clearly on her still-veiled face. Beatrice now has an even stronger effect on Dante than when she was before him in her first life. And it is here that "tutte altre cose" ["all other things"] (2.31.86) that had held such attraction for Dante after Beatrice's death become repellent. Dante's remorse before Beatrice's reproofs and her beauty is such that he faints: "… ch'io caddi vinto" ["… that I fell overcome"] (2.31.89).

Of course this is not the first time Dante has fainted in the *Commedia* before a beautiful lady who has been addressing him. In *Inferno* 5, as Francesca's sad tale reached its climax and abruptly ended, the pilgrim was so overcome by the strong spell it apparently cast over him that he fainted: "E caddi come corpo morto cade" ["And I fell as a dead body falls"] (1.5.142).[3]

The verb "cadere" ["to fall"] in the first person singular past remote "caddi" ["I fell"] in *Purgatorio* 31, with Dante as subject, is the first such repetition since *Inferno* 5.[4] Furthermore, in both episodes the "caddi," Dante's fainting, is the result of his reaction to words spoken to him by a beautiful lady, once the object of courtly love, and in both episodes these words follow Dante's response to the question within the formula of repetition "disse: 'che pense?' "

The configuration of the formula of repetition within its configuration in *Purgatorio* 31 signals the reader to turn back to its first occurrence, so let us take that backward glance with all the understanding that comes from having reached the point in the text where Beatrice responds to Dante's wayward behaviour, and more closely scrutinize the context within which it first appears in *Inferno* 5.

It is in the tercet midway through *Inferno* 5 and on the point of encountering Paolo and Francesca that Dante the pilgrim's "pietà" towards the noble lovers of this second circle of Hell is such that he is nearly lost:

> Poscia ch'io ebbi 'l mio dottore udito
> nomar le donne antiche e ' cavalieri,
> pietà mi giunse, e fui *quasi smarrito*.

[When I heard my teacher name the ladies and the knights of old, pity overcame me and I was as one bewildered.]

(1.5.70–2)

Dante's state of being almost lost reflects that described in the first tercet of the *Commedia*,

> Nel mezzo del cammin di nostra vita
> mi ritrovai per una selva oscura,
> ché la diritta via era *smarrita*,

[Midway in the journey of our life I found myself in a dark wood, for the straight way was lost,]

(1.1.1–3)

midway through his life,[5] when that ten-year period in which Beatrice was obscured to him finally reaches its crisis point. Dante's soul is still very much in a precarious state, as he happens upon "que' due che 'nsieme vanno" ["those two that go together"] (1.5.74), Paolo and Francesca with whom he would gladly speak.

Caretti, in his perceptive commentary on *Inferno* 5, highlights the words "pietà" and "amore" contained in Francesca's first utterances to Dante when she requests that he have pity on them (v. 93).[6] Indeed "amore" and "pietà" are the leitmotifs in this second half of the canto. With Francesca's first words her noble breeding is evident despite her fallen state. She displays the qualities of a courtly lady, a lady to whom Dante would feel he must show courtesy, not to mention "pietà," lest he appear "vile" ["base"], lest he appear an enemy of love, one who does not possess the "cor gentil" ["gentle heart"]. And this is precisely the courtly language that Francesca employs as her tale unfolds, from the lady, the *domina* with the "gentle heart," to the pilgrim, here very much the courtly lover.[7]

In the first of the three tercets initiated by the "Amor," Francesca describes in what she presumes to be Guinizzellian terms how Paolo fell in love with her and why, as one with the "cor gentil," it was beyond his control to resist: "Amor, ch'al cor gentil ratto s'apprende, / prese costui de la bella persona ..." ["Love, which is quickly kindled in a gentle heart, seized this one for the fair form ..."] (1.5.100–1); however, Musa argues that what Francesca and the seduced pilgrim do not appear to understand is that Paolo's response has nothing to do with courtly love and the "cor gentil." It is a sensual love, conceived out of Paolo's desire for Francesca's beautiful body.[8] Whether sensual love or Guinizzellian courtly love, the fact remains that they are both sinful. Otherwise Guinizzelli would be in Paradise in the sphere of Venus and not burning for his lust in the fire of the seventh terrace of Purgatory.

In Guinizzelli's famous canzone, *Al cor gentil rempaira sempre amore* [*To the gentle heart love always returns*], he states: "Foco d'amore in gentil cor s'apprende" ["The fire of love is ignited in the gentle heart"] (v. 11), which suggests that any attempt to avoid love will be in vain if one possesses the gentle heart, hardly an excuse in the eyes of God. Guinizzelli's words influenced not only Francesca in the three "Amor" tercets, but also the younger Dante in his sonnet from the *Vita Nuova* xx: *Amore e 'l cor gentil sono una cosa* [*Love and the gentle heart are but one thing*]. It is perhaps not so surprising that Dante the pilgrim and the poet of this sonnet would have tremendous pity for the tragedy that resulted from the love between Paolo and Francesca. It should come as no surprise that Dante the pilgrim would be seduced by Francesca's eloquent presentation of the way love was kindled between herself and Paolo, because in his lost state it seemed much like the way he describes the genesis of love in the second part of his sonnet:

> Bieltade appare in saggia donna pui,
> che piace a gli occhi sì, che dentro al core
> nasce un disio de la cosa piacente;
> e tanto dura talora in costui,
> che fa svegliar lo spirito d'Amore.
> E simil face in donna omo valente.

[Then beauty in a virtuous woman's face pleases the eyes, striking the heart so deep a yearning for the pleasing thing may rise. Sometimes so long it lingers in that place Love's spirit is awakend from his sleep. By a worthy man a woman's moved likewise.]

(*VN* xx)

Dante the poet of this sonnet would also pity Paolo and Francesca's wretched state, because he himself has written what becomes

Francesca's excuse, that love between those of the gentle heart is inevitable when they are offered something pleasing ("cosa piacente"). Dante the pilgrim in *Inferno* 5 seems unable to grasp what that something pleasing really is and mistakenly thinks it is Francesca and her once-beautiful body. He feels pity for Paolo and Francesca because he believes love was destined to result between two of the gentle heart no matter how much they strive to resist.[9] If love between Paolo and Francesca was bound to occur, then how could it be their fault? The poet of the *Commedia* no longer accepts Francesca's argument as once he would. However, the pilgrim has not yet forsaken the tenets of courtly love and the implicit gray areas that surround it or else he would not show such compassion for Paolo and Francesca's plight. So the pilgrim may well consider that it is not their fault. He still believes that love inevitably develops as Francesca describes it: Paolo, being of the gentle heart, was drawn to the beauty in noble ladies, Francesca was such a lady, therefore he cannot but fall in love with her; at the same time, Love also dictates that she who is loved by one of the gentle heart who possesses all Paolo's charms cannot help likewise falling in love with him.

In the tercet following the three "Amor" tercets, the compassionate pilgrim is caught up in the words of Francesca's final "Amor" tercet, which describes their tragic end. His sympathies seem entirely with this damned pair and he fails to understand that their punishment is just. As he pauses with eyes downcast, Virgil inquires: "che pense?" The formula comes in the midst of what might be called a figurative "fall" on the pilgrim's part, before the literal one awaiting him at the end of the canto. For what is Dante thinking? The response is immediate and clear. He is attempting to fathom the complexities of a courtly love and comprehend how "sweet thoughts" and "desire," words typical of courtly love poetry, relate to the "doloroso passo" ["woeful pass"] (v. 114), in this case the sexual act and its consequence: their murder and damnation. Dante the pilgrim's following words to Francesca reflect a curiosity regarding one he seems to consider his equal, from one of the "fedeli" of Love to another, with no hint of negative judgment on his part:

> Poi mi rivolsi a loro e parla' io,
> e cominciai: "Francesca, i tuoi martìri
> a lagrimar mi fanno tristo e pio.
>   Ma dimmi: al tempo d'i dolci sospiri,
> a che e come concedette amore
> che conosceste i dubbiosi disiri?"[10]

[Then I turned again to them, and I began, "Francesca, your torments make me weep for grief and pity; but tell me, in the time of the sweet sights, by what and how did Love grant you to know the dubious desires?"]

(1.5.115–20)

Dante the pilgrim, as an equal to Francesca, has reacted and responded exactly as would any damned soul, fixed on the "tempo d'i dolci sospiri" ["time of the sweet sighs"], in other words the mortal life. To the condemned souls mortal life is remembered as sweet life, that is forever sweet in their memories now that they are in eternal darkness and torment.[11] Indeed Francesca's first words in answer to Dante's question mirror his reference to the "tempo d'i dolci sospiri": "Nessun maggior dolore / che ricordarsi del tempo felice / ne la miseria ..." ["There is no greater sorrow than to recall, in wretchedness, the happy time ..."] (1.5.121–3). Dante's words, his thoughts, when he answers Virgil's question "che pense?", suggest one whose soul is at grave risk as he is lulled into a state of sympathy with these two damned souls, to the point of seeing only the first life as the "sweet one," seduced as he is under the eloquent spell of Francesca the beautiful noble lady.

As the articulate Francesca recounts the day when she and Paolo read of the love of Lancelot and Guinevere, how upon reading the book they both turned pale ("scolorocci il viso" v.131), and unable to control themselves began to imitate what they were reading, so too Dante the pilgrim, now more moved than before, is on the verge of losing control of his senses. With Francesca's final words: "... quel giorno più non vi leggemmo avante" ["... that day we read no more"] (v. 138), all the pieces of the story come together, and Dante can imagine their last moment before the outrage was done to Francesca's beautiful body by her husband when he murdered her: "... la bella persona / che mi fu tolta; e 'l modo ancor m'offende" ["... the fair form that was taken from me – and the way of it afflicts me still"] (vv. 101–2).[12] As Francesca now ceases, Dante is overcome: "... io venni men così com' io morisse. / E *caddi* come corpo morto cade" ["... I swooned, as if in death, and fell as a dead body falls"] (vv. 141–2). As Paolo and Francesca died, so too Dante faints as if dying, and falls both literally and figuratively as one dead. He falls before the first soul with whom he interacts on his journey, a fall which almost leads to the death of his soul, at this very early juncture on his journey to salvation. But, although Dante "fell as a dead body falls," unlike Paolo and Francesca he regains his senses in the very next verse, verse 1 of *Inferno* 6. Dante recovers from his fall and moves on, but perhaps only because

Francesca, like Beatrice, is no longer physically before him, no longer exercising the control which as a seductive courtly lady she could continue to hold over him by her presence.

Readers of the *Vita Nuova* are familiar with the episode of Dante turning pale and losing his senses before the gentle and beautiful Beatrice. And Dante sees her for the first time since her death in 1290 in *Purgatorio* 30 continuing into *Purgatorio* 31 without a break, with the repetition of the formula "disse: 'che pense?'" within its configuration in the latter canto. Dante should have remained true to what he had ultimately learned from his experiences by the end of the *Vita Nuova*, to continue to keep Beatrice and all she represented uppermost in his thoughts, all the more now that she has passed on to the next life, to her "seconda etade" (2.30.125). But, once Beatrice was no longer near, once he could no longer gain sustenance from her beautiful visage, her "volto: / mostrando li occhi giovanetti a lui" ["countenance: showing him my youthful eyes"] (2.30.121–2), as she points out:

> "... fu' io a lui men cara e men gradita;
> e volse i passi suoi per via non vera,
> imagini di ben seguendo false,
>   che nulla promission rendono intera."

["... I was less dear and less pleasing to him and he turned his steps along a way not true, following false images of good, which pay no promise in full."]

(2.30.129–32)

Dante fell so low:

> "Tanto giù *cadde*, che tutti argomenti
> a la salute sua eran già corti,
> fuor che mostrarli le perdute genti."

["He fell so low that all means for his salvation were now short, save to show him the lost people."]

(2.30.136–8)

Dante's fall during the ten-year interval between Beatrice's death in 1290 and the spring of 1300 requires that this journey be undertaken. It is only by being shown the "perdute genti" that Dante can be saved. And what happens when Dante encounters the first of the "perdute genti" beyond Minos? He was so moved by Francesca's defence of herself and her sin that he literally fell before her: "caddi come corpo morto cade" ["I fell as a dead body falls"] (1.5.142).

Through Dante's love for Beatrice, by the end of the *Vita Nuova* he should have learned to distinguish between true images of good and false images that only appear good, and he should have remembered what he had learned. The harsh and bitter tone of Beatrice's pointed reproach in these two cantos is easily understood when we realize that Dante ignored or forgot for ten-years what he had learned after her death, a ten year period which culminated in his lost state in the dark wood. And then, although Beatrice journeyed down into Limbo to urge Virgil to rescue him, Dante fell at the feet of the first soul encountered on his way to salvation, a soul who just happened to be a "courtly lady."[13]

As *Purgatorio* 31 opens, Dante is still across the Lethe from Beatrice, with his memory intact, with Beatrice demanding that he openly acknowledge his sin, that he publicly confess his sins of the last ten years: "dì, dì se questo è vero; a tanta accusa / tua confession conviene esser congiunta" ["Say, say, if this is true; to such an accusation your confession must be joined"] (2.31.5–6).[14] Dante's attempts at enunciating a confession are in vain. The formula within its configuration is repeated here, indicating that Dante's voice, which should have uttered a confession, "si *spense*" ["became extinct"], that Beatrice, who did not countenance this silence on Dante's part, "*disse: 'Che pense?'*" ["said: 'What are you thinking?'"], and that before Beatrice allows Dante to respond she adds that there is no reason for this silence since Dante still has these memories, they have not yet been "*offense*" ["destroyed"] by the waters of the Lethe.

After Dante voices a weak "sì," he is overcome and breaks down. His tears and his sighs do not allow him to utter any further word of response, allowing Beatrice to continue her charge. She demands to know what ditches ("fossi" v. 25), what chains ("catene" v. 25) blocked Dante on his way to salvation. Furthermore, what attractions presented themselves to him such that he was led to desire them: "… quali agevolezze o quali avanzi / ne la fronte de li altri si mostraro, / per che dovessi lor passeggiare anzi?" ["… what attractions or what advantages were displayed on the brow of others, that you were obliged to dally before them?"] (2.31.28–30). Implicit in these questions is of course a condemnation of Dante's wayward behaviour during the preceding ten years, which is no doubt reflected in Dante's backsliding in both Hell and Purgatory while under Virgil's guidance, some unnecessary lingering on his journey back to Beatrice. Beatrice recalls a simpler time, back in the *Vita Nuova* when Dante's desires for her led him to love the good: "… 'Per entro i mie' disiri, / che ti menavano ad amar lo bene'" ["… 'Within your desires of me that were leading you to love that Good …"] (2.31.22–3).

It is not the intention here to wade into the wider debate regarding Dante's sinful behaviour in the 1290s and whether his backsliding was principally moral, intellectual, religious, or amorous.[15] Suffice it to say that the repetition of the formula within its configuration along with the repetition of "caddi" suggests that the reader not overlook the role Dante's amorous escapades played in his backsliding. Can Dante's encounter with Francesca be literally a ditch or chains ("fosso" or "catene") which block the pilgrim in his military-like advance down through Hell?[16] While Francesca did not actually block Dante's way, as a distraction she slowed him down, temporarily causing him to change course and lose precious time. That encounter is the first major one in the *Commedia*, encompassing some seventy verses of *Inferno* 5, plus the duration of the "dead" faint, during which time his mind had "closed itself" (1.6.1) and we do not know how long the dead faint lasted before he gained his senses. Longer, one imagines, than had the lady not appeared young and beautiful, had she been deformed and unappealing like the "Femmina Balba" as she first appeared to him in his dream in *Purgatorio* 19. Further, there is Beatrice's use of the expression "passeggiare anzi" (v. 30). Michele Barbi, citing passages in which the expression is found in the *Decameron*, interprets "passeggiare anzi" as the lovers passing back and forth below the windows of the beloved's house, in order to show their devotion to her: "Passeggiare anzi; come 'passar davanti' stanno a indicare l'uso degli innamorati per dimostrare il proprio affetto alla donna amata e per sodisfare il desiderio di vederla" ["To dally before; like to 'pass before' describes the custom of the male lovers of demonstrating their affection for the beloved lady and of satisfying their desire to see her"].[17]

While Dante was concentrating on pursuing other women in the 1290s, idling his days and nights beneath their windows, surely he was not thinking about Beatrice, or about his journey back to her and to salvation. He was wasting his time, as he wasted his time before Francesca.[18] Indeed the very expression "passeggiare anzi" suggests a movement which goes nowhere. Constantly going back and forth brings one no further along on the way.

Dante finally utters a confession after Beatrice's last words, which were "passeggiare anzi":

> Piangendo dissi: "Le presenti cose
> col falso lor piacer volser miei passi,
> tosto che 'l vostro viso si nascose."

[Weeping I said, "The present things, with their false pleasure, turned my steps aside, as soon as your countenance was hidden."]

(2.31.34–6)

As soon as Beatrice had died, Dante began his "passeggiare anzi" before "present things with their false charm," and these "present things" turned his steps ("passi") away from what had been forward steps towards salvation under Beatrice's guidance. But with Beatrice no longer present, Dante strayed from his course even while still moving, with his "passeggiare anzi." He no longer allowed himself to be guided by Beatrice now on high, but instead by other ladies, still in the flesh, whom he desired to look down on him mercifully from on high, from their windows above.

Is it possible to read Dante's brief "dalliance" with Francesca into Beatrice's indictment of Dante's past bad behaviour? Only in the most oblique sense. Singleton suggests that Beatrice's use of the term "piacer" within the context of the "presenti cose" is meant to be ambiguous, signifying both "beauty" and, like the Provençal term "plazer," "charm" or "attraction." He further points out that the same ambiguity exists in the Paolo and Francesca episode in *Inferno* 5.104 with regard to Paolo's "piacer."[19] In both instances, whether the meaning is "beauty" or "charm" or "attraction," it seduces the individual from the true way, to a "smarrimento," in Paolo and Francesca's case to their death and damnation, and in Dante's case to risk of the same in the dark wood: "... mi ritrovai per una selva oscura, / che la diritta via era smarrita" ["... I found myself in a dark wood, for the straight way was lost"] (1.1.2–3).

In response to Dante's confession, Beatrice warns him that when next he hears the siren call of earthly pleasures he must be stronger: "... e perché altra volta, / udendo le serene, sie più forte ..." ["... and another time, hearing the Sirens, may be stronger ..."] (2.31.44–5). The only previous appearance of the word "serena" occurred in *Purgatorio* 19 with the siren call of the "Femmina Balba": "Io son dolce serena ..." ["I am the sweet Siren ..."] (2.19.19), in Dante's second night's dream in Purgatory. The "Femmina Balba" is representative of the sins that Dante the pilgrim is about to encounter on the upper three terraces of Purgatory: avarice, gluttony, and lust. Of these three sins it is lust which would be Dante's siren call. Indeed the only pain Dante feels on this journey is the pain of the fire through which he must pass before he leaves the seventh and last terrace behind him.[20] The "Femmina Balba" as she first appeared to Dante was as repellent as Francesca was appealing, and as inarticulate as Francesca was eloquent. However, as he continued to gaze upon her, her tongue became fluent, she straightened up and her face was transformed into that of a courtly lady. And her song was so beautiful that it would have been difficult for Dante to reject her had Virgil not intervened, at the behest of a lady (whose possible identity will be discussed later). Dante would have succumbed to the siren call of the "Femmina

Balba" as he would have yielded to Casella's song of love, had Virgil not intervened in the former instance and Cato in the latter. But the beautiful courtly lady to whom Dante does succumb, whose voice ensnares the pilgrim, is neither the "Femmina Balba" nor the Lady Philosophy of Casella's love song. She is the first one encountered on the journey, Francesca, whose beauty was so great that her brother-in-law fell madly in love with her, despite the inherent risks, and whose eloquence is such that when she finishes her tragic story, Dante falls in a death-like faint before her. The eloquent and beautiful Francesca best embodies the type of lady whose voice can, and did, turn a vulnerable Dante from his appointed path; hence Beatrice warns him that he must stop weeping and better fortify himself when next he hears such "serene."

As Beatrice proceeds to describe how Dante should have followed her "in contraria parte" ["in opposite direction"] (v. 47), her "piacer," her "beauty," her "attraction," is juxtaposed with that "piacer" of the courtly lovers in *Inferno* 5, or the false "piacer" of the "presenti cose," which now by Dante's admission were the siren call that he followed after Beatrice's death:

> "Mai non t'appresentò natura o arte
> *piacer*, quanto le belle membra in ch'io
> rinchiusa fui, e che so' 'n terra sparte;
>   e se 'l sommo *piacer* sì ti fallio
> per la mia morte, qual cosa mortale
> dovea poi trarre te nel suo disio?"

["Never did nature or art present to you beauty so great as the fair members in which I was enclosed and now are scattered to dust. And if the highest beauty thus failed you by my death, what mortal thing should then have drawn you into desire for it?"]

(2.31.49–54)

Just as it was Beatrice's "piacer" which first ensnared Dante, again in its ambiguous meaning of "beauty," "charm," and "attraction,"[21] Dante is likewise subject to the "piacer" in others and is briefly ensnared by the "piacer" of Paolo and Francesca. But he seems unable to distinguish between the true "piacer" of Beatrice, which he should have kept uppermost in his thoughts after his death, and the superficial, false "piacer" of the "serene," one of whom is unmasked as such by Virgil in the "Femmina Balba" episode of *Purgatorio* 19.

Since Dante was unable to distinguish between true and false beauty, after Beatrice's death in 1290s and the departure of her "belle membra" from his sight, Dante, being of the "cor gentil," was attracted to the "piacer," to the "bellezza" of ladies like Francesca. Indeed there is little difference between what attracted Dante to other ladies in the 1290s and what attracted Paolo to Francesca. In the tradition of Guinizzelli's best-known *canzone, Al cor gentil rempaira sempre amore* [*To the gentle heart love always returns*], both Paolo and Dante possessed the "cor gentil," thereby rendering them helpless before the power of love. And Francesca's description of Paolo's attraction to her beauty could have been Dante's: "Amor, ch'al cor gentil ratto s'apprende, / prese costui de la bella persona / che mi fu tolta ..." ["Love, which is quickly kindled in a gentle heart, seized this one for the fair form that was taken from me ..."] (1.5.100–1). But there is a great difference, as Dante is in the process of learning, between Francesca's "bella persona," which was suddenly taken from her when she was murdered, and Beatrice's once "belle membra," taken from her when she suddenly died, still in the flower of youth. It is the difference between falseness, embodied in the surface beauty of the "Femmina Balba," and truth, embodied in the genuine beauty of Beatrice, reflecting the splendour of God.

Dante's fall was immediate after Beatrice's soul was no longer "rinchiusa" ["enclosed"] in her "belle membra" ["fair members"]. Not only did he betray Beatrice by no longer following her, but he also turned to other young women:

> "Non ti dovea gravar le penne in giuso,
> ad aspettar più colpo, o pargoletta
> o altra novità con sì breve uso."

["Young damsel or other novelty of such brief enjoyment should not have weighed down your wings to await more shots."]

(2.31.58–60)

Although scholars point out that the reference to "pargoletta" (referred to specifically in Dante's *Rime* 87 and 89) is purposefully vague, perhaps there is more to "pargoletta" within the context of the *Commedia* than the generic reference to the ladies Dante loved during the 1290s.[22]

If one follows the signal of the formula of repetition within its configuration of rhyme words plus the "caddi" in this episode back to the Paolo and Francesca episode in *Inferno* 5, is it possible that "pargoletta" actually makes an appearance in the *Commedia*? If so then "pargoletta" in the guise of Francesca came forth right at the moment of Dante's very first encounter with a condemned soul, right at the onset of his journey back to Beatrice. By delaying with this "pargo-letta" and then remaining in a "dead" faint because of the power of her presence over him, Dante took longer than was necessary to fly up and reach Beatrice on high, for with his "wings weighed down" ("le penne in giuso") he was in no shape to carry on at that precise juncture.

As Dante fixes his eyes upon Beatrice, now even more beautiful than she had been in life, he finally rejects the other ladies to whom he had turned in the 1290s:

> Di penter sì mi punse ivi l'ortica,
> che di tutte altre cose qual mi torse
> più nel suo amor, più mi si fé nemica.

[And the nettle of remorse so stung me there that of all other things, that which had most turned me to love of it became most hateful to me.]

(2.31.85–7)

To all of which Dante had turned after Beatrice's fair members were scattered in dust; all those seemingly beautiful ladies who had capti-vated Dante and obscured his love for Beatrice have lost their power to entice him, just as the "Femmina Balba," first so seductive in Dante's eyes, became repellent once her fraud was unmasked.

The remorse Dante feels for his sins is so great that he faints: "ch'io *caddi* vinto" ["that I fell overcome"] (2.31.89), but this time his loss of consciousness is entirely different from the other occasion back in *Inferno* 5. After Francesca's seductive story of how that day their death at the hands of her husband put an end to their reading, Dante, feel-ing something of what they were feeling, fainted and fell as one who had literally died, as indeed his soul was at death's door ("caddi come corpo morte cade" ["I fell as a dead body falls"] 1.5.142). But here before Beatrice it is not a question of the soul dying. It is the sin-ful life that is about to die, so that when Dante returns to his senses he is reborn, innocent and pure, in the waters of the Lethe.

The repetition of the formula "disse: 'che pense?'" within its con-figuration of rhyme words along with "caddi" draws together two episodes in the *Commedia*, which are at some considerable distance textually. And it is only by reading of Dante's "reunion" with Beat-rice and then taking the retrospective journey back to the Francesca episode that one understands the peril Dante's soul was in under the spell of her siren call, his pilgrimage on a course to shipwreck after he had barely left port. When Dante lapsed through remaining trans-fixed by the pointless fray between Sinon and Master Adam in *Inferno*

30, Virgil was there to scold the truant pilgrim; otherwise even more time would have elapsed before they moved on to the tenth *bolgia*. When Dante was wasting time, "fixed and attentive" before Casella's love song in *Purgatorio* 2, Cato was there to hasten him and the others along their way. When the dreaming Dante was seduced before the "Femmina Balba," Virgil, urged by a lady, was at hand to expose the ugly truth of her, after which Dante finally awakened so that Virgil and Dante could continue their journey. Herman Gmelin has suggested that the lady who entreated Virgil to expose the "Femmina Balba" was Beatrice.[23] If the lady was Beatrice, and I believe that she was, then for a second time Beatrice has interceded on Dante's behalf. The first was when she went down into Limbo to urge Virgil to rescue Dante from near death ("la morte che 'l combatte" ["the death that assails him"] 1.2.107). Beatrice intervened to save Dante's soul from death because "amor" moved her ("amor mi mosse" 1.2.72). Beatrice begins the line with "amor" just as Francesca did at the start of the three tercets in *Inferno* 5.[24]

By pursuing the alternate journey across textual space from *Purgatorio* 31 back to *Inferno* 5, it is possible to pinpoint the cause of Dante's fall, from "ch'io *caddi* vinto" before Beatrice to "e caddi come corpo morto cade" before Francesca, within the context of their "amor." Beatrice's "amor" moves her to rescue Dante from death, the death of his soul. Francesca's "amor" caused both her physical and her spiritual death, a death Dante himself narrowly escaped at the end of the canto. But Beatrice was not so quick this time to rescue Dante as she was in *Inferno* 2. This time Dante had to prove to Beatrice that he was capable of recognizing why he was prone to fall, something Beatrice is determined to make Dante acknowledge when she says "what are you thinking?": "disse: 'che pense?'" This time Dante will not answer "Oh lasso, quanti dolci pensier" ["Alas! How many sweet thoughts ..."] as once he did when Virgil asked him that same question in *Inferno* 5.111. He is beginning to fathom his own error. And when Dante's "amor" (2.31.87) for all that is false is finally crushed, the repetition of "caddi" with Dante as subject occurs, for the first time since *Inferno* 5, destroying the old Dante for the new, who has now turned his back on the siren call, as he will prepare to rise with Beatrice to the stars.

5 Linguistic Patterns and Internal Structure in Five Cantos in the *Inferno*: From Political *degni* to Political Sinners

PART ONE

When Dante meets Ciacco in *Inferno* 6 he is curious to find out whether the political worthies of the early and mid-thirteenth century, Farinata degli Uberti, Tegghiaio Aldobrandi, Iacopo Rusticucci, Arrigo, and Mosca de' Lamberti, also reside in Hell or if they have been saved. With Ciacco's response that they are all in Hell, but much deeper down than Ciacco, the reader is prepared for a group of episodes which will delineate these individuals as politicians. While it is obvious to the readers of the *Commedia* that they comprise a group, being defined as such in *Inferno* 6, it is the thesis of this chapter that they are also defined within another larger group by means of a series of signposts which the reader is invited to follow on a concurrent journey.

The poet adopts formulas of linguistic repetition which guide the reader from one pertinent episode to the next, and in so doing he accentuates their links in an indisputable, yet not readily apparent manner. He introduces words or phrases in *Inferno* 6 which are repeated in the Farinata episode in *Inferno* 10, or in *Inferno* 16 with Tegghiaio and Iacopo. But in a further instance when Dante meets Catalano and Loderingo in *Inferno* 23, linguistic formulas are also present. This encounter between Dante and these two hypocrites in *Inferno* 23 is not one that *Inferno* 6 anticipates. Why were Catalano and Loderingo not named by Dante in *Inferno* 6 along with the others? Because unlike the other politicians mentioned they were neither "degni" ["worthy"] nor did they put their minds to "ben far" ["doing good"] when they ruled Florence. For that matter they were not even Florentine. Nonetheless the presence of linguistic formulas here, which act as a beacon shining a light on these two souls, call on the reader to bring them into the equation when considering the political worthies of the previous cantos. Likewise, with the linguistic formulas adopted by the poet linking the Catalano and Loderingo episode with the Mosca de' Lamberti episode in *Inferno* 28, the reader is induced to investigate what it is that Catalano and Loderingo have in common with Mosca, something he/she might otherwise have missed. In total I have isolated nine formulas which function as canto links: "dir chi tu se'" ["to tell who are you"], "de la gola" ["of gluttony"/"of the throat"], "nel dolce mondo" ["in the sweet world"], "guardommi un poco e poi" ["he looked at me for a moment and then"], "O Tosco" ["O Tuscan"], "tosca" ["Tuscan"], "aspetta" ["wait"], "quando fuor giunti" ["when they had reached"], and "per l'aura fosca" ["through the dusky air"], formulas which will be surveyed after an examination of the context in which they occur.

Ciacco is only the second soul with whom Dante converses on his journey to salvation, and Dante is not getting off to a particularly good start. He has only just returned to his senses at the beginning of this canto, after having been overcome by Francesca (as he had been overcome by any number of ladies in the previous ten years), when he is moved to weep ("ch'a lagrimar mi 'nvita" v. 59) before the anguish ("angoscia" v. 43) of Ciacco's condition as a glutton condemned to the third circle of Hell. Although Ciacco's sin of gluttony does not fascinate Dante as did Francesca's sin, perhaps Ciacco can still be of use, by providing information that for Dante is even more intriguing than anything Francesca could yield. The unknown Ciacco stresses that he was still alive at the time of Dante's birth, and apparently he was still somehow involved in the civic affairs of Florence up to Dante's adolescence.[1] Just as a younger might seek from an elder a glimpse into ages long past, so Dante hopes that Ciacco can tell him what lies ahead for the divided city of Florence. More important for the concurrent journey which is about to commence, Dante is seized by a great desire to look back and learn what became of his political forebears:

"Farinata e 'l Tegghiaio che fuor sì degni,
Iacopo Rusticucci, Arrigo e 'l Mosca
e li altri ch'a ben far puoser li 'ngegni,
    Dimmi ove sono e fa ch'io li conosca;
ché gran disio mi stringe di savere
se 'l ciel li addolcia o lo 'nferno li attosca."

["Farinata and Tegghiaio, who were so worthy, Jacopo Rusticucci, Arrigo, and Mosca, and the others who set their minds on doing good, tell me where they are and give me to know them, for great desire urges me to learn whether Heaven soothes or Hell envenoms them."]

(1.6.79–84)

Dante establishes from the onset that he has the highest regard for these six individuals, described as "degni" and as having put their minds to "ben far." To Dante the pilgrim the three realms of the afterlife are unfamiliar territory and he has not yet learned that souls are not always where one might expect to find them; nonetheless he suspects that these political worthies might have some kind of taint, that even though they were good politicians, they were not necessarily good Christians.[2] Although in the spring of 1300 Dante himself is immersed in Florentine politics, his question reflects an awareness on his part that politicians, even such noble ones as these, might have been distracted from giving the necessary care to their immortal souls, care that at the very least would have allowed a last-minute conversion, bringing them to Antepurgatory instead of to Hell. Ciacco confirms Dante's doubts by relating that they are among Hell's darkest souls:

E quelli: "Ei son tra l'anime più nere;
diverse colpe giù li grava al fondo:
se tanto scendi, là i potrai vedere."

[And he, "They are among the blackest souls, and different faults weigh them down toward the bottom; if you descend that far, there you can see them."]

(1.6.85–7)

Dante will descend that far and encounter each one, with the exception of Arrigo,[3] in precisely the same order in which he named them when he put his initial question to Ciacco.

How could Dante the pilgrim have known the order in which he would encounter these souls when he listed their names in his question? He could not possibly know where they would be, and even hoped that they might be in Paradise. Yet, here is a unique moment in the *Commedia*, where the pilgrim in essence foresees the order in which he will face specifically named souls. There is an explanation. Dante the pilgrim's ordering is one that follows a chronology of events well known to him, events when each of these politicians dominated the political scene in Florence looking back over the earlier two-thirds of the thirteenth century: from Farinata at the Council of Empoli just after the defeat of the Florentine Guelfs at Montaperti in 1260, to Tegghiaio, whose voice before Montaperti went unheeded, to Iacopo Rusticucci, renowned for his peace initiatives that culminated in the rule of the *Primo Popolo* in the 1250s, to the days just before the murder of Buondelmonte in 1216 when Mosca advised that he be killed.

One might even include Ciacco in this chronology. After all, Ciacco is the first Florentine to appear in the *Commedia* and he pronounces on civic affairs in Florence, reflecting his own involvement therein, just like the "degni" lower down. Ciacco's pronouncements reveal him as one who knows the Florence of Dante, having lived his span of years nearest to Dante's own time. That Ciacco lived in a time contemporary with Dante is a point he stresses with his first words to him:

"O tu che se' per questo 'nferno tratto,"
mi disse, "riconoscimi, se sai:
tu fosti, prima ch'io disfatto, fatto."

["O you that are led through this Hell," he said to me, "recognize me if you can: you were made before I was unmade."]

(1.6.40–2)

Of course the location of individual souls in Hell should have nothing to do with a chronology of events. They are where they are based on their sins, whose gravity increases the further Dante descends into Hell to fathom his own sins. But this political context embodies also a journey back in time, back to an earlier age when Florence ironically was less degenerate than in Dante the pilgrim's time, precisely while he is plumbing the depths of human sin.

The first of the five Florentine politicians whom Dante names and subsequently meets is Farinata degli Uberti. He is relegated to the sixth circle of the epicureans of *Inferno* 10 and establishes first that Dante too is of the "nobil patrïa" of Florence and then, once Dante stands before his tomb, with his initial words, "Chi fuor li maggior tui?" ["Who were your ancestors?"] (v. 42), that he and Dante were not contemporaries, that he was of an earlier age than Dante. If Farinata, unlike Ciacco, was unmade before Dante was made, through his neighbour who shares the tomb, Cavalcante de' Cavalcanti, Farinata can also be linked directly to Dante and those of his generation. While Cavalcante was one of the leading Guelfs and thus opposed to the Ghibelline leader Farinata, he was also the father-in-law of Farinata's daughter Beatrice, through her marriage to his son: Dante's "primo amico," Guido Cavalcanti.[4] Dante's dialogue with Farinata takes up almost all of the canto, save for the mini-drama played out between

Dante and Cavalcante in the middle. This consists in the first section of a fiercely partisan debate between two opposing politicians, one Guelf and one Ghibelline; and in the second section of two individuals who realize that they have more in common than first thought, owing to the perpetually stormy nature of Florentine politics. Farinata's sin of epicureanism could have been addressed in their conversation, but such weighty discussion might have marginalized the political debate.[5] Thus explicit consideration of the immortal soul forms no part of the interchange between two obsessed politicians who play out in Hell the same divisive politics rampant in Florence and cut to the quick in their first exchange:

> ... poi disse: "Fieramente furo avversi
> a me e a miei primi e a mia parte,
> sì che per due fïate li dispersi."
>   "S'ei fur cacciati, ei tornar d'ogne parte,"
> rispuos'io a lui, "l'una e l'altra fiata;
> ma i vostri non appreser ben quell'arte."

[... then he said, "They were fiercely adverse to me and to my forebears and to my party, so that twice over I scattered them." "If they were driven forth, they returned from every quarter, both times," I answered him, "but yours have not learned that art well."]

(1.10.46–51)

This verbal skirmish is not unlike that between Master Adam and Sinon in *Inferno* 30, which interests Dante too much, for which he is reprimanded by Virgil. Here, however, Dante's behaviour is more significant because he is not simply the witness to a skirmish, but an active participant, reflecting his own participation in the partisan politics of Florence in 1300.

Farinata's final volley must wait because Cavalcante breaks in to ask after the whereabouts of his son Guido, and why he is not at Dante's side. Suddenly the episode takes on a poignancy within a contemporary context. Guido is no longer at Dante's side because now, in 1300, their friendship has cooled and is not what it had been when Dante dedicated the *Vita Nuova* to him, his "primo amico."[6] And in two month's time Dante will distance himself even further from Guido. As prior Dante will vote with his colleagues to exile Guido to Sarzana and rid Florence of him and other leading Whites and Blacks in the vain hope that Florence will thus find some peace from factional extremes.[7] Guido will contract malaria while in Sarzana and be dead by the end of August of that same year.[8] But all that is still some months in the future. In the meantime Guido is very much alive, and thus Cavalcante is mistaken when he takes Dante's "ebbe" to signify that Guido's eyes no longer see the sweet light of day, that he in fact is already dead. That Dante remained silent and did not correct Cavalcante in his confusion is only understood later when, with Farinata's response that souls are aware of future events but blind to present ones, Dante explains his hesitation before Cavalcante. He said nothing because he assumed that if souls were allowed a future vision they were also allowed to see the present and therefore Cavalcante should have been well aware that his son was still alive. Later in the canto Dante recognizes that through his inaction he was at fault in needlessly letting Cavalcante believe that his son was dead ("Allor, come di mia colpa compunto / dissi ..." ["Then, compunctious for my fault, I said ..."] v. 109).

It is difficult to say exactly how these initial exchanges with Cavalcante regarding Guido (and later in the canto Dante's recognition that he unwittingly led Cavalcante to believe that Guido was already dead) can be reconciled with Dante the prior's indirect role in causing Guido's death some months hence. What is clear is that a shift occurs with the interruption of Cavalcante, from a glimpse of partisan politics between Guelf and Ghibelline of almost a half-century before to the question of whether or not Guido Cavalcanti is dead right now in the spring of 1300. This cannot help but turn the attention of the reader, who knows what awaits Guido, to factional politics between White Guelfs and Black Guelfs and exile and death and the active role Dante the politician plays in unfolding events.

When Farinata resumes speaking after Cavalcante's interruption, to return the volley, he compares Dante's fate, when his White Guelfs will lose control of the government, to that of his own descendants, all exiled from Florence:

> ... e sé continüando al primo detto,
> "S'elli han quell'arte," disse, "male appresa,
> ciò mi tormenta più che questo letto.
>   Ma non cinquanta volte fia raccesa
> la faccia de la donna che qui regge,
> che tu saprai quanto quell'arte pesa."

[... "and if," he said, continuing his first discourse, "they have ill learned that art, that fact torments me more than this bed. But the face of the Lady who rules here will not be kindled fifty times before you shall know how much that art weighs."]

(1.10.76–81)

If Farinata's descendants have lost the ability, the "arte," of returning to Florence from exile, so fifty months on in the year 1304, Dante (himself now an exile) will appreciate how the frustrated desire to return to Florence will likewise gnaw at him. In fact in the early years of exile he does make common cause with other White Guelfs in the hope of returning to Florence, but they will fail miserably, and by June of 1304, the month to which Farinata refers, Dante will have severed all ties with them.[9]

With Farinata worrying about his offspring and about why after all these many years they still are not allowed to return to Florence, this episode's defining moment in time becomes clear. In September of 1260 the pride of Florence was shattered when the Florentine Guelfs were routed at the Battle of Montaperti at the hands of the Tuscan Ghibellines, and their leader Farinata degli Uberti. The loss of Florentine lives was enormous, and the Arbia river ran red with blood. For Dante's generation memories of the massacre at Montaperti are still all too fresh, and so the Uberti, descendants of Farinata, must continue to pay the price. But Farinata is quick to point out that Montaperti was not his responsibility alone. He was only one of many Ghibellines involved. However, he was alone at the Council of Empoli where the victorious Ghibellines convened shortly after their victory. The Ghibellines of Tuscany were urging that for the good of their faction Florence be destroyed while they had the opportunity. Farinata the Florentine alone faced down his fellow Ghibellines and declared that he would take up his sword to defend Florence against his own faction, fighting alone if necessary.[10] In order to preserve harmony among the ranks of the Ghibellines, the others reluctantly agreed to spare Florence. Farinata is "degno" because in the face of factional bloodshed at its most extreme, he looked beyond partisan politics, beyond what would have been best for his fellow Ghibellines, to the well-being, indeed the very survival, of Florence.[11]

Political rivalry between Farinata and Dante is now over, as Dante expresses his wish that Farinata's seed be allowed to return to Florence one day: "Deh, se riposi mai vostra semenza" ["Ah, so may your seed find repose"] (v. 94). What remains after Farinata's departure is the echo of his words to Dante, that he like the Uberti will also experience exile from Florence, and both Dante the pilgrim and we ourselves are left with the echo that there may not be all that much difference between Dante and the first of the "degni" we encounter. Farinata's words so affect Dante that Virgil describes him as "so lost": "Perché se' tu sì smarrito?" ["Why are you so lost?"] (v. 125). The last time "smarrito" appeared in the text was in *Inferno* 5 when Dante was "almost lost" ("quasi smarrito" v. 72) after hearing the names of the noble lovers in the second circle of the lustful, lovers for whom Dante, himself a courtly lover, had much empathy. His first encounter with one of the "degni" has left him "lost" because Farinata foresees that Dante's politics will lead him to exile and, like the once great Uberti, he will try in vain to return to Florence.[12]

Farinata is the first of those worthy politicians whom Dante encounters, described by Dante in *Inferno* 6 as one of the six "degni" who put his mind to "ben far," to do well for the citizenry of Florence. If we follow Dante's journey, within a political context a journey back in time, then the first of those politicians is perforce the one closest to Dante's own age and accordingly the last of the line of "degni" to enter the political stage. In the forty-year period which led up to 1260 there were six "degni." If Farinata is the last of the worthy politicians and his time ended shortly after 1260, then the final forty years of the century will see no more "degni," no more politicians like Farinata who will put their minds to "ben far" and fight if necessary for the well-being of Florence before that of their own faction. If the age has declined even since Farinata's day, already fraught with partisan violence, what does that tell us about the world in which Dante must operate as a politician now in the spring of 1300?

While it is not my intention here to wade into Dante's political world in the years 1300 and 1301, there is a tangential relationship between what that world exacts from Dante as politician and the question Dante as pilgrim puts to Ciacco in *Inferno* 6 regarding the "degni" who put their minds to "ben far." The words "ben far" resurface in *Inferno* 15 now with Brunetto Latini as spokesperson, and they frame a very similar discourse:[13]

"Ma quello ingrato popolo maligno
che discese di Fiesole ab antico,
e tiene ancor del monte e del macigno,
Ti si farà, per tuo *ben far*, nimico ..."

["But that thankless, malignant people, who of old came down from Fiesole, and still smack of the mountain and the rock, will make themselves an enemy to you because of your good deeds ..."]

(1.15.61–4)

This passage forms part of Brunetto's prediction of Dante's imminent exile, a prediction that no longer unsettles Dante as it did in the Farinata episode, obviously because he has heard it before.

Noteworthy here though is the reason why Dante will incur the wrath of a certain segment of his fellow citizens. Here there is no mincing of words. In the year 1300, at virtually the same time as Dante the pilgrim in *Inferno* 6 is evoking the past political worthies who put their minds to "ben far," as prior of Florence he is endeavouring to emulate their politics. Sapegno in his gloss on "tuo ben far" refers to Dante's unwillingness to put factional hatred before the good of Florence: "... del tuo onesto operare di cittadino, estraneo agli odi di parte ..." ["... of your honest conduct as a citizen, having nothing to do with factional hatreds ..."].[14] Dante's own "ben far" is apparent in his vote in June of 1300 to exile his "primo amico" and fellow White Guelf, Guido Cavalcanti, to Sarzana, along with the other factional leaders, in an attempt to bring peace to his city.

It appears that there has thus arisen on the political horizon at the very end of the 1200s another "degno," another politician who put his mind to "ben far": Dante himself. With the repetition of "ben far" in *Inferno* 15, it is almost as if Dante's own politics has placed him among the other six "degni," now the seventh in their company, just as his poetry placed him among the five ancient poets of Limbo, temporarily to become the sixth in their group.

Indeed in the subsequent canto Dante is sorely tempted to join two of the six "degni," Tegghiaio Aldobrandi and Iacopo Rusticucci, who like Brunetto Latini also dwell among the sodomites of the seventh circle. They recognize Dante as a Florentine by his clothing and wish to detain him out of a curiosity to converse with a fellow citizen who appears to be moving alive and securely through Hell: "... che i vivi piedi / così sicuro per lo 'nferno freghi" ["... that thus securely move living feet through Hell"] (1.16.32–3). Dante might not have stopped, had Virgil not insisted that these souls were worthy of his courtesy. The approach of these two "degni" is reminiscent of that of the first "degno": Farinata. Farinata also recognized that Dante was Florentine, but from his speech not his apparel, and likewise hoped that the still living Dante might pause in his journey through Dis, so that he might learn more from this fellow Tuscan: "O Tosco che per la città del foco / vivo ten vai ..." ["O Tuscan, who go alive through the city of fire ..."] (1.10.22–3). In *Inferno* 10 as well Dante stops and addresses Farinata, but only after some urging from Virgil. Even before Iacopo Rusticucci identifies himself, the reader who recognizes that the stage is set in almost exactly the same way as in the Farinata episode might already be anticipating another encounter with one of the "degni." When Iacopo reveals his name and that of one of the others distinguished as "degno," Tegghiaio Aldobrandi, and the greatly admired Guido Guerra,[15] Dante the pilgrim's reaction is in stark contrast to his reluctant stance before Farinata. With Farinata, even after his identity was revealed Virgil still had to coax Dante to his tomb. In the case of these three politicians Dante's reaction is immediate. He would have jumped down into the fire to embrace them, only held back by his fear of being burned and cooked by it.

In juxtaposition with *Inferno* 10 where Farinata's sin is all but swept aside, here the *contrapasso* of the three politicians' sin is ever present. The reader is aware that while Iacopo speaks, he forms part of a wheel with the other two shades, a wheel that rolls along keeping pace with Dante (who walks with Virgil safely on the embankment above), greased and naked like wrestlers with their necks always turning so that they can maintain eye contact with Dante. On the one hand the poet imprints in the reader's consciousness the image of the constantly turning necks of the sinners while Iacopo converses with Dante, reflecting literally at every turn the sin itself. On the other hand the words that Dante the pilgrim directs to Iacopo, and by extension to Tegghiaio and Guido, are not full of reproach as they were to Farinata. Based on the present dialogue, there is nothing to suggest that these souls acted in any way that was deleterious to the well-being of Florence. Therefore, in contrast to Farinata, they are not put on the defensive by Dante the pilgrim.[16]

Why so much excitement? Why so much enthusiasm on Dante the pilgrim's part towards these shades who were by no means as important in the political arena as Farinata, and who now appear before Dante wretched and humbled? Because the politics of Iacopo and Tegghiaio more closely resemble Dante's own than that of Farinata or any other politician Dante comes across. Santini notes the similarity:

Insomma nei documenti del tempo si muovono e rivivono le figure di Tegghiaio e di Iacopo: uomini di non grande stato, appartenenti cioè al patriziato minore, condizione che si avvicina a quella degli Alighieri; rappresentanti della parte schiettamente popolare della cittadinanza, aliena dalle cieche passioni faziose.[17]

[In short in the documents of the time the personages of Tegghiaio and of Iacopo move and reappear: men of not high station, belonging that is to the lesser nobility, a social class near that of the Alighieri; representing the genuinely popular segment of the citizenry, alien to the blind passions of the factions.]

Starting in the 1230s, Iacopo and Tegghiaio, both Guelfs, often worked together and proved themselves time after time as masters of diplomacy.[18] They were keen and careful negotiators who succeeded over two decades in peacefully negotiating with neighbouring cities pacts which were favourable to Florence. Their careers reached a climax in the 1250s when Florence was governed by the *Primo Popolo*, seen by many Florentines as an all too brief interlude, a golden age of relatively benign Guelf rule.[19] And perhaps this age could have lasted, even for the balance of the century right up to Dante's day, had Tegghiaio's words of warning succeeded in calling off the march on Siena in the late summer of 1260. Tegghiaio, like Farinata, stood at odds with his constituency and spoke words which they did not wish to hear. As Iacopo indicates, his voice should have been appreciated, and it should have been heeded: "... Tegghiaio Aldobrandi, la cui voce / nel mondo sù dovria esser gradita" ["... Tegghiaio Aldobrandi, whose voice should have been prized up in the world"] (1.16.41–2). While Farinata's words just after Montaperti were heeded, albeit by a reluctant audience, and Florence was saved, Tegghiaio's words just before Montaperti went unheeded. So the age of the *Primo Popolo* died on the battlefield of Montaperti, where the Arbia river ran red with Florentine blood, and with defeat came the end of that more conciliatory Guelf rule. The cycle of destruction and exile returned to Florence with a vengeance. Partisan Ghibellines held sway only to be replaced by the even more partisan Guelfs six years later.

If we were to trace the ordering of the "degni" announced by Dante the pilgrim to Ciacco in *Inferno* 6 and continue on that appointed route back in time, only one would remain, one politician for Dante still to encounter: Mosca de' Lamberti. But the reader who has been noting the formulas of repetition and following the concurrent signposted journey, which until now has mirrored the overt journey from "degno" to "degno," must here detour to *Inferno* 23, more precisely to the episode of Catalano and Loderingo. This detour is all the more surprising because Catalano and Loderingo are not "degni" and were politically active later than Tegghiaio and Iacopo, not earlier, even though they are lower down in Hell. Yet this will be a rewarding detour for the reading traveller, who will gain insights into the political drama unfolding in Florence during the course of the 1200s.

Catalano calls after Dante and Virgil, who are making their way down through the sixth *bolgia* of the hypocrites, because he recognizes by Dante's speech that he is Tuscan:

> E un che 'ntese la parola tosca,
> di retro a noi gridò: "Tenete i piedi,
> voi che correte sì per l'aura fosca!"

[And one who caught the Tuscan speech cried after us, "Stay your steps, you who run thus through the dusky air!"]

(1.23.76–8)

These lines are reminiscent of those in *Inferno* 10 where Farinata recognizes that Dante is a fellow citizen by his Tuscan speech, and they also recall the words of the three politicians in *Inferno* 16 who are able to identify Dante as Florentine from his attire.

Like Farinata and Iacopo Rusticucci before him, Catalano calls out to Dante and acknowledges that he appears to be a living man ("Costui par vivo a l'atto de la gola ..." ["This man seems alive, by the action of his throat ..."] v. 88) journeying down through Hell. Catalano begs Dante to stay his steps, and as in the previous two episodes it is Virgil who responds and facilitates the meeting by calling on Dante to wait and slow his pace so that he can converse with the two hypocrites. By now these elements are a clear signal that once again Dante, a Florentine politician in the present, will converse with a condemned shade who was a Florentine politician of the past, a "degno" worthy of Dante's respect, whose sin seemed unrelated to his politics. But not this time: the respectful conversation between Dante and one of his political heroes fails to take place once Dante realizes that these are Catalano and Loderingo. This pair, whose hypocrisy as politicians condemned them to the sixth pouch, are the very negation of those worthy politicians Dante has met up to now.[20] Catalano de' Malavolti and Loderingo degli Andalò were from Bologna not Florence, and they were not "degni" politicians. After the Guelf victory over the Ghibellines at the battle of Benevento in 1266 these men did not put their minds to "ben far" and place the well-being of Florence over factional politics when they were sent there to oversee the peaceful return of Guelf rule. So now they languish in Hell among the hypocrites because as *Frati godenti* they were supposed to maintain the peace between factions, not fan the flames of factional hatred. Indeed, when the Guelf Catalano and the Ghibelline Loderingo were jointly *podestà* of Bologna in 1265, they had managed to bring calm to that city.[21] But when they were brought to Florence the following year, again to share the office of *podestà* and repeat their success in Bologna, Pope Clement iv had other ideas for them, namely to return to the old cycle of factional hatred, which never served Florence well, ridding the city of its Ghibellines and burning down their homes, the ruins of which remained a symbol of factional hatred to Dante's day.[22] Catalano and Loderingo complied with Clement's wishes. Villani sums up their aims as follows:

Questi due frati per lo popolo di Firenze furono fatti venire, e misongli nel palagio del popolo d'incontro alla Badia ... sotto coverta di falsa ipocrisia furono in concordia più al guadagno loro proprio che al bene comune.

[These two friars were brought to Florence by the people, and they put them in the palace of the people facing the Badia ... under the cover of false hypocrisy they were more in harmony with their own gain than with what was good for the people.]

(*Cronica* VII 13)

Such behaviour on the part of Catalano and Loderingo reflects the antithesis of a "ben far" politician. Once Catalano identifies himself and Loderingo and points out that the result of their "peace mission" can still be seen around the Gardingo in the ruins of the Uberti houses, Dante the pilgrim's response is terse. The consequence of their political misdeeds, self-evident to any contemporary Florentine reader, is embodied in that heap of rubble that remains in the core of the city as a constant reminder. But Dante's few words to those whose complicity reinstituted factional hatred in Florence, the result of which continues to cause pain and suffering to Dante and his fellow citizens, speak volumes: "O frati, i vostri mali ..." ["O Friars, your evil ..."] (v. 109).

The formulas of repetition which signalled the reader to take a detour, to an encounter with Catalano and Loderingo, off the main route that leads from "degno" to "degno," now point the reader back to that route, to the last of the "degni": Mosca de' Lamberti, who is condemned to the ninth *bolgia* of the disseminators of discord in *Inferno* 28. The reader who has taken that detour will be able to place Catalano and Loderingo into the equation among those who played key roles on the political stage of thirteenth-century Florence. He/she can also compare their roles with that of Mosca, who is connected to Catalano and Loderingo via the formulas of repetition and also to the other "degni," as the sixth in their company, the last one named by Dante back in *Inferno* 6. What makes Mosca a more complex character is that he can be linked not only with Catalano and Loderingo, the very antithesis of the "degni" politicians, but also with the "degni," on account of his many constructive activities while in civic politics. To be connected to both the one group and the other seems a contradiction in terms; like Catalano and Loderingo he fanned the flames of factional hatred, indeed one might say that he lit the torch. But like the "degni" he put his mind to "ben far" and endeavoured to do his utmost, as he saw it, for the good of his city.

Mosca had a long career in Florentine politics: from 1202 when, along with his father, he and others succeeded in taking Montepulciano from Siena.[23] Many years later he led the Ghibelline army fighting for Florence against the Sienese from 1229 to 1235, and as an elder citizen he became *podestà* of Reggio in 1242. In short his long service to Florence earns him the term "degno" in Dante's eyes. But in 1216 a seemingly trivial matter in the greater scheme of things intervened, a matter which was destined to determine Florentine history for the balance of the century and beyond.

Buondelmonte de' Buondelmonti had promised to marry the daughter of Lambertuccio Amidei; however, at the eleventh hour he broke his pledge and turned away from her to marry instead the daughter of Gualdrada Donati. Buondelmonte had thus dishonoured the Amidei and such a crime could not go unavenged. And so Mosca uttered his famous words: "Capo ha cosa fatta," a thing done has an end. In other words Buondelmonte must be killed. For Mosca it was a simple matter of family honour. The reader of the *Commedia* is well familiar with family honour. Pride in family informs the texture of the dialogue between Farinata and Dante in *Inferno* 10. Later in the text too Dante will put words in the mouth of his great-great-grandfather Cacciaguida, of whom he is so manifestly proud, that refer to the "giusto disdegno" (3.16.137) of the Amidei towards Buondelmonte, and will further point out the ill Buondelmonte wrought by breaking his marriage promise: "o Buondelmonte, quanto mal fuggisti / le nozze süe per li altrui conforti!" ["O Buondelmonte, how ill for you that you did fly from the nuptials at the promptings of another"] (3.16.140–1).[24] With Buondelmonte's murder and the resultant hatred between families, the "viver lieto" ["glad living"] (3.16.138) that Florentines had enjoyed prior to 1216 came to a sudden end. In its place came conflict between Ghibelline and Guelf families and exile, as seen in the Farinata episode, and the destruction of his houses, as seen in the Catalano and Loderingo episode. Ironically the one guilty of disseminating this discord is one deemed a "degno": Mosca de' Lamberti.

Mosca had no idea that in defending family honour he would betray the city that he loved, and furthermore that by unwittingly unleashing factional hatred his own family would pay the ultimate price: exile in 1268 from the city that they loved and to which, like the Uberti, they would never learn the art of returning. When Mosca identifies himself to Dante, he repeats his words, which brought such ill to Florence:

> gridò: "Ricordera'ti anche del Mosca,
> che disse lasso!, 'Capo ha cosa fatta,'
> Che fu mal seme per la gente tosca."

[cried: "You will recall Mosca too who said, alas! 'A thing done has an end!' which was seed of ill to the Tuscan people."]

(1.28.106–8)

But it is left to Dante to remind Mosca that his words will in the end cause the ruin of his own family as well: "E morte di tua schiatta" ["and death to your own stock"] (1.28.109). Dante's reminder proves too much for Mosca, left like Farinata to mourn the ill he caused his descendants, who have lost the status of a powerful Florentine family of which they were once so proud.

Let us now turn back to *Inferno* 6 and retrace these episodes, but with the focus squarely on the formulas of repetition. Early on in Dante's encounter with the glutton Ciacco, Dante fails to recognize him, owing to his *contrapasso*, and asks:

> "Ma *dimmi chi tu se'* che 'n sì dolente
> loco se' messo, e hai sì fatta pena,
> che, s'altra è maggio, nulla è sì spiacente."[25]

["But tell me who you are, who are set in a place so grievous and who suffer such punishment that, if any is greater, none is so loathsome."]

(1.6.46–8)

The poet repeats the verb "dire" plus the interrogative "chi" plus the "tu se'" in two other cantos. It is used in *Inferno* 16, with only one variation: dir > dimmi, when Tegghiaio Aldobrandi, Iacopo Rusticucci, and Guido Guerra (not mentioned by Dante in *Inferno* 6) wish to understand Dante's identity. Iacopo begins:

> ... "Se miseria d'esto loco sollo
> rende in dispetto noi e nostri prieghi,"
> cominciò l'uno, "e 'l tinto aspetto e brollo,
>   la fama nostra il tuo animo pieghi
> a *dirne chi tu se'*, che i vivi piedi
> così sicuro per lo 'nferno freghi ..."

[... "If the wretchedness of this sandy place and our blackened and hairless faces," one began, "bring us and our prayers into contempt, let our fame move you to tell us who you are, that thus securely move living feet through Hell ..."]

(1.16.28–33)

In *Inferno* 23 Catalano and Loderingo also want Dante to identify himself:

> Poi disser me: "O Tosco, ch'al collegio
> de l'ipocriti tristi se' venuto,
> *dir chi tu se'* non avere in dispregio."

[Then they said to me, "O Tuscan, who are come to the assembly of the sad hypocrites, do not disdain to tell us who you are."]

(1.23.91–3)

What does this pattern of thematically unimportant words,[26] repeated in *Inferno* 6, *Inferno* 16, and *Inferno* 23, communicate to the reader? It signals that these episodes are more closely linked than can be gleaned from Dante's words to Ciacco alone, because a version of "dire" plus "chi" plus "tu se'" in this pattern is unique to these three cantos in the *Commedia*.

Further on in *Inferno* 6, Ciacco answers Dante by identifying himself:

"Voi cittadini mi chiamaste Ciacco:
per la dannosa colpa *de la gola*,
come tu vedi, a la pioggia mi fiacco.
    E io anima trista non son sola,
ché tutte queste a simil pena stanno
per simil colpa." E più non fé *parola*.

["You citizens called me Ciacco: for the ruinous fault of gluttony, as you see, I am broken by the rain; and I, in my misery, am not alone, for all these endure the same penalty for the same fault." And he said no more.]

(1.6.52–7)

I draw the reader's attention to the genitive "de la gola" which ends verse 53. Dante repeats this exact formula in *Inferno* 23 when Catalano and Loderingo, with considerable curiosity, observe Dante:

    … mi rimiraron sanza far *parola*;
poi si volsero in sé, e dicean seco:
"Costui par vivo a l'atto *de la gola*;
    e s'e' son morti, per qual privilegio
vanno scoperti de la grave stola?"

[… they gazed at me awhile without uttering a word; then, turning to each other, they said, "This man seems alive, by the action of his throat; and if they are dead, by what privilege do they go divested of the heavy stole?"]

(1.23.86–90)

Dante employs this formula of repetition in only these two cantos in the *Inferno*. Furthermore, in both cases the "gola" rhymes with another substantival verse terminator, "parola," in *Inferno* 6.57 and in

Inferno 23.86. "De la gola" cannot be considered a thematic signifier, since in Ciacco's episode "gola" means gluttony, while Dante's "gola" in *Inferno* 23 simply refers to his throat. I would rather talk in terms of circumstantial contexts; that is, the use of the "gola" references as identifiers. In *Inferno* 6 the pattern "de la gola" mobilizes Ciacco into identifying himself and in *Inferno* 23 (again accompanied by "dir chi tu se'") it impels Dante to do the same.

Ciacco concludes his dialogue with Dante by begging to be remembered when Dante returns to the world above:

> "Ma quando tu sarai *nel dolce mondo*,
> priegoti ch'a la mente altrui mi rechi:
> più non ti dico e più non ti rispondo."

["But when you shall be in the sweet world I pray you recall me to men's memory. More I do not tell you, nor do I answer any more."]

(1.6.88–90)

The locative "nel dolce mondo" is repeated in *Inferno* 10 when the heretical Farinata refers to Dante's return to the only world that matters, the "sweet world" above:

> "E se tu mai *nel dolce mondo* regge,
> dimmi: perché quel popolo è sì empio
> incontr' a' miei in ciascuna sua legge?"

["And, so may you return some time to the sweet world, tell me, why is that people so fierce against my kindred in all its laws?"]

(1.10.82–4)

Thematically the passages are parallel. In each case a sinner is speaking to Dante with reference to his return to the world above, and in each case the contraction plus adjective plus noun pattern "nel dolce mondo" is employed, a pattern unique to these two episodes in the *Commedia*.

The poet ties *Inferno* 6 more closely to *Inferno* 10 when in *Inferno* 6 five lines past "nel dolce mondo" he describes Ciacco's last sight of the pilgrim, just before Ciacco falls back among the other suffering "ciechi":

> Li diritti occhi torse allora in biechi;
> *guardommi un poco e poi* chinò la testa:
> cadde con essa a par de li altri ciechi.

[Thereon he twisted his straight eyes asquint, looked at me a little, then bent his head and fell down with the other blind ones.]

(1.6.91–3)

The poet repeats exactly the same pattern, "guardommi un poco e poi," in *Inferno* 10. However, the formulas each function differently. In *Inferno* 6 the formula closes the episode with Ciacco now silent, while in *Inferno* 10 the formula opens the Farinata episode:

Com'io al piè de la sua tomba fui,
guardommi un poco, e poi, quasi sdegnoso,
mi dimandò: "Chi fuor li maggior tui?"

[When I was at the foot of his tomb, he looked at me a little, then, as if in disdain, asked me, "Who were your ancestors?"]

(1.10.40–2)

The particular pattern of this repetition, unique in the *Commedia*, is striking in its length and structure. It is the longest of its kind among the ones analysed in these cantos, as well as the most intricate (verb plus object pronoun plus indefinite article plus adverb plus conjunction plus adverb). The proximity of a second "un poco" in both cases, *Inferno* 6.102 and *Inferno* 10.45, is also worthy of notice.

When Farinata overhears a fellow Tuscan traversing Hell while still in the flesh, he addresses him with the vocative:

"*O Tosco* che per la città del foco
vivo ten vai così parlando onesto,
piacciati di restare in questo loco."

["O Tuscan, who go alive through the city of fire speaking thus modestly, may it please you to stop in this place."]

(1.10.22–4)

The only other occasion in the *Commedia* when "O Tosco" is adopted occurs in *Inferno* 23, when Catalano and Loderingo address Dante and wish to know his identity. They begin their address as Farinata had already done with "O Tosco":

Poi disser me: "*O Tosco*, ch'al collegio
de l'ipocriti tristi se' venuto,
dir chi tu se' non avere in dispregio."

[Then they said to me, "O Tuscan, who are come to the assembly of the sad hypocrites, do not disdain to tell us who you are."]

(1.23.91–3)

The vocative "O Tosco" is the first pattern of repetition in this chapter of thematic significance, with an explicit bearing on the action of these encounters, in so far as they deal with Florentine leaders.

In *Inferno* 16, when Tegghiaio Aldobrandi, Iacopo Rusticucci, and Guido Guerra recognize a fellow Tuscan by his attire, they shout after Dante to stop:

A le lor grida il mio dottor s'attese;
volse 'l viso ver' me, e "Or *aspetta*,"
disse, "a costor si vuole esser cortese.
   E se non fosse il foco che saetta
la natura del loco, i' dicerei
che meglio stesse a te che a lor la *fretta*."

[My teacher gave heed to their cries, then turned his face to me and said, "Now wait: to these one should show courtesy; and were it not for the fire which the nature of this place darts, I should say that haste befitted you more than them."]

(1.16.13–18)

The imperative "aspetta," along with Virgil's "disse," is repeated in *Inferno* 23. When Catalano and Loderingo hear that Dante is Tuscan and one of them requests that he slow down, again Virgil reacts:

Onde 'l duca si *volse* e *disse*: "*Aspetta*,
e poi secondo il suo passo procedi."
Ristetti, e vidi due mostrar gran *fretta*
   de l'animo, col viso, d'esser meco;
ma tardavali 'l carco e la via stretta.

[At which my leader turned to me and said, "Wait, and then proceed at his pace." I stopped, and saw two show by their look great haste of mind to be with me, but their load and the narrow way retarded them.]

(1.23.80–4)

In each canto the past remote "volse" is adopted, then the past remote "disse," which follows the imperative in *Inferno* 16 and precedes it in *Inferno* 23, with the imperative "aspetta" as the verse terminator both times. Furthermore, the "aspetta" rhymes with the same verse terminator, "fretta," in both *Inferno* 16.18 and *Inferno* 23.82. There is not another instance in the *Commedia* when the imperative "aspetta" is used by Virgil, or Beatrice, to request that Dante stop.

Just after the "aspetta" in *Inferno* 16, when Tegghiaio, Iacopo, and Guido reach Dante and Virgil, the poet adopts the pluperfect of the verb "giungere," preceded by "quando":

> Ricominciar, come noi restammo, ei
> l'antico verso; e *quando* a noi *fuor giunti,*
> fenno una rota di sé tutti e trei.

[As we stopped, they resumed their ancient wail, and when they reached us, all three made of themselves a wheel.]

(1.16.19–21)

In *Inferno* 23 the moment is described when Catalano and Loderingo reach Dante and Virgil, and again the pluperfect of "giungere" is employed, preceded by "quando":

> *Quando fuor giunti* assai con l'occhio bieco
> mi rimiraron sanza far parola;
> poi si volsero in sé, e dicean seco ...

[When they came up, with eye askance they gazed at me a while without uttering a word; then, turning to each other they said ...]

(1.23.85–7)

The duplication of this formula in the *Commedia* is unique to these two cantos.

How clear are the signposts that direct the reader to take the detour from *Inferno* 16 to *Inferno* 23, instead of following the line of "degni" directly from Tegghiaio and Iacopo to Mosca in *Inferno* 28? I believe that the directional arrow that points the reader to take the detour to Catalano and Loderingo is obvious for those with the eyes to see, because of language which is either repeated verbatim or which conveys the same meaning, as can be seen below.[27]

In *Inferno* 16 the three politicians saw by Dante's dress that he was Tuscan, and they shouted after him ("ciascuna gridava" v. 7) to stay his steps so that they could catch up to him. Virgil deemed the encounter between pilgrim and sinners worthwhile and he turned ("volse" v. 14) towards Dante and commanded him to wait ("aspetta" v. 14). When ("quando" v. 20) the sinners reached ("fuor giunti" v. 20) the poets, they showed their faces to Dante ("ciascuno il visaggio / drizzava a me" vv. 25–6) and Iacopo Rusticucci addressed him. He hopes that the wretchedness of the place ("miseria d'esto loco" v. 28) will not cause Dante to disdain them ("rende in dispetto noi" v. 29) and that their fame is such that Dante will say who he is ("a dirne chi tu se'" v. 32), Dante whose living feet ("vivi piedi" v. 32) move safely through Hell.

In *Inferno* 23 when the two politicians recognized by Dante's speech that he was Tuscan, one of them shouted after Dante and Virgil and asked them to slow their steps ("piedi" v. 77) so that they could catch up. Virgil deemed this encounter worthwhile, turned ("si volse"v. 80) to Dante and commanded him to wait ("aspetta" v. 80). The two "frati godenti" showed by their faces ("col viso d'esser meco" v. 83) that they wished to address Dante and when ("quando" v. 85) they reached ("fuor giunti" v. 85) the two poets they addressed Dante. They too manifest the hope that their place among the damned will not cause disdain in Dante ("avere in dispregio" v. 93) and stop him from telling them who he is ("dir chi tu se'" v. 93), almost an exact duplication of Iacopo's "dirne chi tu se'."

And what of Mosca de' Lamberti in *Inferno* 28? While it has been clear through almost all the *Inferno* that he would be the last of the "degni" to be encountered by Dante, as his name is the final one on Dante the pilgrim's list of political "degni" from *Inferno* 6, Mosca will never be reached by a reader who pursues the concurrent signposted journey but is blinkered by Dante's list and does not seek the linguistic signs in any other cantos but those that include one of the worthy politicians. The reader who matches the formulas of repetition with "degni" cantos alone will reach a dead end at *Inferno* 16. The destination that is the Mosca episode in *Inferno* 28 will never be reached, because there are no formulas repeated in *Inferno* 28 from *Inferno* 16, nor from *Inferno* 10 or *Inferno* 6. The way of the concurrent journey to Mosca is via the detour from *Inferno* 16 to *Inferno* 23. *Inferno* 23 is the only canto which contains formulas both from the "degni" cantos which precede it and the "degno" canto which comes after it.

In a brief passage Mosca de' Lamberti presents himself:

E un ch'avea l'una e l'altra man mozza,
levando i moncherin *per l'aura fosca*,
sì che 'l sangue facea la faccia sozza,
   gridò: "Ricorda'ti anche del Mosca,
che disse, lasso! 'Capo ha cosa fatta,'
che fu mal seme per la gente *tosca*."

[And one who had both hands lopped off, raising the stumps through the murky air so that the blood befouled his face, shouted, "You will recall Mosca too who said, alas! 'A thing done has an end!' which was seed of ill to the Tuscan people."]

(1.28.103–8)

The formula "per l'aura fosca" occurs in only one other instance in the *Commedia*, and that is in *Inferno* 23 when one of the two hypocritical politicians recognized a fellow Tuscan, and here too it is a verse terminator:

E un che 'ntese la parola *tosca,*
di retro a noi *gridò*: "Tenete i piedi,
voi che correte sì *per l'aura fosca!*"

[And one who caught the Tuscan speech shouted after us, "Stay your steps, you who run thus through the dusky air!"]

(1.23.76–8)

In both cases the "per l'aura fosca" rhymes with the feminine adjective "tosca." It is surprising but true that "tosca" is found in these two cantos alone in the *Commedia*. As well, in each passage the past remote "gridò" is used with reference to one who "shouted" in order to gain the attention of Dante and Virgil. While the very common form "gridò" is used on numerous occasions throughout the *Commedia*, the "gridò" used as a *verbum dicendi* in the Catalano and Loderingo episode is not repeated again until it is used here to introduce "Ricordera'ti anche del Mosca" ["You will recall Mosca too"], some five cantos later.

In retrospect two types of formulas of repetition have been singled out in these cantos. We have seen those linguistic signals with thematic significance such as "O Tosco," "tosca," "nel dolce mondo," and "per l'aura fosca" where the repetition indicates sinners still obsessed with their political life, that worldly life which had centred on Florence and which ultimately accounted for their spiritual downfall. Then there are the other more hidden formulas of repetition such as "dir chi tu se'," "de la gola," "guardommi un poco e poi," "aspetta," and "fuor giunti," which function as linguistic signals alone.

While the very existence of these signals on their own merits our attention, what do they reveal that has not been conveyed by means of the overt journey from "degno" to "degno"? They frame two politicians who were not among the "degni": Catalano and Loderingo. If one divides the thirteenth century into two ages, the initial one when "cortesia" and "valor" could still be found, when there were political leaders who were "degni" and put their minds to "ben far," and the latter which knew no "cortesia" and "valor," with no political "degni" who put their minds to "ben far," what is the cut-off date between the two ages? Of the "degni," Farinata was the last, whose rhetoric at Empoli was nearer in time to Dante's age than any of the others. Farinata died in 1264, one year before Dante was born. Catalano and Loderingo were on the political stage a mere two years later in 1266. Even though the "viver lieto" ["glad living"] of Cacciaguida's day ended in Florence with the murder of Buondelmonte in 1216, it was still possible to find "cortesia" and "valor" after that year. There were still Florentines willing to put the welfare of Florence above factional interests. But that age was irretrievably lost with the arrival of Catalano and Loderingo on the scene. They ushered in the new age, the age with which Dante and his near contemporary Ciacco were all too familiar, an age so different from that which Tegghiaio and Iacopo knew but suspect is no more when Dante is asked:

> "Se lungamente l'anima conduca
> le membra tue," rispuose quelli ancora,
> "e se la fama tua dopo te luca,
>   cortesia e valor dì se dimora
> ne la nostra città sì come suole,
> o se del tutto se n'è gita fora."

["So may your soul long direct your limbs, and your fame shine after you," he then replied, "tell us if courtesy and valor abide in our city as once they did, or if they are quite gone from it."]

(1.16.64–9)

Dante confirms their suspicion that in Florence "cortesia" and "valor" are now but a memory.

By following signals, repeated words as ordinary in meaning as "aspetta" or "fuor giunti" from *Inferno* 16 to *Inferno* 23, the reader observes the directional sign and takes the detour along the concurrent journey to the episode of Catalano and Loderingo, who oversaw the end of an age in Florence, when "cortesia and valor" would be absent from the streets of Florence, replaced by heaps of rubble where the houses of the great families once stood, such as that around the Gardingo. From *Inferno* 23 the formulas "per l'aura fosca" and "tosca" point to Mosca de' Lamberti, who called for the murder of Buondelmonte and put a quick end to an even earlier and far superior age, the age of the "viver lieto" ["glad living"] in Florence.

Signals often so banal in meaning as these become subtle clues, hitherto overlooked, to canto links and some as yet little explored facets of the medieval mind that forged them.

·

PART TWO

To recap, Dante's encounter with Ciacco in *Inferno* 6 initiates another less obvious journey concurrent with his physical descent to the centre of Hell, a journey that has so far gone unnoticed by Dante scholars. The stages of this journey are signalled by nine linguistic formulas which pinpoint its beginning in *Inferno* 6 and lead through *Inferno* 10, *Inferno* 16, and *Inferno* 23 to its end in *Inferno* 28.[28]

The presence of these linguistic formulas ensures that seven political figures are both singled out from the other sinners and associated with each other: Farinata degli Uberti (*Inferno* 10), Tegghiaio Aldobrandi, Iacopo Rusticucci, Guido Guerra (*Inferno* 16), Catalano de' Malavolti, Loderingo degli Andalò (*Inferno* 23), and Mosca de' Lamberti (*Inferno* 28).

The nine formulas used to link these politicians are outlined below, together with the cantos in which they appear in the *Inferno*:

1	"dimmi chi tu se'"	6.46	Ciacco (gluttony)
	"dirne chi tu se'"	16.32	Tegghiaio, Iacopo, Guido (sodomy)
	"dir chi tu se'"	23.93	Catalano, Loderingo (hypocrisy)
2	"de la gola"	6.53	Ciacco (gluttony)
	"de la gola"	23.88	Catalano, Loderingo (hypocrisy)
3	"nel dolce mondo"	6.88	Ciacco (gluttony)
	"nel dolce mondo"	10.82	Farinata (heresy)
4	"guardommi un poco e poi"	6.92	Ciacco (gluttony)
	"guardommi un poco e poi"	10.41	Farinata (heresy)
5	"O Tosco"	10.22	Farinata (heresy)
	"O Tosco"	23.91	Catalano, Loderingo (hypocrisy)
6	"aspetta"	16.14	Tegghiaio, Iacopo, Guido (sodomy)
	"aspetta"	23.80	Catalano, Loderingo (hypocrisy)
7	"quando ... fuor giunti"	16.20	Tegghiaio, Iacopo, Guido (sodomy)
	"Quando fuor giunti"	23.85	Catalano, Loderingo (hypocrisy)

8 "tosca"	23.76	Catalano, Loderingo (hypocrisy)
"tosca"	28.108	Mosca (dissemination of discord)

9 "per l'aura fosca"	23.78	Catalano, Loderingo (hypocrisy)
"per l'aura fosca"	28.104	Mosca (dissemination of discord)

The scheme illustrates several fundamental points. Formulas 1, 3, 4, 5, 7, 8, and 9 are used exclusively in these cantos. Formula 2, the only one that appears elsewhere in the *Commedia*, is in the *Inferno* found only in these cantos. Formula 6, as an imperative directed to Dante by one of his guides, is unique to *Inferno* 16 and *Inferno* 23. This scheme also shows that what binds these sinners together as a group is not one common sin which would have placed them all in the same circle in Hell, and consequently also in close textual proximity. Rather, they are linked together by the part they played in the unfolding conflict between Guelfs and Ghibellines in thirteenth-century Florence. Their political association, stated by Dante in *Inferno* 6.79–81 ("Farinata e 'l Tegghiaio, che fuor sì degni, / Iacopo Rusticucci, Arrigo e 'l Mosca / e li altri ch'a ben far puoser li 'ngegni ..." ["Farinata and Tegghiaio, who were so worthy, Jacopo Rusticucci, Arrigo, and Mosca, and the others who set their minds on doing good ..."]), is reconfirmed subtly by the linguistic formulas. As can be expected, Catalano and Loderingo, whose political actions proved destructive to the well-being of Florence, are excluded from this association. Unlike other rhetorical devices of repetition, these formulas appear with an unexpected narrative. They outline another journey hidden alongside the overt one, a concurrent journey which Dante pursues to trace the evil of divisive politics in Florence back to its inception in 1216.

After his encounter with Ciacco, forewarned that the political worthies of thirteenth-century Florence are to be found among the blackest souls, Dante continues his progress downward through Hell. Concurrently he is starting to map a journey back towards the "mal seme" ["evil seed"]: Mosca's utterance (*Inferno* 28.108), whose poisonous fruits are the continuing factional strife in Florence. These formulas act as signposts to the significant encounters which are the essence of this concurrent journey. The encounter with his contemporary Ciacco provides Dante with the initial "pointing of the way." Subsequent encounters with Farinata, Tegghiaio, Iacopo, Guido, Catalano, and Loderingo lead the poet to the original seed of responsibility: Mosca.

Formulas 8 and 9 are particularly revealing for the attribution of political responsibility. The role of these formulas in the encounter with Mosca has seminal importance in this itinerary and therefore requires close scrutiny:

E un ch'avea l'una e l'altra man mozza,
levando i moncherin *per l'aura fosca*,
sì che 'l sangue facea la faccia sozza,
    gridò: "Ricordera'ti anche del Mosca,
che disse, lasso! 'Capo ha cosa fatta,'
che fu mal seme per la gente *tosca.*"
    E io li aggiunsi: "E morte di tua schiatta;"
per ch'elli, accumulando duol con duolo,
sen gio come persona trista e matta.

[And one who had both hands lopped off, raising the stumps through the murky air so that the blood befouled his face, cried, "You will recall Mosca too who said, alas! 'A thing done has an end!' which was evil seed for the Tuscan people" – "and death to your own stock," I added then; whereat he, heaping sorrow on sorrow, went off as one crazed with grief.]

(1.28.103–11)

These formulas, "per l'aura fosca" and "tosca," in their position as verse terminators, focus the reader's attention on the third verse terminator, "Mosca," which they frame. They also enclose a description of Mosca's face, his own identification of himself, his quote of the fateful words ("capo ha cosa fatta"), and his own evaluation of the consequences they had for the Tuscan people ("che fu 'l mal seme"). The formulas mark the end of this concurrent journey by revealing Mosca's words as the torch which lit the flame, inaugurating factional politics in Florence. They shift the focus of the indictment away from the person of Mosca, to his unfortunate utterance and its effects as the seed of evil on generations of Tuscans to come, truly a political original sin. Since formulas 8 and 9 link Mosca exclusively with Catalano and Loderingo, they oblige the reader to recognize Catalano and Loderingo's destructive politics as the "issue" of Mosca's words. This link, reinforced by the basic, genetic, acceptation of "seme," presents these two figures as true political offspring of Mosca's "tainted seed."

"Mal seme" in *Inferno* 28 turns the reader's attention back to *Inferno* 3.115: "similemente il *mal seme* d'Adamo" ["so there evil seed of Adam"]. This linguistic formula provides a point of contact between the inflexible structure of the overt journey of Dante, the framework of the *Commedia*, and the separate, more private journey discussed above. In fact it is a formula that appears only these two times in the *Commedia*, thereby suggesting the link between theological original sin and political original sin in Florence.

Mosca, "mal seme d'Adamo," like Adam, issued forth "mal seme," his words in this case. The consequences of his words ("Capo ha cosa fatta"), like an original stain, sullied all facets of political life in Florence and affected all subsequent generations. Even politicians like Farinata, Tegghiaio, Iacopo, and Dante, who practised politics of "ben far," were not exempt from this political original sin and had to grapple with the evil of factional strife. Just as, in Eden, Adam existed in a state of grace before original sin, so too before the original sin of Mosca's words did Florence exist in a political state of grace in its Eden, in Cacciaguida's words, "in pace, sobria e pudica" (3.15.99).

The two journeys are parallel in another fundamental way. Dante's overt journey leads him downward to the source of the evil that had corrupted Adam. Similarly, Dante's concurrent journey leads him backward to the source of political evil in Florence: Mosca's words that had ushered in an age which would be racked by violence, destruction, and exile. Both journeys are the necessary prerequisites for regaining what Singleton refers to as a condition of grace or justice. In the overt journey this is symbolized by reaching Earthly Paradise, and in the concurrent journey by reaching Cacciaguida in the fifth Heaven, where Dante learns of the earthly paradise that was Florence some years before Mosca's words sowed the seed of discord in 1216.[29]

6 Dante's Fear of the Fire: Unperceived Links between *Inferno* 15–16 and *Purgatorio* 26–27

When Iacopo Rusticucci identifies Guido Guerra, Tegghiaio Aldo-brandi, and himself, he also refers to Guido's great wisdom and swordsmanship and to Tegghiaio's voice, which should have been heeded before the disaster at Montaperti.[1] Dante's reaction is imme-diate. Dante would have jumped down to embrace the great worthies who had been on the political scene in the days when the *Primo Popolo* governed Florence, such was the esteem in which he holds them. He is only restrained from taking the leap by his fear of being burned and cooked by the fire:

> S'i' fossi stato dal foco coperto,
> *gittato mi sarei* tra lor di sotto,
> e credo che 'l dottor l'avria sofferto;
>   ma perch' io mi sarei brusciato e cotto,
> vinse paura la mia buona voglia
> che di loro abbracciar mi facea ghiotto.

[Had I been sheltered from the fire I would have thrown myself down among them, and I think my teacher would have permitted it; but since I should have been burnt and baked, fear overcame my good will which made me greedy to embrace them.]

(1.16.46–51)

In Purgatory, immediately upon the conclusion of Dante's encoun-ter with the repentant love poets, Guido Guinizzelli and Arnaut

Daniel, Virgil coaxes Dante into the wall of fire which divides the seventh terrace of the lustful from Earthly Paradise by reminding his reluctant charge that only this now separates him from Beatrice. The pain from the fire is so intense that Dante "would have thrown himself" into boiling glass, had he been able, which would have felt refreshing by comparison:

> Sì com' fui dentro, in un bogliente vetro
> *gittato mi sarei* per rinfrescarmi,
> tant'era ivi lo 'ncendio sanza metro.
> Lo dolce padre mio, per confortarmi,
> pur di Beatrice ragionando andava,
> dicendo: "Li occhi suoi già veder parmi."

[As soon as I was in it I would have flung myself into molten glass to cool me, so without measure was the burning there. My sweet father, to encourage me, went on discoursing of Beatrice, saying, "Already I seem to behold her eyes."]

(2.27.49–54)

In both instances the poet adopts the same formula, "gittato mi sarei," a verbal expression reserved only for these two episodes in the *Commedia*.[2] It is the thesis of this chapter that the repetition of the formula "gittato mi sarei" is a signal to the reader to view these two moments in the *Commedia* together. They highlight the unrepentant sodomites of the second round of the seventh circle,[3] who were once worthy politicians in Florence, and the repentant lustful love poets of the seventh terrace, who were once Dante's "betters who ever used sweet and graceful rhymes of love" (2.26.98–9). They were all Dante's heroes, and in the years preceding his journey in 1300 Dante had endeavoured to emulate them. Now their shortcomings as Christians are self-evident. Alerted by the repeated formula and viewing the distant textual passages as though they were in close textual proximity, one can see two of Dante's key preoccupations – politics and poetry – now bound together. These are two preoccupations which inform Dante the pilgrim's current state as he sets out on his present journey to salvation in *Inferno* 1.

The context of the two verbal expressions is marked by contrasts. In *Inferno* 16 Dante is treading on a raised surface, well protected from the fire, but of his own free will he would have thrown himself *in* had he not feared being seared and burned by it. In *Purgatorio* 27, however, Dante is not protected from the fire. Instead he has been coaxed into the flames, where he feels the sting of the fire as if he were truly being scorched and burned. The pain is of such intensity that he would gladly have thrown himself *out* into boiling glass, which would be cool and refreshing by comparison. In both instances Dante is not "coperto" or shielded from the fire. The effects of the first fire he can avoid entirely, since he is not a sodomite. The second fire he cannot escape if he hopes to continue onward to Beatrice and beyond.[4] In the first instance Virgil's role is purely passive, since he is unaware that Dante is even thinking of casting himself into the fire. Nonetheless Dante believes that Virgil would have allowed him to jump down among the three sodomites, had he asked permission to do so. By contrast, Virgil's role is active and prominent in *Purgatorio* 27 when he insists that Dante pass through the wall of fire.[5] While Virgil's capacity as guide makes it clear why he must compel Dante to pass into the fire in *Purgatorio* 27, why does Dante believe he would have allowed him to jump down into the fire in *Inferno* 16 and embrace Guido, Tegghiaio, and Iacopo? A partial explanation is that Dante takes his cue from earlier in the canto when Virgil recognizes the worth of these three politicians and obliges Dante to pause in his journey because they merit his courtesy:[6]

> A le lor grida il mio dottor s'attese;
> volse 'l viso ver' me, e "Or aspetta",
> disse, "a costor si vuole esser cortese."

[My teacher gave heed to their cries, then turned his face to me and said, "Now wait: to these one should show courtesy."]

(1.16.13–15)

What does Virgil know about these three politicians? Only what he has heard from Dante himself. Virgil is aware that Tegghiaio and Iacopo were among the most worthy politicians in Florence, because when in *Inferno* 6.79–81 Dante asked Ciacco of their whereabouts, he described them as "degni" who put their minds to "ben far."[7] And when at Dante's side, Brunetto Latini referred to Dante's own "ben far" in the previous canto, Virgil learned that such politicians are descendants of the "holy seed of those Romans" ("la sementa santa / di que' Roman" 1.15.76–7), the same noble seed he himself traced further back in his *Aeneid*.

If Virgil would have allowed Dante to jump down into the fire, what does that say about his guiding capabilities? It does not make sense that a guide should allow his over-enthusiastic charge to do himself harm. Perhaps the Roman Virgil, who in his second *Eclogue* wrote of the shepherd Corydon and his desire for the slave boy

Alexis, would be incapable of comprehending that within a Christian context now in medieval Europe the practice of sodomy was an act against nature. Virgil, of an earlier age, is unlikely to deem a sexual relationship between two men as necessarily sinful.[8] Herein lie the strengths and weaknesses of Virgil. His strength as a Roman is his awareness of moral rectitude in the politics of his day, which by extension enables him to judge the worth of politicians of Dante's day as well. His weakness as a Roman is his ignorance of the theology and intolerance of Dante's time, and the gravity of the sin of sodomy in this particular context, which by extension makes him ill equipped to measure these men's worth as Christians.[9]

Dante's wish to jump down and embrace these three shades, worthy politicians after whom he modelled his own behaviour as politician, suggests that his admiration for their politics is such that, with the presumed support of Virgil, who also appreciates their merit as politicians, he momentarily lapses into pre-Christian thinking and overlooks the gravity of their sin. It is ultimately Dante's own recognition of the *contrapasso* of the fire and all it signifies,[10] with no help from Virgil, which overcomes his "buona voglia" and restrains him from taking the leap. It is a lesson which Dante now on the way to salvation absorbs, even if the doomed Virgil cannot.

The time is the spring of 1300, when Dante has already been immersed in Florentine politics for five years and is poised to serve a two-month term as prior,[11] and only yesterday, as he tells Brunetto Latini, he found himself lost in the dark wood of sin:

"Là sù di sopra, in la vita serena,"
rispuos'io lui, "mi smarri' in una valle,
avanti che l'età mia fosse piena.
    Pur ier mattina le volsi le spalle:
questi m'apparve, tornand'ïo in quella
e reducemi a ca per questo calle."

["There above, in the bright life," I answered him, "I went astray in a valley, before my age was at the full. Only yesterday morning I turned my back on it. He appeared to me, as I was returning into it, and by this path he leads me home."]

(1.15.49–54)

Truly committed politicians like Farinata (also a "degno" in the Ciacco episode), Brunetto Latini, Guido, Tegghiaio, and Iacopo – and Dante himself – are so engrossed in their work and are so distracted by their political aims that they do not recognize when or how they entered their own dark wood of sin. Such was Dante's state the day he found himself in the "valle," before he turned his back on it to begin his journey "a ca":

Io non so ben ridir com' i' v'intrai,
tant'era pien di sonno a quel punto
che la verace via abbandonai.

[I cannot rightly say how I entered it, I was so full of sleep at the moment I left the true way.]

(1.1.10–12)

The difference between Dante and these other condemned souls, including Virgil, is that he is just beginning to recognize that practising good politics is not an end in itself, as he idealized it had been in Virgil's world. Therefore he does not now interrupt his journey "a ca," to God. If Dante the pilgrim is to persevere in his journey home, the decision not to jump down and embrace the three sinners must be his, even had Virgil allowed it.

If Dante's obsession with practising good politics distracted him from recognizing *how* and *when* he entered the dark wood of sin, was there a particular sin that took hold of him while he was fixated on civic politics in Florence? Without delving into this complex issue, two sins are more directly addressed by Dante in the *Commedia*: lust and pride.[12] However, throughout Dante's journey, it is only on the terrace of the lustful in Purgatory that Dante must share the pain of other suffering souls before he can pass beyond, and the pain, highlighted by the repetition of the formula, is so intense that Dante would have thrown himself into boiling glass, which would have actually cooled him by comparison. We learn early in the *Commedia* from Charon in *Inferno* 3 that upon death Dante will be bound for Purgatory not Hell ("Per altra via, per altri porti / verrai a piaggia, non qui, per passare: / più lieve legno convien che ti porti" ["By another way, by other ports, not here, you shall cross to shore. A lighter bark must carry you"] 1.3.91–3); therefore, as an eventual penitent Dante feels some of the pain of the fire in Purgatory that his fellow pilgrims withstand, but none of that endured by the damned souls in Hell.[13]

While there is an easily understood connection between the repentant heterosexual lustful of the seventh terrace in *Purgatorio* 26 and 27 and the unrepentant of the second circle in *Inferno* 5, connections that include the unrepentant homosexual lustful of the seventh circle in *Inferno* 15 and 16 are problematic. Yet these are the cantos linked by the formula of repetition. And if the repentant homosexuals described in *Purgatorio* 26 are added into the equation, how do they have any bearing on Dante's own journey to salvation and his sin of lust if he is not homosexual?

Dante's evident sympathy for Francesca's tale in *Inferno* 5, which leads to his subsequent fall, is the first reminder to the reader that Dante was writing poetry about precisely the kind of love that existed between Paolo and Francesca before their carnal union. The first intimation that Dante's encounter with the sodomites might have more to do with his own sinful past than merely the politics he discusses with like-minded, obsessed politicians alone comes in *Inferno* 14 when he first sets out on the bank over the fiery plain. While there are also blasphemers and usurers on this plain, the rain of fire is most pertinent to the sodomites. Indeed, just as the rain of fire which fell upon Sodom and Gomorrah (Genesis 19:24) punished the biblical sodomites, so too does a rain of fire punish all unrepentant sodomites in Hell. In this description of the rain of fire, commentators have noted that the words "Sovra tutto 'l sabbion, d'un cader lento, / piovean di foco dilatate falde, / come di neve in alpe sanza vento" ["Over all the sand huge flakes of fire were falling slowly, like snow in the mountains without a wind"] (1.14.28–30) recall verse 6 of Guido Cavalcanti's *Biltà di donna*: "e bianca neve scender senza venti" ["and white snow falling without winds"]. However, to my knowledge they have not looked at the context of this description and the general sin of lust implicit in courtly love poetry, of which Cavalcanti's *Biltà di donna* is an example. The contrast between the cold beauty of softly falling snow and the horror of the softly falling embers suggests the enormous distance that exists between the grotesqueness of the infernal world and one of the most coolly beautiful and peaceful phenomena of the living world.[14] Yet, Guido Cavalcanti, the one who first described the phenomenon of the slowly falling snow and who, according to Dante, has overtaken Guido Guinizzelli as the most famous courtly poet ("Così ha tolto l'uno a l'altro Guido / la gloria de la lingua ..." ["So has the one Guido taken from the other the glory of our tongue ..."] 2.11.97–8),[15] will in all probability span a similar distance in the very near future. Cavalcanti is to die four months after Dante's journey, and it is unlikely that he will end up among the repentant lustful of the seventh terrace of Purgatory, alongside the other Guido from whom he had taken the glory of the language, because like his father he is guilty of the graver sin of heresy of which he appears unrepentant.[16] Like the repetition of the verbal expression "gittato mi sarei," which, I submit, draws the reader in these two episodes to compare and contrast the state of Dante the pilgrim's soul midway on his journey through Hell with that near the top of Purgatory, so too the poet's adoption of an image from one of Guido Cavalcanti's sonnets should remind the reader (just four cantos after *Inferno* 10, where Guido's father asked of his son's whereabouts) of Guido Cavalcanti's disdainful attitude towards a journey to salvation such as that undertaken by Dante. The fame of Cavalcanti in the spring of 1300 as the best-known writer of love poetry obscures his lurking heretical beliefs, just as the fame that Iacopo, Tegghiaio, and Guido enjoyed as some of thirteenth-century Florence's greatest politicians masked their sin of sodomy that lurked within. Since Dante is the poet most likely to replace Guido in the "nido" of famous poets after Guido's death in August of 1300 ("... e forse è nato / chi l'uno e l'altro caccerà del nido" ["... and he perchance is born that shall chase the one and the other from the nest"] 2.11.98–9), it is timely that he journey "a ca" ["home"] and fathom the sins that his own budding fame obscures.

As Dante sets out behind Virgil in *Inferno* 15 on the poorly constructed bank, he draws a parallel between the Flemings' fear that the tide will overwhelm their dikes and his own present fear that the flames lapping on both sides of these banks will engulf him. So too on the terrace of the lustful in Purgatory, Dante is on a narrow path and fears that the nearby flames will engulf him: "... e io temëa 'l foco / quinci, e quindi temeva cader giuso" ["... and on the one side I feared the fire and on the other I feared I might fall off"] (2.25.116–17). Because of this fear, even when Dante learns that he is conversing with his poetic "father," Guido Guinizzelli, he dares not move any nearer to him.

After the initial description of the fiery plain in *Inferno* 15, Brunetto Latini recognizes Dante and grasps the edge of his clothing:

> Così adocchiato da cotal famiglia,
> fui conosciuto da un, che mi prese
> per lo *lembo* e gridò: "Qual maraviglia!"

[Eyed thus by that company, I was recognized by one who took me by the hem, and cried, "What a marvel!"]

(1.15.22–4)

"Lembo" is repeated only once elsewhere in the *Commedia*, with reference to cloth, when Virgil tells Dante in *Purgatorio* 27 to test the fire with the "lembo": "... fatti far credenza / con le tue mani al *lembo*" ["... try it with your hands on the edge of your clothing"] (2.27.29–30).[17] Dante regards Brunetto so highly that, unaware of the consequences, he suggests pausing in his journey if Virgil will allow it.

Before Virgil can respond, Brunetto points out that the *contrapasso* will exact a heavy price on souls who stay their steps, but he can temporarily run off from his group. Brunetto refers to Dante's "panni," which he will gladly trail, while Dante and Virgil continue on their way along the embankment above, safe from the fire and harm's way:

> "O figliuol," disse, "qual di questa greggia
> s'arresta punto, giace poi cent' anni
> sanz' arrostarsi quando 'l foco il feggia.
>   Però va oltre: i' ti verrò a' *panni*;
> e poi rigiugnerò la mia masnada,
> che va piangendo i suoi etterni danni."

["O son," he cried, "whoever of this flock stops even for an instant must then lie a hundred years without brushing off the fire when it strikes him. Therefore go on: I will come at your skirts, and then will rejoin my band who go lamenting their eternal woes."]

(1.15.37–42)

Not only is Brunetto's adoption of the word "lembo" repeated in the episode of the wall of fire in *Purgatorio* 27, but also his reference to Dante's "panni," a reference which is unique to these two cantos. In *Purgatorio* 27, after the angel of God announces that Dante cannot proceed further without passing through the fire, Dante is terrified because he remembers images of burning bodies. Perhaps the memory of such images also comes to Dante's mind in *Inferno* 16, when he realizes that if he were to jump down to embrace the three politicians he would not be shielded from that fire. In any event, in *Purgatorio* 27 Virgil suggests to Dante that he test the wall of fire with the edge of his "panni" so that he can prove for himself that this fire does not burn materially:

> "Credi per certo che se dentro a l'alvo
> di questa fiamma stessi ben mille anni,
> non ti potrebbe far d'un capel calvo.
>   E se tu forse credi ch'io t'inganni,
> fatti ver' lei, e fatti far credenza
> con le tue mani al *lembo* d'i' tuoi *panni*."

["Be well assured that if within the belly of this flame you should stay full a thousand years, it could not make you bald of one hair. And if perchance you think that I deceive you, go close to it and try it with your hands on the edge of your garments."]

(2.27.25–30)

In both *Inferno* 15 and *Purgatorio* 27 "anni" appears in the rhyme position with "panni."[18] In *Inferno* 15 the reference is to the "cent'anni" (v. 38) that Brunetto would have to lie on the burning plain without being able to brush off the flame should he stop and visit with Dante, and in *Purgatorio* 27 the reference is to the "mille anni" that Dante, according to Virgil, could remain in the flame without it burning one hair from his head. Brunetto's reference suggests not just the increased pain he would endure for a hundred years, but implicitly also the extent to which his already "cotto aspetto" ["cooked features"] (1.15.26) and "viso abbruciato" ["scorched face"] (1.15.27) would further burn materially. Virgil's words ignore the pain Dante in fact would feel for a thousand years, while maintaining that Dante would not burn materially.

Even if "lembo" and "panni" were identifiers alone, they would still further substantiate the link between the two episodes, highlighted by the repetition of the formula "gittato mi sarei." But if one also takes into consideration what these identifiers imply, it becomes clear that the fire is not the only element that repeats itself in both scenes. For it is only in these two instances in the *Commedia* that the edge of Dante's clothing has its own small role to play in the evolving plots, with the reader wondering each time whether the "lembo" of Dante's "panni" will catch fire. In *Inferno* 15 Dante's extended conversation with Brunetto would not have taken place had Brunetto not followed the "lembo" of Dante's "panni." Brunetto is spared the pain that he would otherwise have suffered had he sat with Dante, and Dante is well out of harm's way in remaining on the bank above, with the lower hem of his clothing leading Brunetto along. This reference is a portent of the episode in *Purgatorio* 27 when Virgil suggests that the "lembo" of Dante's "panni" be used to test a fire which will cause Dante great pain, a pain felt by Brunetto but not by Dante in *Inferno* 15, and a pain felt by Iacopo, Tegghiaio, and Guido in *Inferno* 16 but not by Dante because he checks his desire to jump down on to the burning plain and embrace them.

As the three politicians were Dante's political heroes, so Guinizzelli was Dante's poetic hero: "… il padre / mio e de li altri miei miglior che mai / rime d'amor usar dolci e leggiadre" ["… the father of me and of others my betters who ever used sweet and gracious rhymes of love"] (2.26.97–9). In both situations Dante would have preferred to approach these figures and express his respect and gratitude more directly, but in each case it is the fire that restrains him. In *Inferno* 16 Dante states openly that he would have liked to embrace his political heroes. In *Purgatorio* 26, while he does not expressly state that he wished to embrace Guinizzelli, Dante's reference to the story of

Lycurgus, as commentators point out, manifests his desire to brave the barrier, as Hypsipyle's sons did for their mother, and embrace his poetic "father." But he holds back on account of the fire:

> Quali ne la tristizia di Ligurgo
> si fer due figli a riveder la madre,
> tal mi fec' io, ma non a tanto insurgo
>   quand' io odo nomar sé stesso il padre
> mio e de li altri miei miglior che mai
> rime d'amor usar dolci e leggiadre;
>   e sanza udire e dir pensoso andai
> lunga fïata rimirando lui,
> né, per lo foco, in là più m'appressai.

[As in the sorrow of Lycurgus two sons became on beholding their mother again, so I became, but I do not rise to such heights, when I hear name himself the father of me and of others my betters who ever used sweet and gracious rhymes of love; and without hearing or speaking, I went pondering, gazing a long time at him; nor did I draw nearer to him, because of the fire.]

(2.26.94–102)

Although Dante managed to avoid the fire in *Purgatorio* 26, he is inevitably drawn to confront it in *Purgatorio* 27, for in order to leave this terrace Dante must first feel the sting of its flames. The angel of God, the custodian at the exit from the last terrace of the lustful,[19] requires that Dante, along with Statius and all the other "anime sante," pass through the wall of fire which will cause Dante such intense pain that he "would have jumped" into molten glass to escape it. Dante fears the fire, despite Virgil's reassurance that he need not: "Pon giù omai, pon giù ogne temenza ..." ["Put away now, put away all fear ..."] (2.27.31).[20] The penitent lustful back in *Purgatorio* 25 asked in their song *Summae Deus clementïae* for a fitting flame to purify them,[21] so it should come as no surprise that Dante, guilty of the same sinful lust, thinks that molten glass would be preferable to the heat of the purging fire. Dante's turning to other women, to women like "pargoletta," was a reflection of his own sinful lust, something Beatrice makes clear when she berates him in *Purgatorio* 31:

> "Non ti dovea gravar le penne in giuso,
> ad aspettar più colpo, o pargoletta
> o altra novità con sì breve uso."

["Young damsel or other novelty of such brief enjoyment should not have weighed down your wings to await more shots."]

(2.31.58–60)

The shame Dante feels when Beatrice berates him in *Purgatorio* 30 and 31 and the pain he feels in the wall of fire point him and the reader back to his past sins, back to the territory he has already traversed in his life's journey with Virgil, such as his encounter with Francesca, before he forgets his sins in the Lethe.[22] This overt invitation to look back is given greater emphasis by the subtle signposts which are the repetition of the verbal expression "gittato mi sarei" and the repetition of the "lembo" of Dante's "panni." When these expressions are repeated a second time (love poets), they guide the reader back to the time they first appeared (Florentine politicians) and draw necessary links between Dante's backsliding in his life's journey since Beatrice's death in 1290, for which Beatrice will soon take Dante to task.

The repetition of "gittato mi sarei," along with the repetition of the "lembo" and Dante's "panni," turn the reader's attention from the seventh terrace, where Guido Guinizzelli and finally Dante feel the sting of the purging flame, back to the blazing plain of the violent against nature, to the place where the supposedly worthy politicians now suffer eternally for their sin as they burn and cook, thereby accentuating the link between Dante the love poet and Dante the politician of the years leading up to and including 1300. By overcoming the textual space of some forty-three cantos which stands between these two episodes, we can draw conclusions regarding the commonality of effect of these fires on Dante the pilgrim. Dante would have stopped and sat with Brunetto Latini, his "father,"[23] to speak at leisure with him, but for the fire. Dante "would have jumped down" to embrace Guido, Tegghiaio, and Iacopo but for the fire. Dante would have embraced his "father" Guido Guinizzelli if not for the fire. Dante would have moved forward at the angel's request without fear but for the fire and his recollection of seeing burning bodies.

But this last fire is different. Unlike the one that rains down on the sodomites or the part of this last fire that purges Guinizzelli of his lust, this final part of the fire is here for Dante. Dante must not shrink from its flames, in which he must suffer the pain he managed to avoid on the two earlier occasions, if he wishes to find Beatrice and leave behind the life he lived these last ten years in that infernal city of Florence.

Dante must soon leave Virgil behind, and when first he stands before Beatrice and fearfully turns back towards Virgil like a child seeking his mother, Beatrice berates him for still clinging to one he should no longer need. By contrast, three cantos earlier in *Purgatorio* 27 it is only by looking forward at Virgil's request and imagining Beatrice beyond the wall of fire that Dante agrees to move into the fire and on towards Beatrice. Virgil's earlier suggestion that Dante test the fire with a "lembo" of his "panni," inevitably a look back to the Brunetto episode, has no effect on Dante, who remains "fermo e duro" ["unmoved and stubborn"] (2.27.34). Once Dante is in the fire it is only Virgil's comforting words about Beatrice that keep him focused on his appointed journey, Dante who "would have thrown himself" out into boiling glass to escape, which would have been his gravest backsliding of all.

The reminders "gittato mi sarei" and "lembo"/"panni" all highlight the old life when Dante, a respected citizen of Florence, had turned away from Beatrice. The repetition of the formula "gittato mi sarei" and "lembo"/"panni" in *Purgatorio* 27, where Dante suffers the exquisite pain of the fire for his past sins, guides the reader temporarily back to *Inferno* 15 and 16, and the vivid reminder of worthy political souls lost, before returning to the seventh terrace where repentant love poets are purged of their sins. Dante's heroes, his "fathers," burning in their flames, who once so influenced him that he followed them right into his own dark wood, have nothing more to teach "their son." That their example can now best be considered a negative one is a point not lost on Guido Guinizzelli, when he declares that the experiences Dante has had in his journey through their world will teach him how to die a good death:

> "Beato te, che de le nostre marche,"
> ricominciò colei che pria m'inchiese,
> "per morir meglio, esperïenza imbarche!"

["Blessed are you," he began again who had questioned me before, "who in order to die better do ship experience of our regions!"]

(2.26.73–5)

Dante has taken an important step in overcoming that past, in preparing for a good death when finally he enters the wall of fire, and sets his sights firmly on his saviour, Beatrice, a citizen of Florence no longer, who awaits Dante on the other side, ready to guide him home.

7 Florentine Politicians as Fallible Archers: *Purgatorio* 6 and *Purgatorio* 31

Among those who died violently in Antepurgatory, Dante and Virgil encounter the Provençal poet Sordello and approach him in the hope that he may indicate to them the best way to ascend the mountain. Sordello appears aloof and displays little concern for the poets' plight until he learns that Virgil, like himself, is a Mantuan. Sordello is so moved when he encounters a fellow Mantuan that they successfully embrace. Dante the poet is so taken by Sordello's deep passion for this Mantuan, who is otherwise a complete stranger, that he digresses for the next seventy-six verses (exactly half of *Purgatorio* 6).[1] He inveighs against the disorder that reigns throughout the ungoverned land of Italy and has led to the violent death of so many who arrive here in Antepurgatory. Sordello's emotion for Mantua is matched by Dante's own grief for his unhappy Florence. Like the rest of ungoverned Italy, in turmoil she is awaiting the firm and just hand of the Emperor. In the meantime those who seek political office in Florence govern unjustly and sow disunity among its people:

> Fiorenza mia, ben puoi esser contenta
> di questa digression che non ti *tocca*
> mercé del popol tuo che si argomenta.
> Molti han giustizia in cuore, e tardi *scocca*
> per non venir sanza consiglio a l'arco
> ma il popol tuo l'ha in sommo *de la bocca*.

Molti rifiutan lo comune incarco;
ma il popol tuo solicito risponde
sanza chiamare, e grida: "I' mi sobbarco!"

[O my Florence, you may indeed rejoice at this digression which does not touch you, thanks to your people who are so resourceful. Many others have justice at heart, but slowly it is let fly, because the shaft does not come without counsel to the bow; but your people has it ever on its lips! Many others refuse the public burden; but your people answers eagerly without being called, crying, "I'll shoulder it!"]

(2.6.127–35)

In Earthly Paradise, Dante is still separated from Beatrice by the Lethe and is held to account for his backsliding during the ten-year period, from Beatrice's death in 1290 to 1300 when in vain Dante attempts in *Inferno* 1 to climb out of the "selva oscura" on his own. Dante must declare before Beatrice and her attendants that her accusations are true, but such is his confusion and fear that the simple word "sì" comes so weakly from his mouth as to be inaudible:

Confusione e paura insieme miste
mi pinsero un tal "sì" fuor *de la bocca*,
al quale intender fuor mestier le viste.
    Come balestro frange, quando *scocca*
da troppa tesa la sua corda e l'arco,
e con men foga l'asta il segno *tocca*,
    sì scoppia' io sottesso grave carco,
fuori sgorgando lagrime e sospiri,
e la voce allentò per lo suo varco.

[Confusion and fear, together mingled, drove forth from my mouth a *Yes* such that the eyes were needed to hear it. As a crossbow breaks its cord and the bow when it shoots with too great tension, and the shaft hits the mark with less force, so did I burst under the heavy load, pouring forth tears and sighs, and my voice failed along its passage.]

(2.31.13–21)

It is only in the above two passages that the formula "de la bocca" appears, and in each instance it is accompanied by the same configuration of rhyme words "scocca" and "tocca,"[2] albeit in opposite order. Furthermore, in both passages "l'arco" appears, also in the rhyme position, signalling the succeeding "-arco" rhyme endings after the second repetition of the "-occa" rhyme. The greater configuration appears as follows:

2.6.128–35	2.31.14–21
… tocca	… de la bocca
…	…
… scocca	… scocca
… l'arco	… l'arco
… de la bocca	… tocca
… (in)carco	… carco
…	…
… -arco	… -arco

It is the thesis of this chapter that the repetition of the formula "de la bocca," within a configuration of common rhyme words and rhyme endings, is a clear signal to the reader to pause and explore the relationship between two denunciations: that of Dante the poet in *Purgatorio* 6 on the disunity and injustice which afflict contemporary Florence and that of Beatrice in *Purgatorio* 30 and 31 on the sinful life that Dante led in Florence during the ten-year period between 1290 and 1300.[3]

How does Dante's invective against Florence in *Purgatorio* 6 relate to his description of Dante the pilgrim's inability to put voice to his confession in *Purgatorio* 31? Both episodes relate to the sin of those Florentines who are directly involved in the governance of their city.[4] In the first instance the sin appears to be that of the people of Florence, the "popol tuo," of which Dante may or may not be one, depending on whether the reference includes the period leading up to Dante's exile or the post-exile phase of Dante's life alone. On the face of it, for Dante to inveigh against a people which includes himself in their number seems unlikely. In the second instance, if one takes the retrospective journey from *Purgatorio* 30/31 back to *Purgatorio* 6 then it becomes necessary at least to entertain the possibility that, just as Beatrice denounces Dante for his recent behaviour, so too Dante indirectly denounces himself for his recent political involvement.[5]

What makes "de la bocca" a more interesting signpost is that its very repetition might explain what it in its ambiguity is not self-evident in *Purgatorio* 6: namely whether Dante can in any way be tied to the "popol tuo" on whose lips ("bocca"), the poet says sarcastically, is the word justice. In *Purgatorio* 31 there is no ambiguity. The mouth from which the "sì" inaudibly flies forth is Dante's own. If the possessive adjective "tuo" is ambiguous, the "mia" which follows "Fiorenza" is not: Florence is claimed by Dante as his, just as Mantua was claimed by Sordello and Virgil, just as Casella was claimed by Dante as "Casella mio" in *Purgatorio* 2.[6] Commentators rightly dwell upon the irony and the sarcasm of this apostrophe.[7] After all, Florence, ironically described as rich and at peace, is at the centre of the disunity plaguing the Italian peninsula. However, Bosco and Reggio also point out the love of country that permeates the sarcastic and ironic digression, evident in the vocative "Fiorenza mia."[8] And it is precisely this love of country which helps fuel Dante's bitterness towards those who rush to take on public office and then rule unjustly. To drive home the contrast between the "molti," who are just and rule elsewhere, with the "popol tuo," who are unjust and rule in Florence, Dante repeats them, here in close textual proximity. "Molti" appears twice in verses 130 and 133 and each time is juxtaposed with the repeated formula "ma il popol tuo" (vv. 132 and 134), as follows:

Molti ...

...

ma il popol tuo

Molti ...

ma il popol tuo.

Dante uses the familiar image, readily understandable to his contemporaries, of the archer shooting an arrow, to better communicate his message concerning the unjust way the "popol tuo" rule Florence, in opposition to the "molti."[9] The word justice is ever on their tongue, but not in their heart. In the metaphor of the archer, the "molti" are prudent bowmen who bide their time fitting the arrow carefully to the bow, and who take precise aim before letting it fly, while the "popol tuo," shooting hastily and recklessly, are presumably bad shots. Therefore, the "molti" of other lands are the just rulers who consequently judge others with consideration, while the "popol tuo," who hypocritically have the word justice on the tip of their tongue, judge others unjustly, without care.

Eighteen months hence Dante will himself be one of those targeted by careless Florentine archers. Nonetheless, can Dante, involved in the governance of Florence since 1295 and sleepily veering off into the "selva oscura" near the height of his political career, avoid the taint that imbues those ever ready to come forward and take on the responsibility of office? With the possessive adjective "tuo" modifying "popol" in both the first and the second tercet of Dante's invective, it would appear that the group of people being emphasized does not include himself in their number. He willingly claims Florence as his by adopting the possessive adjective "mia," but not the people now drawing the bow. It is the Black Guelfs, quick to respond without being asked, who now rule in Florence: "solicito risponde / sanza chiamare, e grida: 'I' mi sobbarco!'" (2.6.134–5). They rule unjustly with great personal gain, as opposed to (let's say) a "popolo mio," which would have been the government of which Dante had earlier been a member.

If one were simply looking at the issue of Dante's exile, it would seem reasonable to infer that, unlike the "popol tuo," Dante was one of the just rulers. He would have been one of the "molti" who have justice in their heart. Elsewhere they rule, but in Florence they are a small minority, and thus make an easy target for the careless archers, the Black Guelfs who take control of Florence in November 1301. Dante makes particular reference to the months of November and October 1301, along with Florence renewing its members as one faction is sent into exile when the other is brought back:

> Atene e Lacedemona, che fenno
> l'antiche leggi e furon sì civili,
> fecero al viver bene un picciol cenno
>   verso di te, che fai tanto sottili
> provedimenti, ch'mezzo novembre
> non giugne quel che tu d'ottobre fili.
>   Quante volte, del tempo che rimembre,
> legge, moneta, officio e costume
> hai tu mutato, e rinovate membre!

[Athens and Lacedaemon, that framed the laws of old and were so grown in civil arts, offered but the merest suggestion of right living, compared with you that make such subtle provisions that what you spin in October lasts not to mid-November. How many times within your memory have you changed laws, coinage, offices, and customs and renewed your members!]

(2.6.139–47)

According to I. Del Lungo, Dante is referring to the time of the last priorate of the White Guelfs. They had been elected on 15 October 1301, but were forced to resign less than one month later on 7 November because the Black Guelfs had wrested control of Florence from the Whites. And with the sudden shift in members came Dante's exile.[10] This specific reference would support the notion of Dante as victim at the hands of the unjust.

But Dante's exile is not the only issue. There is also the matter of his journey some eighteen months before into the three realms of the afterlife, beginning with his sleepy fall into the dark wood in *Inferno* 1. If one re-evaluates Dante's words here in his invective within the context of the second occurrence of the formula, where he is taken to task by Beatrice, another inference now reveals itself. As a politician in Florence (there where impulsive archers take careless aim, often striking the innocent), Dante must descend into Hell then rise through

Purgatory in order to learn for himself what constitutes true justice. In the archery metaphor of *Purgatorio* 6, Dante must learn how to shoot advisedly and accurately now that he has left Florence behind (here temporarily), now that he journeys through Hell and Purgatory. And in the archery metaphor of *Purgatorio* 31, here where the pilgrim's return to Beatrice is almost completed, he attempts to prove what he has learned along the way: how to shoot advisedly.

Before Dante can cross the Lethe in *Purgatorio* 31, Beatrice sternly commands him to acknowledge his sinful ways of the 1290 to 1300 period, and further to put voice to an admission of guilt. The metaphor of a military encounter between Beatrice and Dante has already been established in *Purgatorio* 30 with Beatrice's reference to the sword ("... ché pianger ti conven per altra spada." ["... for you must weep for another sword."] v. 57), and also the poet's description of her as an admiral ("Quasi ammiraglio che in poppa e in prora ..." ["Like an admiral who goes to stern and bow ..."] v. 58).[11] In the first tercet of *Purgatorio* 31, where Beatrice turns from her attendants back to Dante and insists that he confirm her accusations regarding his backsliding, her sharp words evoke the military metaphor, as they remind the pilgrim of the "altra spada": "... volgendo suo parlare a me per punta, / che pur per taglio m'era paruto acro ..." ["... turning against me the point of her speech, which even with the edge had seemed sharp to me ..."] (2.31.2–3).

Dante is so overcome by the shame of his past sins that his own military volley in response to Beatrice's attack is a "sì" too weak to be audible. Indeed his acknowledgment of guilt would have gone unnoticed had Beatrice not seen his lips mouth the word. The poet likens his response to that of a feeble shot from a crossbow, a shot which fails to reach its intended target, Beatrice's ears, with any force. The lack of force is caused by the archer's apparatus breaking (there is continuing disagreement among commentators on whether it is the bow and bowstring which break or the crossbow itself),[12] due to the extreme tension in the bowstring:

> Come balestro frange, quando scocca
> da troppa tesa, la sua corda e l'arco
> e con men foga l'asta il segno tocca ...

[As a crossbow breaks its cord and the bow when it shoots with too great tension, and the shaft hits the mark with less force ...]

(2.31.16–18)

Accordingly the arrow loses the impetus it would otherwise have had.

In contrast to the arrow of the "popol tuo," Dante's arrow does at least reach the right target; however, his shot proves too weak to be effectual as a military volley. Unlike those Florentines, Dante is attempting to be a capable archer, a just shot. But having led a corrupt life of sin for the previous ten years, Dante is weak and out of shape. He is a weak archer at best, whose arrow – the word – feebly reaches its mark, but inaudibly, hence ineffectually. After Beatrice's military volley in *Purgatorio* 30 she points out to her attendants how close Dante's sinful ways had brought him to the death of his soul:

> "Tanto giù cadde, che tutti argomenti
> a la salue sua eran già corti,
> fuor che mostrarli le perdute genti.
>   Per questo visitai l'uscio d'i morti,
> e a colui che l'ha qua sù condotto,
> li preghi miei, piangendo, furon porti."

["He fell so low that all means for his salvation were now short, save to show him the lost people. For this I visited the gate of the dead, and to him who had conducted him up hither my prayers were offered with tears."]

(2.30.136–41)

Among the "perdute genti" of Hell are the political worthies of Florence who, according to Dante the pilgrim in *Inferno* 6, "a ben far puoser li 'ngegni" ["set their minds on doing good"] (v. 81), politicians Dante had endeavoured to emulate during his own political career in the late 1290s. But they had led lives of sin. They fell even farther than Dante and all are eternally damned in the nether reaches of Hell. Dante was shown these "perdute genti" (all except Arrigo) in order to fathom the deficiencies of his political role models. He has had to relearn how to aim his arrow at the right target, a skill lacked both by the Florentine politicians referred to in *Purgatorio* 6 and by those singled out in *Inferno* 6.

As Dante reflects on his past sins he breaks under the heavy load, unable to voice another word. Following the extended military metaphor, here with the simile of the crossbow, Dante, no longer able to bear the burden of his past sins, would be the broken apparatus of the archer now incapable of attempting another shot:

> ... sì scoppia' io sottesso grave carco,
> fuori sgorgando lagrime e sospiri,
> e la voce allentò per lo suo varco.

[... so did I burst under the heavy load, pouring forth tears and sighs, and my voice failed along its passage.]

(2.31.19–21)

More important, the "carco" or burden of Dante's sin, which now weighs all too heavily upon him, gains further relevance when one considers that its counterpart, "incarco," which appears in the greater configuration in *Purgatorio* 6, refers to the burden of political life readily assumed by the "popol tuo" of Florence, the very same burden Dante himself was taking on as prior of Florence in this year of 1300.

If from *Purgatorio* 31 one takes the retrospective journey back to *Purgatorio* 6 to re-evaluate the message in Dante's invective, one must entertain the possibility that Dante, the failed archer in *Purgatorio* 31, also wielded the very "arco" described in *Purgatorio* 6. The repeated formula within its greater configuration is a call to the reader to look back into Dante's past life right along with Dante the pilgrim, here before he is submerged in the Lethe and forgets. But the call is not to the 1290 to 1300 period in general, when Dante neglected Beatrice, but more specifically to the years between 1295 and 1300 when Dante held public office, thus taking on an occupation which later in *Purgatorio* 6 he condemns with such indignation.

Well beyond the Lethe, in *Paradiso* 17, Dante seeks to learn the truth about his fate from his great-great-grandfather Cacciaguida, as he has already heard "parole gravi" ["grave words"] concerning his future from other souls encountered when still at Virgil's side.[13] When Dante entreats Cacciaguida to tell how his future will unfold, he adopts the image of the archer's arrow, explaining to his ancestor that if an arrow is to be shot at him, he had best be forewarned, so he can see it coming: "ché saetta previsa vien più lenta" ["because an arrow foreseen comes slower"] (3.17.27).[14] In describing his descendant's fate, Cacciaguida pursues the metaphor already suggested by the pilgrim and reveals to him that "quello strale" ["that arrow"] (3.17.56), in flight even now, is the arrow of exile, an unjust exile already being plotted against him by Pope Boniface in Rome:

> "Tu lascerai ogne cosa diletta
> più caramente; e questo è quello strale
> che l'arco de lo essilio pria saetta."

["You shall leave everything beloved most dearly; and this is the arrow which the bow of exile shoots first."]

(3.17.55–7)

The bow and arrow which will soon be targeting Dante belong to the careless Florentine archers described back in *Purgatorio* 6, those Black Guelfs so eager for public office, who have justice on the tip of their tongue, but not in their heart. As Dante is the target of the careless archers, can one therefore conjecture that, were he and not the Blacks controlling the bow and arrow, he would be capable of shooting wisely? While superficially this seems the logical conclusion, the repetition of the formula within its configuration in *Purgatorio* 31 suggests that it could be the wrong one, with Dante's own part as archer included in the equation.

In both *Purgatorio* 6 and *Purgatorio* 31 Florence is the locus of sin.[15] In the former instance it is the sin of those in control of the Florentine government, and in the latter it is the sin of Dante personally, who was distracted by what that city offered and even more so by what it lacked in the years 1290 to 1300 following Beatrice's death. Dante fell so low, while practising politics in Florence, that by the spring of 1300, as he tells Brunetto Latini, he fell into the valley of sin: "mi smarri' in una valle" ["I went astray in a valley"] (1.15.50).[16] By 1302, according to Cacciaguida, Dante will fall into the valley of exile, along with his former colleagues in government ("E quel che più ti graverà le spalle, / sarà la compagnia malvagia e scempia / con la qual tu cadrai in questa valle" ["And that which shall most weigh your shoulders down will be the evil and senseless company with which you shall fall into this vale"] 3.17.61–3). As he stands before Beatrice in *Purgatorio* 31, Dante, who some eighteen months hence will be permanently separated from Florence, must review the sins he committed in that city. These are the sins he has already encountered when journeying down through Hell and up the mountain of Purgatory with Virgil, sins for which he will atone the rest of his life when as an exile he goes down and up another's staircases ("lo scendere e 'l salir per l'altrui scale" ["to descend and mount by another man's stairs"] 3.17.60), before by the grace of God eventually reaching Paradise.

In the literal military sense Dante, along with the other exiled White Guelfs whom he will forswear by 1304 on account of their reckless adventurism,[17] never does learn to shoot accurately, if by being a competent shot one is suggesting that Dante and the others can achieve victory over the Black Guelfs controlling Florence by force of arms. Since the White Guelfs never do regain Florence, Dante remains as impotent in the early days of exile as he is before Beatrice in *Purgatorio* 31. While competence in the strict military sense might gain Dante access to Florence, Florence is hardly the city to which Dante should wish to return, there where he had once fallen so low. What is more important in *Purgatorio* 31 is that Beatrice sees Dante utter his first true confession, even if the first word, the "sì," metaphorically the arrow, is shot with insufficient force. As Dante is poised to cross into Earthly Paradise, he has set his sights on a return to the true city of God, to which he will soon alight at Beatrice's side.

But the invective against Florentine rulers in *Purgatorio* 6, highlighted by the first occurrence of the linguistic configuration, must not be obscured when one examines Dante's initial, tentative steps towards a confession, highlighted by the second occurrence with its parallel archery metaphor. When the reader takes the retrospective journey from *Purgatorio* 31 back to *Purgatorio* 6 and rereads Dante's invective in light of Beatrice's reprimand, then reference to political figures in Florence in the former passage and reference to Dante's own sins in the latter passage draw the reader to focus on the year 1300, not the period after Dante's exile when the "popolo tuo" control the bow and arrow. In that year it was Dante and his fellow White Guelfs who controlled the bow and arrow.[18] These were the same White Guelfs whom Cacciaguida describes as "malvagia e scempia" (3.17.62), hardly words to describe capable political archers. Indeed, in their company Dante fell into the "valley" of sin in the spring of 1300, and two years later in their company he will fall into the "valley" of exile.

Even if the White Guelfs too are bad shots, could one not exclude Dante from this group on the basis that he practises the politics of "ben far," of bridging the differences between the factions?[19] On what basis can such noble politics be considered sinful? I believe Beatrice answers that question when she explains to her attendants in *Purgatorio* 30 that Dante, currently practising politics in Florence, had fallen so low that it was necessary to show him the "perdute genti." These "genti" include Dante's political heroes who had also fallen low despite their own politics of "ben far," of looking beyond factional interests. Their obsession with politics had occupied them to such a degree that they were blinded to other realities. They had neglected the health of their immortal souls, which were now in mortal peril. Just like Dante when he entered the dark wood, they were asleep ("Io non so ben ridir com' i' v'intrai, / tant' era pien di sonno a quel punto ..." ["I cannot rightly say how I entered it, I was so full of sleep at the moment ..."] 1.1.10–11), unaware of their sins, obsessed by their role as politicians. The "perdute genti" were brought low by different sins: for Farinata it was heresy, and for Brunetto, Tegghiaio, Guido Guerra, and Iacopo Rusticucci homosexuality. For all of them, as John Scott suggests, it could have been their pride, the result of ambition.[20] Perhaps if not for their politics they might have found time to take stock of their lives. But they found no time and were lost. Dante the obsessed politician was taking such care to follow in the path of his political predecessors that he too was neglecting the health of his immortal soul, and he too fell low. The sins are different ones. In Dante's case it could have been his love poetry, or his study of philosophy, or his pride. But unlike the other politicians, Dante took some action. When he had fallen so low, he did pause and attempt to climb out of his dark wood, something those other politicians never considered.[21]

Of course Dante was rescued by Virgil, who showed him the "perdute genti," sinners who might well have included Dante in their number. By the time Dante stands before Beatrice in *Purgatorio* 31, for now unencumbered by his life as a politician, he takes stock of his life. And he attempts to confess. He attempts to shoot his arrow with care, something the politicians still in Florence or gone into exile appear incapable of doing. Ultimately Dante will speak the words, thereby alighting with Beatrice to Paradise, but not before she condemns "quella scuola" (2.33.85) Dante followed, which Scott convincingly glosses as the Guelf School.[22] And as has been predicted more than once in the *Commedia*, after Dante's temporary exile on Earth, he will be saved.

In *Paradiso* 1 Beatrice explains to Dante that it is God who as the true archer aims the souls to the place they will rest for eternity:

"Né pur le creature che son fore
d'intelligenza quest' arco saetta,
ma quelle c'hanno intelletto e amore."

["And not only does this bow shoot those creatures that lack intelligence, but also those that have intellect and love."]

(3.1.118–20)

In the end Dante, once a feeble archer in *Purgatorio* 31, a citizen of that city ruled by careless archers, will be as an arrow himself shot from the bow of the infallible archer.[23]

8 Virgil and Caiaphas "ne l'etterno essilio"

As Dante begins to censure Catalano de' Malavolti in *Inferno* 23 for the ill he and the other hypocritical "peacemaker" Loderingo degli Andalò brought to Florence, Dante is distracted by the sight of one crucified. Catalano explains what Dante's guide could not have known. The one crucified flat on the ground is the hypocrite Caiaphas, the high priest of the Pharisees who had urged that the life of Christ be taken for the good of the nation. As Catalano ends his account by pointing to Caiaphas's father-in-law, Annas, and the other Pharisees who are likewise crucified, Dante sees Virgil marvel at this strange sight before them:

> "E a tal modo il socero si stenta
> in questa fossa, e li altri dal *concilio*
> che fu per li Giudei mala sementa."
> Allor vid'io maravigliar *Virgilio*
> sovra colui ch'era disteso in croce
> tanto vilmente *ne l'etterno essilio*.

["And in like fashion is his father-in-law racked in this ditch, and the others of that council which was a seed of evil for the Jews." Then I saw Virgil wonder over him who was thus outstretched, as on a cross, so vilely in the eternal exile.]

(1.23.121–6)

In *Purgatorio* 21, as Dante grieves over the just vengeance wrought upon the penitent souls of the fifth terrace who are likewise prostrate, the newly released Statius catches up with Dante and Virgil and addresses them:

> ... "O frati miei, Dio vi dea pace."
> Noi ci volgemmo sùbiti, e *Virgilio*
> rendéli 'l cenno ch'a ciò si conface.
>   Poi cominciò: "Nel beato *concilio*
> ti ponga in pace la verace corte
> che me rilega *ne l'etterno essilio*."

[... "O my brothers, may God give you peace." We turned quickly and Virgil answered him with the greeting that is fitting thereto; then he began, "May the true court which binds me in the eternal exile bring you in peace to the assembly of the blest."]

(2.21.13–18)

The formula "ne l'etterno essilio" emerges in these two episodes only. Its repetition in *Purgatorio* 21 invites the reader to take the retrospective journey to the context of its first appearance in *Inferno* 23.[1] With light now shed on these two texts, other repetitions reveal themselves. In both instances "ne l'etterno essilio" appears within a configuration which includes "Virgilio" and "concilio," making up the other two words of the *terza rima*. Furthermore, in both instances a configuration of the rhyme words "(con)venia," "via," and "pria" appears two lines before the "Virgilio"/"concilio"/"ne l'etterno essilio" configuration, and in both instances the rhyme words ending in "chia" begin eight lines after it, as outlined below:

Inferno 23. 116–38	*Purgatorio* 21. 8–30
... "convenia"	... "via"
...	...
... "via"	... "venìa"
...	...
... "pria"	... "pria"
...	...
... "concilio"	... "Virgilio"
...	...
... "Virgilio"	... "concilio"
...	...
... "ne l'etterno essilio"	... "ne l'etterno essilio"
[eight lines later]	[eight lines later]
... "cer*chia*"	... "conoc*chia*"
...	...

... "coper*chia*"   ... "seroc*chia*"

...   ...

... "soper*chia*"   ... "adoc*chia*"

Although the positions of "(con)venia" ... "via" and "concilio" ... "Virgilio" in *Inferno* 23 are reversed in *Purgatorio* 21, as can be seen in the outline above, the highlighted "ne l'etterno essilio" appears on both occasions in the same position within its frame: on the tenth line from the beginning, at the end of the two configurations of like rhyme words, and eight lines before the *terza rima* which ends in "chia." Once the twenty-two-line frame of "ne l'etterno essilio" is identified in both cantos, the reader's attention is inevitably drawn to the key repeated configuration: "ne l'etterno essilio," along with "concilio" and "Virgilio" with all that this may signify.[2]

While commentators of the *Commedia* have remarked on the repetition of "etterno essilio," to my knowledge they have not noted that the formula is unique to these cantos, nor have they noted the existence of a repeated configuration of rhyme words and rhyme endings which frames "ne l'etterno essilio."[3] If the repeated rhyme endings form the outer frame of the configuration, it is the repeated rhyme words "essilio," "concilio," and "Virgilio" which guide the reader on an interpretive journey back to *Inferno* 23, by way of the formula "ne l'etterno essilio," and also forward to the ultimate destination of this journey in *Paradiso* 26 where they appear for the third and last time, but without the adjective "etterno":[4]

Paradiso 26.116–20
... essilio
...
... Virgilio
...
... concilio

While Adam is referring here to his own exile, his words in the rhyme position frame "Virgilio" with attendant implications for Virgil's exile in Limbo: "onde mosse tua donna Virgilio" ["whence your lady dispatched Virgil"] (3.26.118).

The linguistic signposts in *Paradiso* 26, with Adam's direct reference to Virgil, again point the reader back to the *Inferno*, the dwelling place of those in eternal exile; more precisely to *Inferno* 23, where the formula "ne l'etterno essilio" first appears, along with "Virgilio" and "concilio."

In *Inferno* 23 after Dante and Virgil have reached a sort of refuge in the sixth *bolgia* from the unruly devils of the fifth one, they find themselves among the hypocrites. Dante describes the heavy, leaden cloaks the hypocrites must endure and adopts the adjective "etterno" to describe how they bear this burden through all eternity ("Oh in etterno faticoso manto!" ["O toilsome mantle for eternity!"] 1.23.67), anticipating the "etterno" which will modify "essilio" later on in the canto. Dante the pilgrim begs of his guide to find him some famous souls: "Fa che tu trovi / alcun ch'al fatto o al nome si conosca" ["Pray find someone who may be known by deed or name"] (1.23.73–4). Two such toiling individuals appear to be Catalano and Loderingo. Though unknown to Virgil, they are well known to Dante, since they had betrayed the peace of his city in the year following his birth, to preserve which peace they had been ostensibly chosen to rule jointly in 1266. Dante begins to rebuke Catalano and Loderingo ("O frati, i vostri mali ..." ["O Friars, your evil ..."] 1.23.109), when he is distracted in mid-sentence by a more amazing sight. It is astounding to find Dante the pilgrim diverted from this sole opportunity to inveigh against these two souls for having exacerbated factional hatred in Florence, considering his obsession with that matter and its ultimate impact on his own life. But Dante, insisting that Virgil find someone who can be recognized by "fatto" ["deed"] or "nome" ["name"], recognizes in the one crucified and prostrate a person whose fame far eclipses that of Catalano and Loderingo.

As Catalano and Loderingo were unfamiliar to Virgil, so too is this new soul, Caiaphas, nor does his *contrapasso* strike a chord. Unlike Virgil, the Christian reader is not surprised to see that one who played a central role in Christ's crucifixion is here crucified himself. Correspondingly, just as Virgil had been ignorant of the momentous event that was the crucifixion, he is likewise ignorant of the changes that that crucifixion brought about within Hell. Virgil had passed this way before, but at a time when Hell was still intact. This very ignorance has compromised his ability to guide Dante through the preceding *bolgia*. In *Inferno* 21, Virgil sought direction from the questionable Malacoda, who told him about another "scoglio" ["crag"] which supposedly had not been destroyed by the earthquake that occurred at the moment of Christ's death (1.21.111). In fact, however, no ridges remain over the sixth *bolgia*.[5] And shortly Virgil, lost again, will once more be obliged to seek direction to the next *bolgia* from an unlikely source, the one whom Dante had been poised to censure: Catalano.[6]

With Dante's attention now riveted on this more famous soul, Catalano identifies Caiaphas for Dante's benefit, even though Dante does not ask his identity. And although Dante does not ask Catalano to relate what he and all Christians know very well, Catalano proceeds to do just that and tells how Caiaphas, the high priest, advised the Pharisees to sacrifice Christ for the good of the people.[7]

Here as self-appointed surrogate guide, Catalano further explains to Dante the unique *contrapasso* meted out to Caiaphas, Caiaphas's father-in-law, Annas, and the other Pharisees of the Council. Yet Dante himself requested no such explanation, presumably because this *contrapasso*, a crucifixion for a crucifixion, is easily understood by all Christians. Although Catalano continues to address his words to Dante, the living "tosco" about whom he has been so curious since verse 76 when he caught Dante's Tuscan speech ("un che 'ntese la parola tosca"), the pilgrim, silent ever since catching sight of Caiaphas, no longer heeds Catalano's words. It is Virgil, in the background throughout this encounter with Catalano and Loderingo, who now comes to the fore and reacts to this strange new sight. With Catalano's gloss of the crucified souls now at an end, Virgil is left marvelling before the sight of the crucified Caiaphas at the point in the text where the formula of repetition within its configuration of rhyme words first appears:

> "E a tal modo il socero si stenta
> in questa fossa, e li altri dal *concilio*
> che fu per li Giudei mala sementa."
> Allor vid'io maravigliar *Virgilio*
> sovra colui ch'era disteso in croce
> tanto vilmente *ne l'etterno essilio.*

["And in like fashion is his father-in-law racked in this ditch, and the others of that council which was a seed of evil for the Jews." Then I saw Virgil marvel over him who was thus outstretched, as on a cross so vilely in the eternal exile.]

(1.23.121–6)

The *terza rima* binds "Virgilio" to the one in "essilio" over whom he is marvelling, but as well to the "concilio" about which he has no understanding.

In the first of the two tercets where Catalano speaks his last words on the subject of Caiaphas and his crucifixion, he adds that Caiaphas is not the only one so crucified. Catalano makes two other references to those who had been in league with Caiaphas. First he refers to an individual, Annas (Caiaphas's father-in-law), and second to a group, the rest of the Council of the Pharisees, for a total of three references, two individuals and one group of individuals.[8] While Virgil marvels at this remarkable sight, he does not respond to Catalano's words.

Being ignorant of the Gospels, he does not know what to make of them. And for Dante as for any Christian of his day the words are so well known that nothing further need be added.

How are we to interpret the fact that Catalano is here the poet's mouthpiece? Why is he the one who tells the familiar story of the actions of Caiaphas, Annas, and the others of the Council of the Pharisees and how they were a "mala sementa" ["seed of evil"] for the Jewish nation?[9] It is ironic that the poet puts these words in Catalano's mouth, because just as the Pharisees took actions which were a "mala sementa" for their people, so also did Catalano for the future citizens of Florence, including Dante. In Catalano's case, however, the evil seed predated him. Catalano was one in a line of rulers in thirteenth-century Florence who fanned the flames of partisan politics (see chapter 5), whose politics sprang from the "mal seme" which was Mosca de' Lamberti's famous utterance ("... gridò: 'Ricordera'ti anche del Mosca, / che disse, lasso! "Capo ha cosa fatta," ' / che fu mal seme per la gente tosca" ["... shouted: 'You will recall Mosca too who said, alas! "A thing done has an end!" ' which was seed of ill to the Tuscan people"] 1.28.106–8), which led to the murder of Buondelmonte in 1216. Catalano left Florence even more divided than it had been prior to his arrival on the political scene, and earlier in the canto he refers to the unfortunate role he and Loderingo played in dividing and literally destroying parts of Florence: "... e fummo tali, / ch'ancor si pare intorno dal Gardingo" ["... and we were such that it still appears around the Gardingo"] 1.23.107–8).

With the second tercet the narrative shifts to Virgil's reaction to what he sees and hears. Why is the focus now squarely on Virgil? Why does Dante the pilgrim remain silent? What reason can there be, here of all places, for the poet to shift his attention to Virgil, keeping Dante the pilgrim well in the background? The punishment of Caiaphas and the other Pharisees is surely more pertinent to Christians than to pagans. Yet, it is Virgil who is now emphasized, whose name is in the rhyme position with "concilio" and "essilio" and whose reaction to what he sees is registered in the text. Further, the reaction of marvelling over a soul in Hell is not typical of Virgil. Indeed, here is the only episode in the *Inferno* where Virgil "marvels" over any soul he encounters.[10]

Virgil remains front and centre for the balance of the canto as he abruptly shifts his attention away from Caiaphas and back to Catalano and resumes his role as guide. After having been misled earlier by Malacoda, he is hopeful that Catalano will point out some passageway that has survived the earthquake, allowing him to guide Dante over the slope from the sixth *bolgia* and on to the seventh. Catalano proves more obliging. But at no point in the remaining tercets of this canto does Dante the pilgrim utter a single word. Now that they have moved beyond Caiaphas, why does Dante not again set his sights on Catalano and complete his speech of condemnation? Why the complete focus on Virgil? I submit that the question cannot be answered within the confines of this episode. It is only by following the signposted journey, signalled by the formula "ne l'etterno essilio" within the central configuration, to the fifth terrace of the *Purgatorio*, and ultimately into the *Paradiso*, signalled by the "Virgilio"/"essilio"/"concilio" rhyme words, that light can be shed on the question.

The prostrate posture of the penitent souls of the fifth terrace of Purgatory is reminiscent of that of Caiaphas, Annas, and the other Pharisees of the Council, even though the two groups would appear to have nothing in common. The *contrapasso* dictates that the avaricious and the prodigals be prostrate, but prone (unlike Caiaphas and the others who lie supine) because they must learn about earthly things in their proper measure, with their hands and feet tied (*Purgatorio* 19.115–26).

Direct reference to Christ's crucifixion is made on this terrace by the once avaricious Hugh Capet to his descendant Philip the Fair. Hugh predicts that like Pontius Pilate, who handed Christ over to the people, Philip will hand Pope Boniface VIII, the Vicar of Christ, over to the Colonna family (which occurs in 1303).[11] And like Christ, Hugh predicts that this Vicar of Christ will be mocked.[12] Philip would also have been considered like Pilate because he too denied responsibility for the result of his actions. Dante may well have heard of Pope Benedict XI's speech in Perugia in 1304 when he referred to Philip as "the new Pilate."[13] But Philip's cruelty is not yet sated, Hugh continues, for the covetous King then sets his sights on the Templar Knights.[14] The Templars were so called because they had been housed at the palace of the Latin Kings, known as "Solomon's temple," harking back to the Temple built by Solomon. A succeeding one had been destroyed when Jerusalem was destroyed in 70 AD, according to Dante in *Purgatorio* 21, to take just vengeance against the people who had played a role in the crucifixion of Christ.[15]

From the first tercet of *Purgatorio* 21 the poet sets the scene for the predominant focus of the canto: events that took place around the time of Christ. The poet refers first to the story of the Samaritan Woman (see John 4: 5–15), and compares Christ's thirsting for water to the pilgrim's thirsting to know the cause of the earthquake felt towards the end of the preceding canto (2.20.127–9): "... quand' io senti', come cosa che cada, / tremar lo monte; onde mi prese un gelo / qual prender suol colui ch'a morte vada" ["... when I felt the mountain shake like something that is falling; at which a chill such as seizes one who goes to his death"]).

Dante's intense curiosity about the earthquake he experienced in *Purgatorio* 20 is mingled with compassion towards the souls who suffer on this terrace, even though he knows that the *contrapasso* is perforce just: "… e condoleami a la giusta vendetta" ["… and I was grieving at the just vengeance"] (2.21.6). The words "giusta vendetta" have greater relevance when the reader looks back to *Inferno* 23, where Caiaphas suffers the *contrapasso* of being crucified for his role in Christ's crucifixion.[16] But the formula "giusta vendetta" does not appear in *Inferno* 23. Instead it appears in *Paradiso* 7 in verses 20 and 50, the only places after *Purgatorio* 21 where the formula "giusta vendetta" is repeated.

In *Paradiso* 7 beginning with verse 19, Beatrice responds to Dante's thirst to understand what Justinian meant in the preceding canto when he referred to Titus wreaking vengeance on Jerusalem for the crucifixion which in turn had avenged original sin.[17] Beatrice explains that those Jews who rejected Christ were obliged to play their necessary role in his crucifixion, and argues that although those "Giudei" and God desired the same outcome for Christ, the Jewish nation had to be punished:

> "Però d'un atto uscir cose diverse:
> ch'a Dio e a' Giudei piacque una morte;
> per lei tremò la terra e 'l ciel s'aperse.
>   Non ti dee oramai parer più forte,
> quando si dice che *giusta vendetta*
> poscia vengiata fu da giusta corte."

["Therefore from one act issued things diverse, for one same death was pleasing to God and to the Jews; thereat the earth trembled and Heaven was opened. No longer, now, should it seem hard to you when it is said that just vengeance was afterwards avenged by a just court."]

(3.7.46–51)

Beatrice's words refer to the action of the Pharisees, when the "mala sementa" (1.23.123: "che fu per li Giudei mala sementa" ["which was a seed of evil for the Jews"]) was planted, resulting in the destruction of Herod's temple in 70 AD. But more important for this study, the repetitions of "giusta vendetta" in *Paradiso* 7 tie *Purgatorio* 21, where "giusta vendetta" first appears and Titus's vengeful act is first recounted, to *Inferno* 23, where Annas and Caiaphas are crucified. This establishes an overt link between those two episodes, which are already linked by the other linguistic signposts under study. Even though "giusta vendetta" does not appear in the text of *Inferno* 23, it is there by example with Annas, Caiaphas, and the other Pharisees. The meaning of "giusta vendetta" in *Purgatorio* 21.6 does not relate to the punishment of the Jewish nation; as an identifier, however, linking *Paradiso* 7 with *Inferno* 23, and also *Purgatorio* 21.82–4, it is very significant.

Paradiso 7 also refers to the earthquake ("per lei tremò la terra e 'l ciel s'aperse" ["thereat the earth trembled and Heaven was opened"] v. 48) which occurred at the moment Christ died, when the veil of the Temple was rent in twain,[18] permitting those Jewish and pagan worthies who had implicit faith in Christ to come to be freed and allowed entry into Paradise. The earthquake also damaged parts of Hell – for instance the sixth *bolgia* where Caiaphas and his Pharisees lie crucified and where Virgil was misled by Malacoda. And when *Purgatorio* 21 opens, thoughts about another earthquake that both Dante and Virgil experienced in *Purgatorio* 20 consume the pilgrim. But Dante does not yet realize that this earthquake too heralds freedom for a soul who has long suffered the "giusta vendetta" of God and who is only now allowed entry into Paradise.[19]

In the third tercet of *Purgatorio* 21, there is further reference to an event from the time of the crucifixion of Christ, but here Dante refers explicitly to the Gospel in which the event is described: "Ed ecco, sì come ne scrive Luca ..." ["And lo, as Luke writes for us ..."] (v. 7).[20] Just as two disciples deep in conversation were overtaken by the newly risen Christ, so too Dante and Virgil are overtaken by one recently risen: Statius. Both pilgrim and guide are unaware of this third presence, distracted as they are by the throng of prostrate penitent souls at their feet.

Statius's greeting in the vocative, "O frati miei, Dio vi dea pace" ["O my brothers, may God give you peace"] (v. 13), gains the attention of Dante and Virgil.[21] "O frati" also appears in *Inferno* 23 when Dante begins to censure Catalano and Loderingo for betraying the peace in Florence but is distracted by the sight of the crucified Caiaphas. However, unlike Dante's brief words of reprimand following the "O frati" in *Inferno*, Statius adds the possessive "miei," assuming that Dante and Virgil are travellers, fellow pilgrims like himself. It is Virgil who returns to Statius's greeting and explains that he is not in fact a pilgrim like Statius, and it is here that the formula "ne l'etterno essilio" is repeated, along with its rhyme words within the greater configuration outlined earlier:

"*O frati* miei, Dio vi dea pace."
Noi ci volgemmo sùbiti, e *Virgilio*
rendéli 'l cenno ch'a ciò si conface.

Poi cominciò: "Nel beato *concilio*
ti ponga in pace la *verace corte*
che me rilega *ne l'etterno essilio.*"

["O my brothers, may God give you peace." We turned quickly and Virgil answered him with the greeting that is fitting thereto; then he began, "May the
true court which binds me in the eternal exile bring you in peace to the assembly of the blest."]

(2.21.13–18)

Virgil corrects Statius's greeting by emphasizing that God cannot
give him peace. As a pre-Christian, Virgil admits to being condemned
to eternal exile in Hell by a true court. He explains in *Inferno* 1 that his
sentence by the Emperor of that court is a result of his rebellion:

"ché quello imperador che là sù regna,
perch' i' fu' ribellante a la sua legge,
non vuol che 'n sua città per me si vegna."

["For the Emperor who reigns there-above wills not that I come into His city,
because I was rebellious to His law."]

(1.1.124–6)

Virgil's exile is eternal because through his "rebellion" he lacked the
necessary implicit faith in Christ to come.[22] The "verace corte" is the
same "corte" which Virgil hopes will allow Statius to go in peace to
the "beato concilio" in Paradise.

If one compares this repeated formula, "ne l'etterno essilio," within
its *terza rima* configuration (all part of the greater configuration), to its
first occurrence, a shift in emphasis can be noted. In *Inferno* 23 Virgil
is simply a spectator, marvelling at the novel sight of one of the "concilio," the Council of the Pharisees, crucified there "ne l'etterno essilio" in Hell. In *Purgatorio* 21, however, Virgil is at pains to explain to
Statius, without even having been asked, that he resides in Hell. He
deliberately stresses his own plight now on centre stage. Here Virgil,
not Caiaphas, is highlighted as the one dwelling "ne l'etterno essilio," and it is now a true court, "la verace corte," not the false one of
the Pharisees, that has condemned this soul, Virgil, to "etterno essilio." Instead of the "concilio" of the Pharisees which had once condemned Christ, we have the "beato concilio" where Christ rules
supreme among the blessed.

In *Inferno* 23 the rhyme word "Virgilio," linked to "concilio" and
"essilio," not only ties Virgil linguistically to the formula "ne l'etterno
essilio" but also draws the attention of the reader to his reaction on

seeing Caiaphas. Dante the pilgrim's reaction is off stage, not even recorded. Virgil's marvelling before Caiaphas is described within the tercets of that configuration, and attention is focused on him alone as he addresses Catalano. Likewise in *Purgatorio* 21 it is the repetition of "Virgilio" within the configuration, again rhyming with "concilio" and "essilio," which once more fixes attention on Virgil, while Dante is again silent and unseen. If Virgil, unlike Statius, is relegated to "etterno essilio," and if unlike Statius he will not reach the "beato concilio," should it not be Dante who responds to Statius's "O frati miei," since both he and Statius share the same destination of the "beato concilio"? As it is Virgil who responds instead of Dante and refers to his own state before mentioning Dante's, Statius understandably mistakes Dante too for a lost soul condemned like Virgil to eternal exile.

With Caiaphas's state of "etterno essilio" emphasized in *Inferno* 23, and Virgil's state of "etterno essilio" emphasized in *Purgatorio* 21, what does this repetition communicate to the reader? The repetition of the formula invites the reader to compare or contrast the two individuals thus highlighted: Caiaphas and Virgil. Beyond the formula itself revealing that they are both condemned to Hell, is there more? If Caiaphas represents those of the Jewish nation who instead of believing in Christ rejected him, then perhaps Virgil can also be seen as representative of a nation that similarly rejected Christ.[23] If Virgil represents Rome, more specifically pagan Rome, we can begin to see the parallel. Virgil's Romans, like Caiaphas's Jews, rejected Christ. Consequently both Caiaphas and Virgil, along with the people they represent, must be condemned by the "verace corte." It is fitting in this context that Virgil be the one who responds to Statius, for Statius also represents the Roman people. But unlike Virgil, Statius, who lived in the first century after Christ, represents those Romans who also believed in him. Thus he is liberated by the same "verace corte" which condemned Virgil to eternal exile.

After Statius queries the right of Virgil and Dante to be in Purgatory, if they are both condemned to eternal exile, Virgil is quick to indicate that Dante is alive and emphasize that there is another key difference between them. Dante will not be exiled to Hell, but saved to reside one day in Paradise ("... ben vedrai che coi buon convien ch'e' regni" ["... you will clearly see that he is to reign with the good"] v. 24). What conclusion may be drawn from this initial conversation between Virgil and Statius (before the one learns the identity of the other), beginning within the repeated configuration? Through Virgil's mouth the poet contrasts Virgil's damnation with his own salvation. Like the other souls condemned to Hell, Virgil can read the future and foresee that Dante, like Statius, will be saved. But there is no hope for Virgil, no reward for this guiding task he has undertaken at Beatrice's behest.[24] He has been sentenced by the true court to an exile which will be eternal.

The episode in *Purgatorio* 21 is not the last which juxtaposes Virgil "ne l'etterno essilio" with one who is saved. While the formula "ne l'etterno essilio" does not reappear, "essilio" within its configuration of rhyme words is repeated by Adam in *Paradiso* 26, when he describes his sin of pride to Dante, the sin that caused his own, long exile in Limbo:

"Or, figliuol mio, non il gustar del legno
fu per sé la cagion di tanto *essilio*,
ma solamente il trapassar del segno.
    Quindi onde mosse tua donna *Virgilio*,
quattromila trecento e due volumi
di sol desiderai questo *concilio*."

["Now know, my son, that the tasting of the tree was not in itself the cause of so long an exile, but solely the overpassing of the bound. In the place whence your lady dispatched Virgil, I longed for this assembly during four thousand three hundred and two revolutions of the sun."]

(3.26.115–20)

Before analysing the text quoted above, two preliminary remarks are in order. Adam's reference to Virgil in verse 118 is the last time that the name "Virgilio" appears in the *Commedia*, here once again in the rhyme position with "essilio" and "concilio."[25] This last repetition draws increased focus, not on Caiaphas and the other Pharisees, not on Statius or even Dante the pilgrim, but on Virgil, whose name, not theirs, remains part of the configuration. Virgil is the one constant in this signposted journey. His fate is here juxtaposed with that of Adam. The "concilio" has been transformed from that of the Pharisees in *Inferno* 23.122 to that of God in *Purgatorio* 21.16 and also here in *Paradiso* 3.26.120. But the "essilio" has lost its modifier "etterno" in *Paradiso* 26.116, an omission which makes all the difference between damnation and salvation. Nothing changes for Virgil. "Virgilio" remains the same "Virgilio," whom the "concilio" of God has condemned to "etterno essilio" in Limbo, a place to which Virgil has already returned by now as Adam addresses Dante.

If one considers the *Commedia* in its entirety, and counts the number of references to "Virgilio," the reference to "Virgilio" in *Paradiso* 26.118 is not just the last of the three, but stands out as the last of a total of thirty-two. Of these thirty-two "Virgilio" references, five in the *Inferno*, twenty-five in the *Purgatorio*, and two in the *Paradiso*,[26] in the rhyme position "Virgilio" only appears once per *cantica*, always with the same rhyme words "essilio" and "concilio," which together make up the linguistic configuration now under scrutiny. So Adam's words quoted above do not just betoken the end of the signposted journey, signalled by the thrice appearing "essilio"/"Virgilio"/"concilio" rhyme words, but also the end of a parallel journey, signalled by the thirty-second and last appearance of the name "Virgilio."

When Adam begins to answer the questions he perceives that Dante wishes put to him, why does he find it necessary to associate Limbo solely with Virgil, who must dwell there in eternal exile? Furthermore, why must he refer to Virgil by name, this being only the second time that Virgil's name has appeared in the *Paradiso*? I submit that the poet wishes to communicate to the reader some last words about Virgil, with direct reference to him by name, and he intends to do so through the words of the first father. Adam for his part reveals that during the 4302 years he was in "essilio" for the sin of pride, in Limbo where Beatrice found "Virgilio" and where Virgil still dwells, he desired more than anything else this "concilio" of the blessed in Paradise. But in order to understand their relevance to Virgil one must take the retrospective journey over ground already traversed. By now the reader is aware that Virgil, like Adam, has also yearned for the "concilio" of God. Virgil has already made this point clear in his greeting to Statius. But unlike Adam whose yearning is in the past tense ("desiderai"), his yearning having been satisfied some 1266 years before when Christ delivered him from Limbo, the exiled Virgil continues to be in awe of the City of "the Emperor" which is forever closed to him, and he communicated his sense of wonder to Dante back in *Inferno* 1:

> "In tutte parti impera e quivi regge;
> quivi è la sua città e l'alto seggio:
> oh felice colui cu' ivi elegge!"

["In all parts is His empire, in that part is His kingdom, there is His city and His lofty seat. Oh, happy he whom He elects thereto!"]

$$(1.1.127-9)$$

And Virgil was there and saw Adam's deliverance by Christ from exile. Virgil was there to witness Adam's fondest wish come true, and described Adam's deliverance to Dante, first among the Old Testament worthies although not referred to by name:

... "Io era nuovo in questo stato,
quando ci vidi venire un possente,
con segno di vittoria coronato.
    Trasseci l'ombra del primo parente,
d'Abèl suo figlio e quella di Noè,
di Moïsè legista e ubidente ..."

[... "I was new in this condition when I saw a Mighty One come here,
crowned with sign of victory. He took hence the shade of our first parent,
Abel his son, and Noah, and Moses, obedient giver of laws ..."]

(1.4.52–7)

While Virgil witnessed this once-only release of some of his fellow
Limbo dwellers, he was but a spectator (see chapter 3). To have been a
participant would have meant being saved. But Virgil was not saved,
because as one who rebelled against God, as one who did not have
implicit faith in Christ to come, he was condemned to "etterno essilio," not temporary "essilio" like the "primo parente."

Virgil's "etterno essilio" juxtaposed with Adam's non-eternal "essilio" is underscored in *Paradiso* 26, if the reader has arrived at this passage by way of the signposted journey. What one can infer in reading
Adam's response to Dante is that Virgil remains in eternal exile despite
his recent service, even though Adam does not explicitly say so. But if
one looks back to the previous stop on the signposted journey in *Purgatorio* 21, the last time the configuration "Virgilio"/"concilio"/"essilio" appeared, the noun "essilio" was still modified by the adjective
"etterno." And it was Virgil himself who expressed his fate, that the
court of God had decreed he be assigned to "etterno essilio" in Limbo.

Virgil, like all humankind before Christ, was condemned to Limbo,
stained by original sin. What is ironic is that in *Paradiso* 26 the poet
chooses to have the "primo parente," the very one who committed that
sin, make this last reference to Virgil by name in the *Commedia*, reminding the reader who has followed the signposted journey that the critical
modifier "etterno" will not be omitted from Virgil's exile. He will remain for eternity among the condemned "mal seme d'Adamo" ["evil
seed of Adam"] to whom the poet had referred in *Inferno* 3.115.

Not all Adam's offspring are condemned. Those who embrace
Christ can be saved, but this Virgil did not do. If one looks back to the
first occurrence of the linguistic configuration in *Inferno* 23, there the
reference is to another evil or ill seed, the "mala sementa" for the
"Giudei," which was the Council of the Pharisees. And the one who
utters these words is that political hypocrite of Florence of the late
1260s, Catalano, who descended from the "mal seme per la gente

tosca" ["seed of evil to the Tuscan people"] (1.28.108), Mosca's words, which were responsible for first unleashing factional hatred and violence in Florence.

For those who sprout from these evil seeds, the result is often exile in earthly life. There was exile for Adam's offspring when he was cast out of Eden. For those of the Jewish nation who did not believe in Christ there was exile, and the destruction of their temple and the whole city of Jerusalem by Titus in 70 AD. For many of the "gente tosca," including Dante himself, there was political exile.[27] In this life, individuals or groups of individuals may be justly or unjustly condemned to exile.

But in the afterlife there will be no exile, provided the reader of the *Commedia* journeys with Dante and learns the lessons Dante is learning. Dante, personally, is journeying to God so as to avoid exile in the next life, even as he learns from his ancestor Cacciaguida that exile awaits him in this one. Those of the Jewish nation who embraced Christ or looked too his coming now live for eternity in Paradise and reap the reward for their past sufferings during the earlier Babylonian captivity, as is outlined by the poet in *Paradiso* 23, where two of the three rhyme words of the configuration also appear: [28]

> Quivi si vive e gode del tesoro
> che s'acquistò piangendo ne lo *essilio*
> di Babillòn, ove si lasciò l'oro.
> Quivi trïunfa, sotto l'alto *Filio*
> di Dio e di Maria, di sua vittoria,
> e con l'antico e col novo *concilio*,
>   colui che tien le chiavi di tal gloria.

[Here they live and rejoice in the treasure which was gained with tears in the exile of Babylon, where gold was scorned. Here, under the exalted Son of God and Mary, together with both the ancient and the new council, he triumphs in his victory who holds the keys of such glory.]

(3.23.133–9)

But just as the lack of the adjective "etterno" there in *Paradiso* 26 emphasizes the difference between salvation for Adam and damnation for Virgil, so too the missing third rhyme word "Virgilio" here in *Paradiso* 23.136 emphasizes the reward that could have also been Virgil's and that of his people, had he not lacked faith in Christ to come, in the "Filio" who replaces "Virgilio" in verse 136 of this linguistic configuration.[29]

9 The Destination: Dante's Eyes Fixed and Attentive

On the shore of Purgatory, Dante asks his newly arrived friend Casella to stop a while so that they can talk. Out of his love for Dante, Casella agrees to stay his steps, which prompts a second request. Provided that no new laws of Purgatory have taken from Casella his ability to remember and reproduce the "amoroso canto" ["amorous song"], would Casella sing Dante a song, like those which used to soothe all his pains?[1] Casella complies, and Virgil and all the penitent souls are stilled, "fissi e attenti" ["fixed and attentive"] to the notes of one of Dante's *canzoni*, *Amor che ne la mente mi ragiona* [*Love that discourses in my mind*], sung sweetly by Casella.[2] They are rapt and oblivious to all their new surroundings until Cato sharply reproaches them for having delayed when they should have hastened to the mountain immediately upon reaching shore.

At the top of the mountain of Purgatory when at the behest of the three theological Virtues Beatrice finally reveals herself fully to her "fedele" ["faithful one"] Dante, his eyes are "fissi e attenti" before the smile that he has been deprived of seeing since her death ten years before. For ten long years Dante's eyes have so thirsted for the sight of Beatrice's face that now, despite his purification in the Lethe, he is left senseless, caught by Beatrice's smile in the same old net of pre-1290 courtly love days.[3] Once more he is roused from his reverie, not by the reproachful Cato this time, but by the three Virtues with the simple words "troppo fiso" ["too fixedly"] which open Dante's senses to all the other wonders that surround him.

In the Empyrean, after Beatrice has taken her seat on high, she looks down on Dante and smiles at him one last time before turning her attention anew to the eternal fountain. Instead of following her gaze upward, Dante looks downward to the newly arrived Bernard of Clairvaux, the "fedele" of the Virgin Mary, and last guide to Dante. Bernard mildly reproaches Dante for looking down at him in curiosity instead of directing his eyes on high where the Virgin Mary, Queen of the Realm, presides smiling and beautiful. And Dante does as he is bidden, lifting his eyes to Mary. His eyes, now "fissi e attenti" on her, are followed by Bernard's. Here there is no one to scold Dante. On the contrary, he gazes all the more ardently, as he beholds the depth of the faithful Bernard's affection for his lady the Virgin Mary.

Only in these three instances in the *Commedia* does Dante adopt the formula "fissi e attenti."[4] Led by the signposts of the repeated formula "fissi e attenti," the reader will come at last to the goal of the pilgrim's journey: the Empyrean. Dante's eyes, his "occhi miei," modified in the latter two instances by "fissi e attenti," reach the same destination, but by a longer route which begins in the *Vita Nuova* where his "occhi miei" first strayed from Beatrice in the direction of the Donna Gentile.

Ultimately the reader will be looking up, following Dante's gaze towards the Virgin Mary on the highest level of the Empyrean. Alongside Dante, "fedele" of Beatrice (2.31.134) and Lucia (1.2.98), stands Bernard, "fedele" of the Virgin Mary, who has directed Dante's gaze upward to where Mary is seated. At long last Dante's "occhi miei" fix upon the Virgin Mary, bringing him back to the one who first recognized his plight in *Inferno* 2. There Mary commended Dante to Lucia, who in turn called on Beatrice to hear Dante's piteous cry and observe his mortal struggle beneath the slope on the shore by: "la fiumana ove 'l mare non ha vanto" ["the flood over which the sea has no vaunt"] (1.2.108). Mary's first words to Lucia identified Dante as a "fedele" who needed the help of her to whom he had been faithful: "Or ha bisogno il tuo *fedele* / di te, e io a te lo raccomando" ["Your faithful one has need of you now, and I commend him to you"] (1.2.98–9). Mary, seeing that Dante's soul was at the point of death, turned to Lucia, thereby opening the way for the faithful Dante to journey upward to salvation, now almost attained.

From the vantage point of the Empyrean, destination of the signposted journey to the Empyrean, and ever mindful of Dante's true goal, the enlightened reader can now look back to the place where the formula first emerges. There at the shore by another slope, Dante's immortal soul is once more in peril. Like Virgil and the newly disembarked souls, he finds himself in an unfamiliar land, and is unsure how to behave. Ignorant, like his pagan guide, of the new laws in effect in this Christian place, Dante nonetheless senses that the singing of amorous songs may be forbidden in Purgatory. What he requests of Casella, however, is slightly different:

> E io: "Se nuova legge non ti toglie
> memoria o uso a l'amoroso canto
> che mi solea quetar tutte mie doglie,
>   di ciò ti piaccia consolare alquanto
> l'anima mia, che, con la sua persona
> venendo qui, è affannata tanto!"

[And I, "If a new law does not take from you memory or practice of the songs of love which used to quiet in me all my pains, may it please you therewith to comfort my soul somewhat, which coming hither with its body is so wearied."]

(2.2.106–11)

If Casella can still remember the words to love songs and is still able to sing them, Dante hopes he will will be pleased to oblige his old friend. What is lacking in Dante's request is an appreciation that laws of the new realm now govern the conduct of penitent souls even though Casella or others may still possess the ability to transgress them.[5] What is stressed by the pilgrim is his own soul's need of consolation. Casella obligingly sings a song from Dante's repertoire:

> "Amor che ne la mente mi ragiona"
> cominciò elli allor sì dolcemente,
> che la dolcezza ancor dentro mi suona.
>   Lo mio maestro e io e quella gente
> ch'eran con lui parevan sì contenti,
> come a nessun toccasse altro la mente.

["Love that discourses in my mind," he then began so sweetly that the sweetness still within me sounds. My master and I and that folk who were with him appeared content as if naught else touched the mind of any.]

(2.2.112–17)

In verse 115 a shift occurs in the narrative. No longer is it just about Dante and his good friend Casella, but about the entire company of souls listening, contented and quieted by the sweetness of the song that the pilgrim asked Casella to sing, even though the pilgrim did not request that Casella console anyone but himself. The reader now looking back at this episode from the vantage point of the Empyrean will be in a position to reconsider it with the benefit of hindsight and scrutinize more carefully its relevance to the difficulties of one particular pilgrim, Dante himself. Consequently, all the others included in the "tutti" which the formula modifies will be seen in the light of the pilgrim's own errant behaviour and by extension the impact this has on them:

> Noi eravam tutti *fissi e attenti*
> a le sue note; ed ecco il veglio onesto
> gridando: "Che è ciò, spiriti lenti?
>   qual negligenza, quale stare è questo?
> Correte al monte a spogliarvi lo scoglio
> ch'esser non lascia a voi Dio manifesto."

[We were all fixed and attentive to his notes, when lo, the venerable old man, crying, "What is this, you laggard spirits? What negligence, what stay is this? Haste to the mountain to strip off the slough that lets not God be manifest to you."]

(2.2.118–23)

The choice of the "amoroso canto" sung by Casella was written by Dante probably for the Donna Gentile of the *Vita Nuova* to whom Dante turned after the death of Beatrice, and only later allegorized as Lady Philosophy in the *Convivio*, where the "canto" appears as the second *canzone*, opening book III.[6] Dante was responsible both for its composition and now for its being sung by Casella to console his soul. This composition of Dante's reflects his erstwhile fixed attention on the "other woman": the Donna Gentile. The song's effect on Dante and all the others in his company is negative in the extreme. It lures them to yield to temptation. The souls, fixed and attentive to its notes, delay their climb towards the mountain for their salvation. And the song that tempts is Dante's old song.

Implicit in Dante the pilgrim's request to Casella is that, for the duration of a song, he wishes to forget that he is at the foot of the mountain of Purgatory and imagine himself back in Florence so that his soul, having just completed a journey down to the depths of Hell, can be consoled.[7] Dante desires ease from the pains that should keep him ever mindful of the truths the journey taught him about his past sinful life. These are the same truths which Casella's singing used to make him forget back in Florence. That ten-year period from the death of Beatrice to Dante's painful journey through Hell was the time when he ceased to be the "fedele" of Beatrice, when his songs like the *canzone* for the Donna Gentile reflected his fallen state. And such songs were also having a contrary effect on those around him.

Implicit in Dante the poet's reference to the fixed and attentive state of all who listen to the song so sweetly sung by Casella is the powerful lure of his poetry which draws its readers to linger fixed and attentive before the wrong kind of song, to love something which they should eschew. What we witness in the Casella episode is an example of that temptation. The poet's praise of the sweetness of his song also suggests that pride in his own poetry holds sway in his soul, reminiscent of Oderisi's former pride in his own accomplishments. Dante will encounter Oderisi, now penitent, on the first terrace of Purgatory proper. Unlike Oderisi, however, Dante does not yet appear to repent of his pride. If Dante still remembers with pleasure the sweetness of his song, then the pilgrim's prediction to Sapia that he will have to return to the terrace of the proud after his death has a further ring of truth to it.

What is it that Dante's songs lure his audience to love? As with all courtly love poetry these songs, now sung even more sweetly in the new style than before, tempt those who read or hear them into a desire for other men's wives. For a condemnation of such poetry one need look no farther than the seventh terrace of Purgatory where we find the father of the "sweet new style," Guido Guinizzelli, being purged of his sin in the burning flames which enclose the penitent lustful. Dante the pilgrim's request that Casella sing a love song prepares the reader for an idle moment when the pilgrim and his fellows turn their thoughts to beautiful courtly ladies. But Casella does not sing a simple "amoroso canto." His choice of *Amor che ne la mente mi ragiona* opens up the discourse by allowing for a very different interpretation.[8] Is the Donna Gentile of the *canzone* the one Dante describes in chapters xxxv, xxxvi, and xxxvii of the *Vita Nuova*?[9] Within the context of the *Vita Nuova* what is depicted is the piteous woman who became the object of Dante's attentions shortly after the death of Beatrice, a woman in whom Dante started to take too much delight, but no more than that. However, one cannot consider the question of the Donna Gentile without looking beyond the *Vita Nuova* to book II of the *Convivio*,[10] where Dante explains that this same Donna Gentile is Lady Philosophy, and it is her praises that he sings in book III of the *Convivio* with the opening *canzone, Amor che ne la mente mi ragiona*. The Donna Gentile is no longer the woman of flesh and blood of the *Vita Nuova*, but has been allegorized to represent philosophy itself. The notes of this *canzone* sung so sweetly by Casella which once consoled only Dante after the death of Beatrice now console all who hear it, including Virgil, seduced by its siren call.

In Dante's journey to salvation he must learn to curb his pride in his own genius. But he begins badly in this new land, as the *canzone* in praise of Lady Philosophy, written by himself, immobilizes all who hear it, "fissi e attenti" to its notes. Dante asks Casella if any new law prevents him from singing love songs, and appears unaware that by asking such a question he has already transgressed the limits of the realm. Juxtaposing Dante's *canzone* with *In exitu Israel de Aegypto*, sung earlier aboard ship by these same pilgrim souls, Robert Hollander points to this episode as another example of Dante's flawed responses: "He, lost in the beauty of his old song, either fails to understand or else forgets the message of the new song which he has heard first, and which should have served as a rein on his enthusiasm. It is as old as Exodus and as new as the dawn which brings it, this Easter Sunday morning at the shore of the mountain."[11]

In *Inferno* 26 Dante himself cautions that he must rein in his enthusiasm and curb his genius:

> Allor mi dolsi, e ora mi ridoglio
> quando drizzo la mente a ciò ch'io vidi,
> e più lo 'ngegno affreno ch'i' non soglio,
> perché non corra che virtù nol guidi;
> sì che, se stella bona o miglior cosa
> m'ha dato 'l ben, ch'io stessi nol m'invidi.

[I sorrowed then, and sorrow now again, when I turn my mind to what I saw; and I curb my genius more than I am wont, lest it run where virtue does not guide it; so that, if a kindly star or something better has granted me the good, I may not grudge myself that gift.]

(1.26.19–24)

The reason for these lines, as Dante enters the eighth *bolgia* of the fraudulent counsellors, appears enigmatic. But not for long. As Ulysses' tale of his voyage beyond the Pillars of Hercules comes to a close at the end of the canto, the reader is left mindful of Dante's earlier words. Dante the poet must curb his "ingegno" ["genius"] to ensure that, unlike Ulysses, he does not transgress the limits placed by God on human quest. The very presence of such cautionary words leads one to question whether Dante is aware that he has ever before overstepped those bounds. This surely occurred when he turned to Lady Philosophy in the guise of the Donna Gentile shortly after Beatrice's death.[12]

The episode here under scrutiny on the shore beside the mountain of Purgatory lends further credence to this conjecture. At the end of

Purgatorio 1, Virgil and Dante are sent by Cato to the shore where Dante is to be girded by the reed that grows there in preparation for the difficult climb ahead. And Virgil performs his task as pleased another ("com' altrui piacque"):

> Venimmo poi in sul lito diserto,
> che mai non vide navicar sue *acque*
> omo, che di tornar sia poscia esperto
>   Quivi mi cinse sì *com' altrui piacque*:
> oh maraviglia! ché qual elli scelse
> l'umile pianta, cotal si *rinacque*
> subitamente là onde l'avalse.

[Then we came to the desert shore, that never saw any man navigate its waters who afterwards had experience of return. There, even as pleased another, he girdled me. O marvel! That such as he plucked the humble plant, even such did it instantly spring up again, there whence he had uprooted it.]

(2.1.130–6)

Commentators have long noted that the formula "com' altrui piacque" also appears in *Inferno* 26, describing the conclusion of another voyage which took place in these same waters some 2500 years prior. Ulysses recounts the delight of all aboard his ship when after so long a time at sea in uncharted waters they spied the dark mountain off in the distance:

> "Noi ci allegrammo, e tosto tornò in pianto,
> ché de la nova terra un turbo *nacque*
> e percosse del legno il primo canto.
>   Tre volte il fé girar con tutte l'*acque*;
> a la quarta levar la poppa in suso
> e la prora ire in giù, *com' altrui piacque*,
> infin che 'l mar fu sovra noi richiuso."

["We rejoiced, but soon our joy was turned to grief, for from the new land a whirlwind rose and struck the forepart of the ship. Three times it whirled her round with all the waters, and the fourth time it lifted the stern aloft and plunged the prow below, as pleased another, till the sea closed over us."]

(1.26.136–42)

The "altrui" in *Inferno* 26 is God, who put an end to the voyage of the proud pagan who had transgressed His limits. In *Purgatorio* 1 the "altrui" refers to Cato, who may be seen as the extension of God's will.

With the repetition of the formula, the reader is invited to juxtapose the doomed journey of Ulysses, who was sent to the bottom by the will of God and never reached the shore, with the journey of Dante the pilgrim, who has seen those depths but whom God has allowed to resurface and proceed safely to that same shore.

Along with the repetition of the rhyme words "acque" and "nacque," now "rinacque" also beckons the attention of the reader. In both cases the "acque" refer to those same waters that surround Purgatory. Indeed in *Purgatorio* 1.130–2, quoted above, there is implicit reference to the failed voyage of Ulysses as one who navigated those waters but did not survive them. Ironically it was the new waters in *Inferno* 26 which rose up and overwhelmed Ulysses and his men. And the storm which churned those waters was born ("nacque") from what for Ulysses was a new land: Purgatory. In *Purgatorio* 1, "nacque" becomes "rinacque," reflecting the theme of rebirth implicit in Purgatory. The rush that grows along those waters is reborn after Virgil picks it, reflecting this rebirth that awaits the penitent souls who, unlike Ulysses, manage to disembark at Purgatory's shore. The repetition of the formula "com' altrui piacque" along with its rhyme words invites a juxtaposition between the result of Ulysses' hubris and the rebirth of Dante the pilgrim now girded with the humble plant by his guide, in both cases "as pleased another."

But *Purgatorio* 2 tells a different story. Do not be misled into thinking at the end of *Purgatorio* 1 that Dante will learn from Ulysses' failed attempt and curb his pride in his own genius. For Dante now girded by the humble plant does not immediately depart from this barren shore. He delays his journey to salvation. He also delays the journey of Casella by asking him to sing an "amoroso canto." Then too he hinders the other newly disembarked souls as they listen transfixed to Casella's song. Like Ulysses' crew, who are urged on to their doom by Ulysses' eloquent words in *Inferno* 26.112–20, the penitent souls are also in thrall to the eloquent words of another. And like Ulysses and his crew, Dante and his fellow pilgrims break the law of this new land. They are fixed and attentive to the seductive words of Lady Philosophy. But unlike Ulysses and his crew, the penitent souls are roused from their reverie by Cato, inevitably "as pleased another," and unlike Ulysses and his crew they are allowed to advance to the mountain.

We must remember that Dante's "ingegno," so prudently restrained at the start of *Inferno* 26, was the source of the eloquent words in praise of Lady Philosophy, so sweetly sung by Casella. These words almost made Dante succumb to temptation, together with the other recently disembarked penitent souls, reflecting the lost state of Dante's soul and his impact on others during the ten-year period leading up to this journey to salvation in 1300.

Despite such incidents of backsliding, Dante is moving back towards Beatrice, something that Cavalcante dei Cavalcanti does not understand in *Inferno* 10 when reference is first made to Dante's "ingegno" within a philosophical context. Cavalcante wrongly assumes that if Dante can journey through Hell by dint of his genius ("per altezza d'ingegno" 1.10.59) then his son Guido should be at Dante's side. Dante responds by indicating Virgil as his guide perhaps to the one Guido disdained, namely Beatrice:[13]

> E io a lui: "Da me stesso non vegno:
> colui ch'attende là, per qui mi mena
> forse cui Guido vostro ebbe a disdegno."

[And I to him, "I come not of myself. He who waits yonder, leads me through here to the one whom perhaps your Guido had in disdain."]

(1.10.61–3)

Dante's return to Beatrice is contrasted with Guido Cavalcanti's rejection of what she represents. Like Dante, Guido could have left his "Donna Gentile," his Lady Philosophy, and been guided by another to his salvation.[14] But Cavalcante knows his son well and realizes that Guido travels through life "per altezza d'ingegno." Like Ulysses, Guido is not one to follow in anyone else's wake. Guido's transgression of the rules, his philosophical exploration beyond his own Pillars of Hercules, will very probably bring him to this sixth circle of the heretics, right alongside his father, Cavalcante, and his father-in-law, Farinata. Unlike Ulysses and Guido Cavalcanti, Dante has broken no such laws. He does not explore the nether reaches of the damned at his own behest. He does not appear in danger of shipwreck, but the siren song of pride in his own genius must be resisted, as he makes clear in *Inferno* 26, lest it temporarily lead him off his course, as happens in *Purgatorio* 2.

In *Purgatorio* 19 Dante is once more spared the fate of Ulysses, but only after almost succumbing and following that negative example. He dreams of the Femmina Balba, who before his eyes is transformed into the sweet siren.[15] As occurred earlier in the Casella episode, once the siren begins to sing Dante is so transfixed that it would be difficult for him to turn away from her:

> Poi ch'ell' avea 'l parlar così disciolto,
> cominciava a cantar sì, che con pena
> da lei avrei mio intento rivolto.

"Io son," cantava, "io son dolce serena,
che ' marinari in mezzo mar dismago;
tanto son di piacere a sentir piena!"

[When she had her speech thus unloosed, she began to sing so that it would
have been hard for me to turn my attention from her. "I am," she sang, "I am
the sweet Siren who leads mariners astray in mid-sea, so full am I of pleasant-
ness to hear."]

(2.19.16–21)

The Femmina Balba sings her own praises, and for a brief time the
slumbering Dante is under her spell. In a dream she almost lures
Dante away from his appointed course, much as Casella's "amoroso
canto" of the "Donna Gentile," allegorized as Lady Philosophy, enticed him at the shore of the mountain, and much as the "Donna Gentile" literally enticed him after the death of Beatrice.[16] The Femmina
Balba did in fact succeed in tempting Ulysses from his course at sea,
or so she claims:[17]

"Io volsi Ulisse del suo cammin vago
al canto mio; e qual meco s'ausa,
rado sen parte; sì tutto l'appago!"

["Ulysses, eager to journey on, I turned aside to my song; and whosoever
abides with me rarely departs, so wholly do I satisfy him."]

(2.19.22–4)

Ulysses, who will transgress the limits imposed on humankind and
follow the siren call of knowledge to his doom near the shore of the
mountain, here reveals his all too human vulnerability to the song of
the seductive siren.

Before encountering Ulysses in *Inferno* 26 Dante has already conveyed to the reader that his genius must not run where virtue does
not guide: "e più lo 'ngegno affreno ch'i' non soglio, / perché non
corra che virtù nol guidi" ["and I curb my genius more than I am
wont, lest it run where virtue does not guide it"] (1.26.21–2). In *Purgatorio* 2 and again in *Purgatorio* 19 the transfixed pilgrim temporarily
turns away from virtue's guidance until in the former instance Cato
arrives on the scene, and in the latter a lady ("santa e presta" ["holy
and alert"] v. 26), possibly Beatrice herself (see chapter 4)[18] urges
Virgil to shake Dante from his slumber while the Femmina Balba is
still in mid-song. On both occasions Ulysses' negative example looms
large just off stage.

In *Purgatorio* 31 Beatrice forces Dante to acknowledge all the impediments and the allurements encountered on his journey back to her by reminding him of the ditches across his path ("fossi attraversati" v. 25), the spurious attractions and advantages ("agevolezze ... avanzi" v. 28) of worldly delights, the sirens ("le serene" v. 45) he must valiantly resist, and the damsels or other fleeting trifles ("pargoletta / o altra novità con sì breve uso" vv. 59–60) which must not hinder him. These references recall Dante's weakness and backsliding during the 1290 to 1300 period after Beatrice's death when he was enticed off course by the call of the Donna Gentile, allegorized in the *Convivio* as the call of Lady Philosophy. The reference to the sirens reminds the reader specifically of the Femmina Balba, who tempted Ulysses off his course and was poised to lure Dante as well. But unlike Ulysses, Dante has managed to get back on course and journey home to his lady, and he confesses his fault:

> ... "Le presenti cose
> col falso lor piacer volser miei passi,
> tosto che 'l vostro viso si nascose."

[... "The present things, with their false pleasure, turned my steps aside, as soon as your countenance was hidden."]

(2.31.34–6)

Dante was tempted off course soon after Beatrice's death and turned, as he says in the *Convivio* II xii, to Lady Philosophy. And she was the subject of Dante's *canzone*, which opens book III: *Amor che ne la mente mi ragiona*, so sweetly sung by Casella that Dante and all his company closed their minds to all else, fixed and attentive until scolded by Cato for their negligence in pursuing their appointed course from the shore of Purgatory to the mountain. Dante might have remained off course, like Ulysses never to reach his true goal, but Cato arrived and scolded as pleased God. Dante has now scaled the height of that mountain, and here acknowledges that all the other things which once held him in thrall are now hateful to him: "tutte altre cose qual mi torse / più nel suo amor, più mi si fé nemica" ["all other things, that which had most turned me to love of it became most hateful to me"] (2.31.86–7). Were Dante not willing to look beyond his own human capacity and seek guidance from others, he would have succumbed to the spell of the sirens, and like Ulysses would have been shipwrecked long before this.

After fainting from remorse Dante regains his senses in the waters of the Lethe where Matelda has drawn him. Approaching the far shore he hears a song quite unlike *Amor che ne la mente mi ragiona* sung at that other shore now far behind him:

> Quando fui presso a la beata riva,
> *"Asperges me"* sì dolcemente udissi,
> che nol so rimembrar, non ch'io lo scriva.

[When I was close to the blessed shore, I heard *"Asperges me"* sung so sweetly that I cannot remember it, far less write it.]

(2.31.97–9)

The songs are so different and yet the tercets that contain them bear some striking similarities. Let us compare the two:

> *"Amor che ne la mente mi ragiona"*
> cominciò elli allor sì dolcemente,
> che la dolcezza ancor dentro mi suona.

[*"Love that discourses in my mind,"* he then began so sweetly that the sweetness still within me sounds.]

(2.2.112–14)

The formula "sì dolcemente" is repeated in both instances and appears nowhere else in the *Commedia*. As well, in both instances what immediately follows is reference to the current state of the poet either remembering or not the words of the songs. While the sweetness of *Amor che ne la mente mi ragiona* still resounds in Dante's memory, the sweetness of *Asperges me* is on a higher plane, too much for human faculties to retain. The sweetness with which the song was sung has erased the very words themselves from Dante's memory, so much so that even now he finds himself unable to transcribe these famous verses from Psalm 50: "Asperges me hyssopo, et mundabor; lavabis me, et super nivem dealbador" ["Cleanse me of sin with hyssop, that I may be purified; wash me, and I shall be whiter than snow"] (50:9). Dante's sins are being washed away as *Asperges me* is being sung, the same sins which had held such attraction for him as he listened to *Amor che ne la mente mi ragiona*. *Asperges me* was sung so sweetly that its words were likewise wiped from Dante's memory. The formula "sì dolcemente" is used to describe both songs, yet the impact from *Asperges me* is far greater. *Amor che ne la mente mi ragiona* may be an enticing tune for humans to remember, but it is fleeting compared with the *Asperges me* sung by the angels. As we see in *Paradiso* 33, what a mere mortal like Dante the pilgrim cannot remember and cannot transcribe is far nobler than what he can.

Once Dante attains the far shore of the Lethe, he should be well beyond the reach of temptation and able to recognize how much sweeter the song is that comes down from on high than any "amoroso canto" produced by mortal man (Dante himself). Dante is now at Beatrice's side and the three theological Virtues sing their song to Beatrice:

"Volgi, Beatrice, volgi li occhi santi,"
era la sua canzone, "al tuo fedele
che, per vederti, ha mossi passi tanti!"

["Turn, Beatrice, turn your holy eyes upon your faithful one," was their song, "who has moved so many steps to see you."]

(2.31.133–5)

The Virtues sing a "canzone" to Dante's true lady of the *Vita Nuova* in which they beseech her to cast her saintly eyes in the direction of her faithful one who has come such a long way to be by her side. Such a *canzone* is in marked contrast to the "amoroso canto" in praise of Lady Philosophy that Casella had sung and which had detained Dante and the company of souls on the shore of Purgatory. Dante is now Beatrice's "fedele," not just as one of the "fedeli d'Amore" (*Vita Nuova* III), but as one who has ultimately proven himself faithful to her through all his trials, despite the ditches, the attractions, the sirens, and the "amorosi canti" that had appeared as roadblocks in his way back to her.[19]

In response to the song of the three theological Virtues, "Volgi Beatrice, volgi li occhi santi," Beatrice turns to Dante and unveils her smiling face. *Purgatorio* 32 opens with the focus on Dante's own eyes, now "fissi e attenti," which have not looked upon Beatrice in ten years:

Tant'eran li occhi miei *fissi e attenti*
a disbramarsi la decenne sete,
che li altri sensi m'eran tutti spenti.

[So fixed and intent were my eyes in satisfying their ten-year thirst, that every other sense was quenched in me.]

(2.32.1–3)

The formula of repetition "fissi e attenti" now describes Dante's eyes, which are making up for some ten years of being deprived of sight of the one alone who could have quenched that thirst.[20]

The saga of Dante's eyes, now again turned to Beatrice here in Earthly Paradise, began in the *Vita Nuova* one year after her death. At the opening of chapter xxxv, Dante was filled with sorrowful thoughts as his mind turned to times past. He raised his eyes to see whether others were witness to his grief:[21]

Poi per alquanto tempo, con ciò fosse cosa che io fosse in parte ne la quale mi ricordava del passato tempo molto stava pensoso, e con dolorosi pensamenti, tanto che mi faceano parere de fore una vista di terribile sbigottimento. Onde io, accorgendomi del mio travagliare, *levai li occhi* per vedere se altri mi vedesse. Allora vidi una gentile donna giovane e bella molto, la quale da una finestra mi riguardava sì pietosamente, quanto a la vista, che tutta la pietà parea in lei accolta.

[Afterwards, for some time, because I was in a place where I remembered days gone by, I became very pensive and filled with such sorrowful thoughts that I took on an appearance of terrible distress. Becoming aware of my condition, I raised my eyes to see if anyone noticed it; and then I saw a gracious lady, young and very beautiful, who was looking at me from a window so compassionately, as it seemed from her appearance, that all pity seemed to be gathered in her.]

(*VN* xxxv)

Dante's eyes met those of the Donna Gentile, in whom he sensed the most noble kind of love. He addressed his first sonnet to her and described how his eyes saw in her a kindred spirit:

Videro *li occhi miei* quanta pietate
era apparita in la vostra figura,
quando guardaste li atti e la statura
ch'io faccio per dolor molte fiate.

[These eyes of mine beheld the tenderness which marked your features when you turned to gaze upon my doleful bearing and the ways I many times assume in my distress.]

(*Videro li occhi miei*, vv. 1–4)

In chapter xxxvi, we are told that the Donna Gentile reminds Dante of Beatrice, who enables the tears of grief to flow from his eyes:

E certo molte volte non potendo lagrimare né disfogare la mia tristizia, io andava per vedere questa pietosa donna, la quale parea che tirasse le lagrime fuori de *li miei occhi* per la sua vista.

[Often indeed when I could not weep or give expression to my sorrow I used to go to see this compassionate being, the very sight of whom seemed to draw the tears from my eyes.]

(*VN* xxxvi)

In chapter xxxvii, Dante's eyes begin to delight too much in the Donna Gentile:

Io venni a tanto per la vista di questa donna, che *li miei occhi* si cominciarono a dilettare troppo di vederla ...

[The sight of this lady had such an effect on me that my eyes began to delight too much in seeing her ...]

(*VN* xxxvii)

He becomes angry with himself and curses his eyes: "Onde più volte bestemmiava la vanitade de *li occhi miei* ..." ["And often too I cursed the vanity of my eyes ..."]. His thoughts address his eyes and point out their error in turning away from the one for whom they used to weep. Now they should weep in guilt for having abandoned Beatrice. At the close of this address, Dante is full of anguish: "E quando così avea detto fra me medesimo a *li miei occhi*, e li sospiri m'assalivano grandissimi e angosciosi" ["When I had spoken within myself to my eyes in this way, I was beset with deep sighs of anguish"]. Dante tells how in his sonnet which follows he will speak to his eyes: "E dissi questo sonetto, lo quale comincia: *L'amaro lagrimar*. Ed hae due parti: ne la prima parlo a *li occhi miei* ..." ["And so I wrote the sonnet beginning: *The bitter tears*. It has two parts. In the first I speak to my eyes ..."]. The sonnet invokes Dante's eyes ("oi occhi miei" v. 2), which once wept for Beatrice. They have forsaken her for the Donna Gentile and now must turn away from the "viso d'una donna che vi mira" ["the face of a lady who holds you"] (v. 11). Dante's heart reminds his eyes never again to forget and turn from Beatrice:

"Voi non dovreste mai se non per morte,
la vostra donna, ch'è morta, obliare."
Così dice 'l meo core, e poi sospira.

["While life endures you should not ever be inconstant to your lady who is dead." So speaks my heart, I hear, and then it sighs.]

(*L'amaro lagrimar*, vv. 12–14)

In *Purgatorio* 32, the reappearance of Beatrice before Dante's "occhi miei," now "fissi e attenti," raises the question of whom they were "fissi e attenti" upon during the ten long years he thirsted for a sight of her. Part of the answer comes in *Purgatorio* 2 when Dante is fixed and attentive to the song *Amor che ne la mente mi ragiona* in praise of Lady Philosophy, Dante who wrote such "amorosi canti" in her honour. And the circumstances at the shore of Purgatory can only be understood if one looks back at chapters xxxv, xxxvi, and xxxvii of the *Vita Nuova*, which explain those earlier circumstances that first caused Dante to wander in the direction of the Donna Gentile.

The retrospective journey signposted by the formula "fissi e attenti" takes the reader from *Purgatorio* 32 back to *Purgatorio* 2 and likewise to those same circumstances, but now from the perspective of Dante's "occhi miei," which have replaced "tutti" as the subject modified by "fissi e attenti." The first tercet of *Purgatorio* 32 announces the return of Dante's wandering eyes to the true goal. Or does it? Let us look at the tercet in relation to the one that follows:

> Tant'eran li occhi miei *fissi e attenti*
> a disbramarsi la decenne sete,
> che li altri sensi m'eran tutti spenti.
>   Ed essi quinci e quindi avien parete
> di non caler – così lo santo riso
> sé traéli con l'antica rete! ...

[So fixed and intent were my eyes in satisfying their ten-year thirst, that every other sense was quenched in me; and they themselves had a wall of indifference, on one side and on the other, so did the holy smile draw them to itself with the old net ...]

(2.32.1–6)

All of Dante's other senses fail him, stilled just as when he could think of nothing but the sweetness of Casella's song to the Donna Gentile, so contented "come a nessun tocasse altro la mente" ["as if naught else touched the mind of any"] (2.2.117). In that episode in *Purgatorio* 2 Dante was fixed and attentive to the song from the old times and was transported back to the irresponsible days of his youth when he looked at the Donna Gentile, his mind closed to all else. Now in *Purgatorio* 32 he is fixed and attentive before the unveiled Beatrice and again he is transported back to those days, his eyes once more ensnared, unable to see anything but the beautiful unveiled face of Beatrice. The siren call of feminine beauty has sounded once again, and as before Dante is helpless, his eyes unable to escape the old net, until the three Virtues intervene and warn Dante that his eyes have been looking upon his beloved too fixedly:

... quando per forma mi fu vòlto il viso
ver' la sinistra mia da quelle dee,
perch' io udi' da loro un "Troppo fiso!"

[... when my face was turned perforce to my left by those goddesses, for I heard from them a "Too fixedly!"]

(2.32.7–9)

It seems curious that Dante's eyes, once more looking upon Beatrice with too much ardour, were similarly described in the episode of the *Vita Nuova* when they began to delight too much in seeing the Donna Gentile after Beatrice's death. Again I quote:

Io venni a tanto per la vista di questa donna, che *li miei occhi*
si cominciarono a dilettare troppo di vederla ...

[The sight of this lady had such an effect on me that my eyes began to delight too much in seeing her ...]

(*VN* xxxvii)

In chapter xxxix Dante's eyes are rescued from the Donna Gentile by a vision of Beatrice in glory:

... mi parve questa gloriosa Beatrice con quelle vestimenta sanguigne co le quali apparve prima a *li occhi miei*; e pareami giovane in simile etade in quale io prima la vidi.

[... I seemed to see Beatrice in glory, clothed in the crimson garments in which she first appeared before my eyes; and she seemed as young as when I first saw her.]

(*VN* xxxix)

Dante expresses the shame he feels for his wandering eyes by announcing the sonnet which will close the chapter:

E dissi allora: *Lasso! Per forza di molti sospiri*; e dissi "lasso" in quanto mi vergognava di ciò, che *li miei occhi* aveano così vaneggiato.

[So then I wrote: *Alas! By the violence of many sighs.* I said "alas" because I was ashamed that my eyes had indulged in such inconstancy.]

(*VN* xxxix)

The return of Dante's eyes to the youthful image of "questa gloriosa Beatrice" in the *Vita Nuova* is echoed by their return to her in *Purgatorio*

32, yet the return cannot be based on past memories. That caused all the trouble in *Purgatorio* 2. However, the reproach of the three Virtues is less severe than that of Cato. The image of a youthful Beatrice in glory rescued Dante's eyes from the trap of temptation in the *Vita Nuova* xxxix, but Beatrice in glory in *Purgatorio* 32 is no longer that young lady of his youth. Thus Dante is forced to withdraw his eyes from the "antica rete" of surface feminine beauty and take in the magnificent whole:

> Ma poi ch'al poco il viso riformossi
> (e dico "al poco" per rispetto al molto
> sensibile onde a forza mi rimossi),
>   vidi 'n sul braccio destro esser rivolto
> lo glorïoso essercito ...

[But after my sight had adjusted itself to the lesser object – lesser, I mean, with regard to the greater from which I was forced to withdraw – I saw that glorious army had wheeled on its right ...]

(2.32.13–17)

The final repetition of the formula in *Paradiso* 31 occurs just after Dante has paid homage to Beatrice, who has guided him beyond temptation to liberty and is now in her rightful seat in the Empyrean. Dante is now with another "fedele," Bernard, his final guide and "fedele" of the Virgin Mary:

> "E la regina del cielo, ond' ïo ardo
> tutto d'amor, ne farà ogne grazia,
> però ch'i' sono il suo fedel Bernardo."

["And the Queen of Heaven, for whom I am all afire with love, will grant us every grace, since I am her faithful Bernard."]

(3.31.100–2)

It is now only the Virgin Mary who can intervene on Dante's behalf and grant every grace. The Virgin Mary has already interceded once before. In *Inferno* 2 we learn that it was the Virgin Mary who first noted Dante's plight in the dark wood. Adopting the term "fedele," she commended the beaten Dante to Lucia as Lucia's "fedele": "Or ha bisogno il tuo fedele / di te, e io a te lo raccomando" ["Your faithful one has need of you now, and I commend him to you"] (1.2.98–9).

However, for the moment Dante appears more interested in the "sene," Bernard, than in looking up and beholding the vast array of souls in their blessed state and ultimately the Virgin Mary on high ready to consider the request of her "fedel Bernardo." With the mildest reproach Bernard directs Dante's eyes away from himself:

> "Figliuol di grazia, quest' esser giocondo,"
> cominciò elli, "non ti sarà noto,
> tenendo li occhi pur qua giù al fondo ..."

["Son of grace, this joyous being," he began, "will not be known to you if you hold your eyes only down here at the base ..."]

(3.31.112–14)

Dante has been concentrating on Bernard and is taken to task for it. In each of the three episodes highlighted by the formula "fissi e attenti" Dante is reprimanded, but in each succeeding episode the reprimand becomes milder: from Cato's harsh words when Dante is lulled by the siren call of Lady Philosophy, to the three theological Virtues' concern that Dante is too taken with feminine beauty, to Bernard redirecting Dante's curious eyes from himself to the Virgin Mary on high.

And Dante immediately does as he is bidden and follows Bernard's gaze:

> Io *levai li occhi*; e come da mattina
> la parte orïental de l'orizzonte
> soverchia quella dove 'l sol declina,
>   così, quasi di valle andando a monte
> con li occhi, vidi parte ne lo stremo
> vincer di lume tutta l'altra fronte.

[I lifted up my eyes; and as at morning the eastern parts of the horizon outshine that where the sun declines, so, as if going with my eyes from valley to mountain-top I saw a part on the extreme verge surpass with its light all the rest of the rim.]

(3.31.118–23)

Dante lifted his eyes once before to take in new sights after Beatrice had left him. In the *Vita Nuova*, Dante, full of sorrow, looked about to see whether anyone had noticed his distressing appearance:

> Onde io, accorgendomi del mio travagliare, *levai
> li occhi* per vedere se altri mi vedesse. Allora vidi
> una gentile donna giovane e bella molto ...

[Becoming aware of my condition, I raised my eyes to see if anyone noticed me; and then I saw a gracious lady, young and very beautiful ...]

(*VN* xxxv)

If the earlier appearance of the formula "levai li occhi" announced the departure of Dante's eyes, straying from the correct path in the valley of temptation and sin, its repetition here in the Empyrean highlights that he has learned to resist all temptation and turn his eyes upward to the highest summit where reigns the true Lady, Queen of the Realm.

As Dante the pilgrim lifts his eyes towards the summit, a final reference is made to Phaeton's misguided flight at the reins of the Chariot of the Sun, a reference which has appeared on four previous occasions in the *Commedia* and always signifies the incorrect journey which can befall us if we seek human quest and reject guidance as pleases God.[22] The reference to Phaeton and his fall is a reminder of what awaits those who take a wrong turn in their life-journey, like Ulysses, who listened to the siren call and was sent down to the bottom "as pleased another." At the foot of the mountain of Purgatory Dante was lulled by the siren call of an all too worldly song, but was rescued by the reproachful Cato and sent on to commence his climb, "as pleased another." Here in the Empyrean, as Dante's eyes travel upward from valley to summit just as he himself has done, he sees angels singing songs in celebration of the Virgin Mary. These are the right songs, sung at the summit as pleases God.

And so, as they inevitably must, his eyes reach the culmination of their journey up the Celestial Rose:

> Bernardo, come vide li occhi miei
> nel caldo suo caler *fissi e attenti,*
> li suoi con tanto affetto volse a lei,
> che ' miei di rimirar fé più ardenti.

[Bernard, when he saw my eyes fixed and intent on the object of his own burning glow, turned his own with such affection to her, that he made mine more ardent in their gazing.]

(3.31.139–42)

With the final repetition of the formula "fissi e attenti," Dante's eyes have reached the peak, the destination of their ascent. His eyes, which had looked upon Beatrice too "fissi e attenti" on top of that other summit, the mountain of Purgatory, now look "fissi e attenti" upon Mary at the final summit. Here Dante is not scolded for being one of those "fissi e attenti" to the unsuitable song as he was in *Purgatorio* 2. Here Dante is not scolded for his "occhi miei" being too "fissi e attenti" on feminine beauty as he was in *Purgatorio* 32. Here Dante's "occhi miei," "fissi e attenti," are joined by Bernard's own, making Dante's even more ardent in their admiration of the Virgin Mary.

The signposted journey through Purgatory has highlighted the detours Dante's life has taken over the years: from his love for feminine beauty, to his love for Lady Philosophy after Beatrice's death, both contributing to his fall into the dark wood in 1300, from which he cannot emerge until the Virgin Mary intervenes on his behalf. The Virgin Mary, the one, according to Bernard, who can help Dante, "quella che puote aiutarti" (3.32.148), is the destination of the signposted journey, she who first took steps to save him from a Phaeton-like demise, she who initiated his overt journey back to herself.

Lastly, in *Paradiso* 33 the Virgin Mary's pivotal role is described by her "fedele" Bernard in his prayer of devotion to her. And Bernard's first reference to Dante in his prayer to the Virgin Mary encapsulates in two tercets what Dante has seen in his journey from the depths of Hell to this high place:

> "Or questi, che da l'infima lacuna
> de l'universo infin qui ha vedute
> le vite spiritali ad una ad una,
>
>   supplica a te, per grazia, di virtute
> tanto, che possa con *li occhi levarsi*
> più alto verso l'ultima salute."

["Now this man, who from the lowest pit of the universe even to here has seen one by one the spiritual lives, implores thee of thy grace for power such that he may be able with his eyes to rise still higher toward the last salvation."]

(3.33.22–7)

Bernard requests of the Virgn Mary that Dante's eyes may be raised to God, the ultimate salvation. His words "li occhi levarsi" recall how far Dante has come since he first raised his eyes to the Donna Gentile so long ago ("levai li occhi per vedere se altri mi vedesse" ["I raised my eyes to see if anyone noticed me"] *VN* xxxv).

The first words to follow Bernard's prayer describe Mary's eyes, "fixed" on Bernard:

> Li occhi da Dio diletti e venerati,
> fissi ne l'orator, ne dimostraro
> quanto i devoti prieghi le son grati ...

[The eyes beloved and reverenced by God, fixed upon him who prayed, showed us how greatly devout prayers do please her ...]

(3.33.40–2)

Mary looks momentarily at her "fedele" (Bernard), just as Beatrice in *Paradiso* 31.91–3 had looked at her "fedele" (Dante), before returning her gaze to God.

Dante is now attempting to fathom the "luce etterna" (3.33.83), "la forma universal di questo nodo" ["the universal form of this knot"] (3.33.91):

Così la mente mia, tutta sospesa,
mirava fissa, immobile e attenta,
e sempre di mirar faceasi accesa.

[Thus my mind, all rapt, was gazing, fixed, motionless and intent, ever enkindled by its gazing.]

(3.33.97–9)

In this final instance where a form of the adjectives "fisso" and "attento" appear in the text, they modify not Dante's eyes this time, but his mind fixed and attentive to the "forma universal" (v. 91), which Dante the poet thinks he saw.[23] Dante now stands before the ultimate goal of the overt journey, the goal beyond the last repetition of the formula, yet still linked to it. Here the subject of "fisso" and "attento" is not Dante along with other souls, as was the case in *Purgatorio* 2, nor is the subject Dante's eyes alone, as it was in both *Purgatorio* 32 and *Paradiso* 31. In this final canto of the *Commedia* Dante's sight and mind both merge. As Porena says in his commentary, "i tre aggettivi, pur riferendosi grammaticalmente alla parola *mente*, nella sostanza dipingono tutto Dante: fisso con gli occhi, immobile col corpo, attento con la mente" ["the three adjectives, although referring grammatically to the word *mente*, in substance ... depict the entire being of Dante: fixed with his eyes, immobile with his body, intent with his mind"].[24] Indeed this description of Dante recalls the formula, the signposts, along the way: Dante "immobile col corpo" ["immobile with his body"] together with the other souls in *Purgatorio* 2, Dante "fisso con gli occhi" ["fixed with his eyes"] in *Purgatorio* 32 and *Paradiso* 31. And here, in *Paradiso* 33, Dante is "attento con la mente" ["intent with his mind"] as he fixes his entire being ("tutto Dante") on the Eternal Light.

The poet now stresses that there is no turning away from a fixed and attentive gaze upon the Eternal Light:

A quella luce cotal si diventa,
che volgersi da lei per altro aspetto
è impossibil che mai si consenta ...

[In that light one becomes such that it is impossible he should ever consent to
turn himself from it for other sight ...]

(3.33.100–2)

The fourth and final appearance of the adjectives "fisso" and "attento," taken together with the first of the three "fissi e attenti," highlights the journey to salvation available to all, including those once
transfixed by the siren call of Lady Philosophy. Now that Dante's
"mente" is turned "fissa, immobile e attenta," to "quella luce," however, his "doglie," referred to back in *Purgatorio* 2 with the first appearance of the formula, can truly be relieved. Dante's "occhi miei,"
repeated for the last time in *Paradiso* 33 (v. 129), have journeyed from
the valley of the Donna Gentile to the lofty heights of the Empyrean
where they are now fixed on the Trinity, and here it is impossible for
the pilgrim who has reached this final goal to fix his gaze upon any
lesser being.

Notes

1 Milman Parry, *The Making of Homeric Verse* 174.

2 Bruce A. Rosenberg, "Oral Literature in the Middle Ages" 443–4: "In nearly all of the applications of the Parry-Lord theory to national literatures, the starting point has been a modification of the original conception, adjusted to suit the demands of the particular language being studied and the tradition in which it was being performed. Old English scholars, for instance, found it necessary to modify the Parry specification of 'a group of words,' since some single words ... appeared to be used formulaically. Creed thought it could be a 'single monosyllabic adverb.' The stipulation that the formula be 'regularly employed' also had problems, particularly if one adhered to Magoun's interpretation of that to mean 'repeated.' The body of Anglo-Saxon verse is slight, the sampling base quite small for such assertions, and few medievalists have been so inflexible. The result has been a series of very flexible interpretations of 'regularly employed,' allowing for inverted word order (in the definiton of Wayne O'Neil) and for the addition of a word at the middle or end of the formula (Lewis Nicholson). And, as H.L. Rogers has pointed out, 'under the same metrical conditions' has come to be rendered as 'under no metrical conditions.' "

3 A well-known example of a single word repeated in close textual proximity which is used to great dramatic effect is Francesca's adoption of "Amore" at the beginning of three tercets in *Inferno* 5 (100, 103, and 106), to juxtapose the considerable control Love held over her fate with the lack of control on her own part. When Christ's name appears in the *Paradiso* in

the rhyme position, perforce it is repeated twice more to complete the *terza rima* scheme and to ensure that "Cristo" rhymes with nothing else. The "Cristo" repetition appears in four instances in the *Paradiso*: 12.71–73–75; 14.104–106–108; 19.104–106–108; 32.83–85–87. For discussion of the key role of the "Cristo" repetition in the rhyme position, see John Freccero, "The Significance of *Terza Rima*."

4 For an example of a repetition of a group of words in close textual proximity, see *Paradiso* 27.22–6: "Quelli ch'usurpa in terra *il luogo mio*, / *il luogo mio, il luogo mio* che vaca / ne la presenza del Figliuol di Dio, / fatt' ha del cimitero mio cloaca / del sangue e de la puzza …" ["He who on earth usurps my place, my place, my place, which in the sight of the Son of God is vacant, has made my burial-ground a sewer of blood and of stench …"]. Peter's thrice repeated "il luogo mio" recalls a comparable passage from Jeremiah 7: 4 where "the temple of the Lord" appears three times. Were the repetitions of "il luogo mio" not near each other, neither the analogue with Jeremiah nor the emphasis on Peter's personal "place" would be so readily apparent. A more complex example of a group of words placed in close textual proximity is the repetition of "Lì si vedrà" ["There shall be seen"] which appears three times in 3.19.115, 118, and 121, followed by the repetition of the single word "Vedrassi" in 3.19.124, 127, and 130, followed by the repetition of the single word "e" in 3.19.133, 136, and 139, all placed at the beginning of their respective tercets. These repetitions at the start of the eagle's invective against those who rule Europe in Dante's day further emphasize the seriousness of their disunity. Di Salvo points out what the first letters of the repeated words spell: "E si noterà che le prime tre terzine cominciano con una L (Lì), le altre tre con una V (Vedrassi) e le ultime tre con una 'e.' Accostate formano un acrostico: LVE da leggere lue, macchia, peste, a designare re e principi, autentici devastatori del mondo civile e sommamente ingiusti." ["And it will be noted that the first three tercets begin with an L (Lì), the other three with a V (Vedrassi) and the final three with an 'e'. Put together they form an acrostic LVE to be read lues, macula, plague, to designate kings and princes, true devastators of the civil world and extremely unjust."]

5 Paul Zumthor, *Oral Poetry: An Introduction* 197, maintains that the necessary memorization to preserve oral texts "remained the only viable means for even graphemic societies" right up to the nineteenth century, "as long as the use of writing was not widespread."

6 Mary Carruthers, *The Book of Memory* 258–60.

7 Carruthers 5.

8 Michael Clanchy, *From Memory to Written Record: England 1066–1307* 268, suggests that even where there was no direct relation between the literary work and the oral tradition, reading was still understood as relating to hearing not seeing.

9 Suzanne Lewis, *Reading Images: Narrative Discourse and Reception in the Thirteenth-Century Apocalypse* 3, sees the shift happening earlier, by the second half of the thirteenth century; Paul Saenger, "Silent Reading: Its Impact on Late Medieval Script and Society," suggests the transformation occurs in the early fourteenth century; Clanchy 278 and Carruthers 170–3 see the shift as most gradual of all.

10 Carruthers 122.

11 See John Ahern, "Singing the Book: Orality in the Reception of Dante's *Comedy*," who argues for the oral transmission of the *Comedy* along with the written. The *Comedy* was already being sung in Dante's lifetime, and it would appear with the approval of Dante, so long as the performance was an accurate one. The fact that the *Comedy* was written in Italian, not Latin, encouraged oral performance; indeed oral performance would have been impossible had the *Comedy* been written in Latin: "Some will think that an exclusively oral reception of the poem runs counter to Dante's self-evident intentions as a poet, even though *comedìa* means 'rustic song,' and its subdivisions' titles, *canto* and *cantica*, also link it with song ... Moreover, the poem's division into easily performable units of about 140 lines in an oft-sung vernacular meter strongly encouraged oral performance" (228).

12 Ahern 226.

13 Ahern 226, 228.

14 See Robert Pogue Harrison, *The Body of Beatrice* 60, who refers to Dante's use of the word "velame" ["veil"] in the *Convivio* and in *Inferno* 9, as the allegory which must be "stripped away" to find the "*other* significance." Only select readers are capable of this exercise.

15 See 3.2.1–6, where Dante points out that only a select group of readers are capable of following where Beatrice (Theology) guides through Paradise.

16 See 2.25.83, where Dante refers to the "intelligenza" along with the "memoria" and the "volontade," following St Augustine in the *De Trinitate* x xi 18: "The memory, the intelligence and the will make one mind" ("Memoria, intelligentia, voluntas una mens").

17 See Chiavacci Leonardi, *Inferno* 366, who notes in *Inferno* 12 that "vo' che sappi" also appeared in *Inferno* 4. 33. She does not refer to the second time the formula appears in that canto, some twenty-nine lines later.

18 It could be argued that the limited number of words ending in "-ilio," for example, leave Dante with little choice but to repeat many of the same words in his *terza rima*, a point which could also be made in reference to other repeated words in the rhyme position highlighted in this study. This being the case, it follows that the poet would either seek diversity and attempt to find new rhyme words to the degree possible or repeat the same words as before. In this chapter the thrice occurring "concilio"/"Virgilio" /"essilio" has been examined, plus one instance where "Filio" is substituted for "Virgilio." If Dante was thus confronting the problem common

to poets of seeking diversity in his rhymes, should it not stand to reason that when diversity was not sought, when on the contrary the same words were repeated, such would be done for a particular reason, as when "Cristo" is repeated? If there was such an awareness on Dante's part, then it ought not to be surprising that repeated *terza rima* words could also relate to each other and act as signals that guide the reader along an alternate journey from one related episode to the next.

19 See H. Wayne Storey, "Canto xxxi," 470, who has noted this repetition.

20 For an application of repeated patterns as signals to the reader see also Charles S. Singleton, "The Vistas in Retrospect," who traces the repetition of "ruina" as a sign; Teodolinda Barolini, *Dante's Poets* 31, who identifies three incipits in the *Commedia*: "As 'Donne ch'avete' was selected from the *Vita Nuova*, so 'Voi che 'ntendendo' and 'Amor che ne la mente' were placed in the *Convivio*. We may reasonably believe, therefore, that Dante intends us to read these incipits in the light of their previous histories; indeed, it seems not unlikely that he chose these poems precisely for the archeological resonance they afford." In Teodolinda Barolini, "Casella's Song" 155–6, Barolini traces the repetition of the verb "consolare" in the *Convivio*, recalling Boethius's *Consolation of Philosophy*, to *Purgatorio* 2, where "consolare" is followed by Casella singing *Amor che ne la mente*, Dante's song from the *Convivio* in praise of Lady Philosophy. More recently Teodolinda Barolini, "Dante and Cavalcanti (On Making Distinctions in Matters of Love): *Inferno* v in Its Lyric Content," identifies a number of textual links, where the same linguistic pattern appears in both the *Commedia* and Dante's lyric poetry. Barolini further examines textual links particularly between Dante and Cavalcanti.

21 Bosco, "La 'Follia' di Dante" 430.

22 Iannucci, "Autoesegesi dantesca" 94.

23 Amilcare A. Iannucci, "Canto xxxi," 471; Iannucci, "Dante's Intertextual and Intratextual Strategies in the *Commedia*: The Limbo of the Children" 83.

24 Amilcare A. Iannucci, "The Mountainquake of *Purgatorio* and Virgil's Story" 54–44; Iannucci, "Dante's Intertextual and Intratextual Strategies" 84, where the episode of the children in Limbo is only fully understood when Dante the pilgrim hears from St Bernard in *Paradiso* 32 the final words on their fate: "Moreover, even though it seems odd at first that Dante the poet should introduce children in the Rose and spend so much time on them, such a poetic strategy, in fact, is consistent with Dante's way of narrating and construction of structurally determining episodes like Limbo."

25 Baranski, "Structural Retrospection" 23.

26 Baranski, "The 'Marvellous' " 73.

27 Baranski, "Structural Retrospection" 14.

28 Singleton, "The Vistas in Retrospect" 66, 71.

29 In Baranski, "Structural Retrospection," retrospection is key to understanding the *Commedia*: "Without its web of connections and
reminiscences the *Comedy* would collapse into a jumble of disconnected
self-contained episodes, and so lose that overall coherence and excellence,
the integration of all the parts in the whole, which reveal, according to its
fiction, the hand of God behind its writing and its goals" (23).

CHAPTER 1

1 For an extensive analysis of *Inferno* 1 see Anthony K. Cassell, *Inferno I,
Lectura Dantis Americana*.

2 See John Freccero, "The Prologue Scene" 10 (repr. his *Dante: The Poetics of
Conversion* 12), who notes another repetition that acts as a signpost. By
means of Dante's repetition of "selva" and "ed ecco" in *Purgatorio* 28, the
juxtaposition between "selva oscura" in *Inferno* 1 and "selva antica" in
Purgatorio 28 comes to the fore: "The resemblance can hardly be fortuitous. Dante's descent into hell and his ascent of the mountain of purgatory bring him to a point from which he can begin his climb to the light,
his entrance into sanctifying grace, without fear of the impediments that
blocked his way before."

3 Charles S. Singleton, "In Exitu Israel de Aegypto" 116: "The guiding and
protecting hand of the Lord is here to drive back the Adversary who
comes. Not so on the prologue scene. The beasts were not driven back."

4 As well in Cassell 25, there is reference to the "pride to which Dante's pro-
jected persona confesses as a besetting sin in *Purgatorio* XII, 1–9" from the
vantage point of Dante's dark wood of sin in *Inferno* 1.

5 Singleton, "In Exitu" 108.

6 The rhyme words "passo"/"lasso"/"basso" also appear in *Inferno* 5.114/
112/110, *Inferno* 8.104/106/108, and *Paradiso* 13.117/113/115, but not in a
configuration with the formula of repetition "persona viva." Both of the
references in the *Inferno* continue the issue first raised in *Inferno* 1.26/28/
30: there are pitfalls before Dante in his journey to salvation which could
threaten its successful outcome. In *Inferno* 5.114/112/110 the pilgrim appears caught in Francesca's web, overly concerned with her "dolci pensier" (see chapter 4), and in *Inferno* 8.104/106/108 the pilgrim is prepared
to turn back because of the devils' threats before the City of Dis. The
rhyme words "basso"/"passo"/"sasso" also appear in *Purgatorio* 3.55/
53/57 and *Purgatorio* 27.66/62/64. Both references in the *Purgatorio* relate
to the theme in *Purgatorio* 11.54/50/52: the indication by others of a passageway through which Dante can ascend to the next level. In *Purgatorio*
3.55/53/57 Virgil is hoping that some soul can show them where one
"senz' ala" like Dante can ascend, and in *Purgatorio* 27.66/62/64 an angel

invites Dante and his companions to ascend the final passageway before it turns dark.

7 I further quote John Freccero, "Dante's Firm Foot and the Journey without a Guide" 248 (repr. in his *Dante: The Poetics of Conversion* 31), for a contextualization of his interpretation of "riva" and its link with "piaggia diserta" on line 29: "The interesting thing about Dante's metaphoric mariner, however, is that he neither drowns nor reaches his port, but rather emerges from the sea onto the shore of a middle ground, from which he looks back, terrified, at the danger he has so narrowly escaped. Further on beyond this simile, the poet refers to the area between the dark wood and the mountain proper as a 'piaggia diserta,' and since the word 'piaggia' may be translated either 'slope' or 'shore,' the two images, the first a glance up to the light, and the second, an emergence from the water, exist side by side, and serve as two analogues from the same conversion, an abrupt movement from sin and ignorance into wisdom and virtue – or so it seems at any rate, until we learn what the pilgrim will soon discover: that this slope or shore is no exit, but rather a dead end for any man left on his own."

8 Sapegno, *Purgatorio* 122, suggests that when *riva* or *ripa* appears elsewhere in *Purgatorio* (see 2.10.29; 2.13.8) it never refers to the ledge or terrace, but always the slope of the mountain. Hence he concludes that in this passage "riva" should be understood to mean "along the wall."

9 Singleton, "In Exitu" 104–5: "The simile, in its first term, puts water, perilous waters, upon the scene, as well as the figure of a man who struggles forth from those waters (surely the figure of a swimmer), panting from his exertions as he stands upon the shore to look back upon that *pelago* where he had almost perished; all of which is matched, in the second part of the simile, by the man (or his *soul*, this being a moral landscape) who, fleeing in fear, now turns to look back upon a *passo* 'that never left anyone alive,' *passo* corresponding to *pelago* of the first part." See John Freccero, "The Prologue Scene" 19, who underlines the repetition of Ulysses' "alto passo" in *Inferno* 26 before the looming mountain of Purgatory and its relevance to the mountain of the prologue scene. The repetition of "passo" in *Inferno* 26 here too points the reader back to its occurrence in *Inferno* 1.

10 Sapegno, *Inferno* 7: "il passaggio; qui la selva. Con lo stesso significato intenso di 'punto cruciale, decisivo,' di 'passaggio dalla vita alla morte dell'anima' " ["the passageway; here the wood. With the same intense meaning of 'crucial and decisive point,' of 'passageway from life to death of the soul' "].

11 Antonino Pagliaro, "... lo passo Che non lasciò già mai persona viva" 109.

12 Freccero, "Dante's Firm Foot" 269. Freccero's probing interpretation of the "piè fermo" is at odds with the traditional view, going back to Boccaccio, which interprets the firm foot as the lower foot that takes most of the

body's weight. Freccero points out: "for if this foot were always the lower, the pilgrim could make no progress at all, as a little experimentation will show"; "His left leg, which even in a normal man does not receive as much of the vital spirit as does the right (it is for this reason the 'firm,' rather than the 'agile,' foot), now so lacks the *spiritus* of the heart that it is unable to respond to the command of the mind, and the pilgrim consequently limps toward his objective" (265–6).

13 "Viso basso" appears only once elsewhere in the *Commedia*, again in a configuration with the rhyme words "passo" and "sasso" in *Purgatorio* 3.52–8:

> "Or chi sa da qual man la costa cala,"
> Disse 'l maestro mio fermando 'l *passo*
> "sì che possa salir chi va sanz' ala?".
>
> E mentre ch'e' tenendo 'l *viso basso*
> esaminava del cammin la mente,
> e io mirava suso intorno al *sasso*,
> da man sinistra m'apparì una gente …

["Now who knows on which hand the hillside slopes," said my master, staying his step, "so that he can ascend who goes without wings?" And while he held his face low, searching his mind about the road, and I was looking up around the rock, on the left appeared to me a company …]
In both instances the reference is to how Dante, weighed down by his flesh before one with "'l viso basso," can "salir," with "man" also repeated on both occasions, but in *Purgatorio* 3 twice, indicating both the direction in which the slope falls for Dante to climb and also the direction in which the penitent souls are moving.

There is also reference in *Inferno* 5, where the configuration "basso"/ "lasso"/"passo" is repeated, to Dante's "viso" as that which is "basso": "China' il viso, e tanto il tenni basso …" ["I bowed my head and held it bowed …"] (v. 110). In this instance the "passo" is modified by "doloroso," the way for Paolo and Francesca to damnation, not salvation.

14 Singleton, "In Exitu" 113; for further discussion and bibliographical reference to Casella's song see chapter 9.

15 While Dante has successfully put some distance between himself and those still waging war against temptations below the Gate of Purgatory, the question of Dante's pride is a more complex one, in that he will be returning to the first terrace once he is divested of Adam's flesh, not on account of Adam's pride in relation to God for which humankind has had to pay ever since, but for his own pride towards other men. See Cassell 40, who points out that "the wayfarer suffers not only from the concupiscence of his lower soul and the original wound of pride common to all mankind, but he suffers also from the sin of his own commission of which

his disordinate seeking of the heights is, in fact, the proof: the personal sin of his own pride expressed in ambition, presumption, and *curiositas*."

16 The imperative "venite" appears only five times in the *Commedia*, therefore making the repetition of "venite" on the first Terrace of Purgatory all the more significant.

17 Both *Inferno* 1, before Dante is driven back by the she-wolf, and *Purgatorio* 12, when the angel encourages him to ascend, share common points: there is reference to the morning star in the prologue, "Temp'era dal principio del mattino, / e 'l sol montava 'n sù con quelle stelle" ["It was the beginning of the morning, and the sun was mounting with the stars"] (*Inf.* 1.37–8), and there is reference to the morning star on the first terrace when the angel appears: "… biancovestito e ne la faccia quale / par tremolando mattutina stella" ["… clothed in white and such in his face as seems the tremulous morning star"] (*Purg.* 12.89–90); "stelle" (*Inf.* 1.38) and "belle" (*Inf.* 1.40) prefigure "bella" (*Purg.* 12.88) and "stella" (*Purg.* 12.90), all in the final position, which oblige the reader to compare and contrast the two scenes.

CHAPTER 2

1 The rhyme words "ambascia"/"fascia"/"lascia" also appear in *Inferno* 33.96/92/94, but without the formula of repetition, "infernale ambascia." Nonetheless, the anguish ("ambascia") is indeed infernal:

Noi passammo oltre, là 've la gelata
ruvidamente un'altra gente *fascia*,
non volta in giù, ma tutta riversata.
    Lo pianto stesso lì pianger non *lascia*,
e 'l duol che truova in su li occhi rintoppo,
si volge in entro a far crescer l'*ambascia* …

[We went farther on, where the frost roughly swathes another people, not bent downwards, but with faces all upturned. The very weeping there prevents their weeping, and the grief, which finds a barrier upon their eyes, turns inward to increase the agony …]

This is the ninth circle, the deepest "anguish of Hell," out of which Virgil and Dante recently came and to which Dante refers when he addresses Marco Lombardo in *Purgatorio* 16.39: "e venni qui per l'infernale ambascia" ["I came here through the anguish of Hell"]. In this instance the "fascia" does not refer to the souls' body or their happiness but to the ice that swathes them. Here it is not a question of smoke not allowing ("lascia") souls to see, but the chill not allowing ("lascia") the condemned souls to cry because the tears pool in their sockets and freeze.

2 Singleton, *Inferno* 641, in his gloss of 34.118 draws the readers' attention to a number of time references made during Dante the pilgrim's journey through Hell, and concludes: "Thus, we realize now, looking back, that

the descent through Hell has required twenty-four hours – the night of
Good Friday and the day of Holy Saturday."

3 See 3.26.119.

4 In Charles S. Singleton, *Dante Studies 1* 11–13, Singleton suggests the importance of Dante's journey through the three realms in the flesh: "A
body here? How is that? Is this body to be taken as the hill and the other
features on this scene, to be understood as we have learned to understand
those things? Have we begun another metaphor here? Not so. This body
is no metaphor. ... This body is tired from the struggle out of that water
and when it moves on across the deserted shore (shore!) it may no longer
be recalled or reduced to metaphor. ... The whole journey beyond exceeds
metaphor. It is irreducible to the kind of allegory in which it had its origin.
As this figure of a living man, this whole person soul and body, moves
through the doorway to Hell, the poem quits the recognizable and familiar double vision in which it began, to come into single and most singular
vision, that is, into single journey; to embodied vision, having a substance
and a persuasion that could not have been expected from this beginning.
There unfolds the line of a literal journey given as real, and it is the body
beyond, the flesh brought into these realms of spirit there, that like a cata-
lyst precipitates everywhere the fleshed, the embodied and incarnate." In
Dante Studies 2 265–83, Singleton links Dante's "return to Eden" from the
seventh terrace of Purgatory to the debatable notion that Adam was
placed in Eden after God had formed him outside of Eden: "Dante did not
take sides there as to whether Adam was fashioned in the Garden or, first,
outside the Garden, but his very hesitation shows clearly enough that he
views the point as a matter of debate in his time. Now it is of some interest
to note, as we are presently concerned to do, that when in his poem Dante
came to represent a 'return to Eden,' he did take a position on this question in the very outline of literal event as he conceived it at the top of the
mountain." For careful analysis of Dante's *in carnem* journey, with *Inferno*
1 as the main focus, see John Freccero, *The Poetics of Conversion* 1–54.

5 In the *Mon.* 1.16 Dante juxtaposes the gentleness of Christ, who came during the once-only peaceful time in history, with the opposite quality in humankind going back to Adam and original sin. The opposite quality,
wrath, is featured here on the third terrace.

6 See Mario Trovato, "Canto xvi," 236, who draws parallels between the
gloom of the terrace of the wrathful and infernal space. The atmosphere of
this terrace within which the penitent wrathful are purged of their sin is a
reminder of the "infernale ambascia" through which Dante so recently
came.

7 Di Salvo, *Purgatorio* 277.

8 See 1.3.115–16: "... similemente il mal seme d'Adamo / gittansi di quel
lito ad una ad una ..." ["... so there the evil seed of Adam: one by one

they cast themselves from that shore ..."] where Dante describes these damned souls as the evil seed of Adam. "Seed of Adam" describes all his descendants, all humanity.

9 Di Salvo, *Purgatorio* 277, suggests that the other meaning of "secondare," along with "seguire," can be: "accompagnarsi a qualcuno" ["to go along with someone"].

10 The *contrapasso* of this sin dictates that the souls remain within the smoke until they are free from their sin. Marco explains this limitation of his movements to Dante at the end of their encounter: "Dio sia con voi, ché più non vegno vosco. / Vedi l'albor che per lo fummo raia / già biancheggiare, e me convien partirmi / (l'angelo è ivi) prima ch'io li paia." ["May God be with you, for I come with you no farther. Behold the brightness that rays through the smoke already whitening, and I must go – the angel is there – before I am seen by him."] (2.16.141–4).

11 In Freccero, "The Prologue Scene" 10, he juxtaposes the "selva antica" (2.28.23) where Adam dwelt before he sinned and the "selva oscura" (1.1.2), the point of departure for Dante's *in carnem* journey: "The resemblance can hardly be fortuitous. Dante's descent into hell and his ascent of the mountain of purgatory bring him to a point from which he can begin his climb to the light, his entrance into sanctifying grace, without fear of the impediments that blocked his way before. That new point of departure, the garden of Eden, was the home of man before the fall. Through Adam's transgression, the prelapsarian state of man was transformed into the state of sin. In poetic terms, Adam transformed the *selva antica* into a *selva oscura*."

12 See Di Salvo, *Purgatorio* 277–8, who interprets "ambascia" by reflecting on how Dante's just completed journey through Hell affects him psychologically, and how his memory of that terrain he has just traversed leaves its mark upon him, Dante who as a sinner himself felt some of the pain of the condemned souls.

13 When Dante refers to Aeneas and St Paul, he does so for fear that, should he agree to embark on the sort of journey last taken by St Paul and before him Aeneas, his journey might be one of folly ("temo che la venuta non sia folle" ["I fear that the coming may be folly"] 1.2.35), for he is hardly on the same footing as such worthy individuals, and he is unsure that his journey, unlike theirs, would be permitted from on high. If it is not allowed from on high, then Dante, seed of Adam, would be transgressing the bounds imposed on him as a living man by God.

14 See Singleton, *Dante Studies* 2 246, who quotes from an English translation of Thomas Aquinas's *Compendium Theologiae ad Fratrem Reginaldum* ch. 152: "but when the soul of man turned from God by sin, fittingly also the human body lost that supernatural disposition through which it was immovably subject to the soul, and so man incurred the necessity of death. If therefore one regard the nature of the body, death is natural; but if one

consider the nature of the soul and the disposition which on the soul's account was in the beginning added supernaturally to the human body,
death is *per accidens* and against nature, since it is natural for the soul to be
united to the body."

15 See Thomas Aquinas, who in the *Summa Theologiae*, 2–2, q. 163, a. 1, points
out that Adam's sin was one of pride because he desired something forbidden to him, and in so doing he tried to be like God, because he desired
something beyond the bounds determined by God.

16 For a good overview of Adam's "trapassar del segno" see Kevin Brownlee, "Canto XXVI" 394.

17 Pride between individuals such as artists on the first terrace is not considered among the gravest sins. In *Purgatorio* 11, for instance, some did not
accept that their artistic skill was limited, their art defective. The sin of
pride between an individual and God, however, is at the root of all sin. So
with Lucifer when he rebelled, thinking himself the equal of God and re-
jecting the limitations placed upon him by God; such was also Adam's sin
when he rebelled against God and tasted of the forbidden tree.

18 After Dante has taken the passage, the "varco," from the first terrace of the
proud to the second terrace of the envious, he declares to Sapia in 2.13.136–
8 that he will have to spend some time among the proud himself: "Troppa è
più la paura ond' è sospesa / l'anima mia del tormento di sotto, / che già lo
'ncarco di là giù mi pesa" ["Far greater is the fear that holds my soul in sus-
pense, of the torment below, so that already the load down there is heavy
upon me"]. Dante's sin is one of pride, as is Adam's; however, Dante's
pride, like those who inhabit the first terrace, is against men not God.

19 Freccero, "Dante's Firm Foot" 269.

20 Beatrice makes a later reference in *Paradiso* 7 to the disobedience of
Adam and his seed and their inability to "ir giuso" in humility on account
of the extreme presumption of Adam: "… quanto disobediendo intese ir
suso; / e questa è la cagion per che l'uom fue / da poter sodisfar per sé dis-
chiuso" ["… so far as in his disobedience he had intended to ascend; and
this is the reason why man was shut off from power to make satisfaction by
himself"] (3.7.100–2). Adam's desire to "ir suso" ["go up"] when he sinned
required that Christ "ir giuso" ["go down"] in humility, so that Christ could
then ultimately ascend, ultimately an "ir suso" on Christ's part, after his
"ir giuso," which Dante imitates when he points out to Marco Lombardo in
Purgatorio 16 that he is going up, "vo suso," and furthermore that his is an
"andar suso," allowed by God, in the flesh of Adam.

CHAPTER 3

1 For a comprehensive discussion of the *descensus Christi* and annotated
bibliography, see Amilcare A. Iannucci, *Forma ed evento nella Divina Commedia* 51–81.

2 There is no theological foundation for adults being left behind in Limbo after the *descensus Christi*. See Amilcare A. Iannucci, "Limbo: The Emptiness of Time," for a study of Dante's departure from theological thought and how that departure affects his Limbo, Virgil, and the *Commedia* as a whole.

3 "Or" precedes the first and third repetition of the formula "vo' che sappi" but not the second.

4 In *Inferno* 21.112–14, there is reference to the time of Dante's journey being some 1266 years later than Christ's descent: "Ier, più oltre cinqu'ore che quest'otta, / mille dugento con sessanta sei / anni compié che qui la via fu rotta" ["Yesterday, five hours later than now, completed one thousand two hundred and sixty-six years since the road was broken here"].

5 See Amilcare A. Iannucci, "Dante's *Inferno*, Canto IV" 300, who sees Virgil as "pushed to the margin," into the "noble castle" of Limbo.

6 As was already discussed in the Introduction, in Singleton, "The Vistas in Retrospect," the repetition of "ruina" is traced as a signal, from *Inferno* 23, to *Inferno* 12, and ultimately back to *Inferno* 5. Here in *Inferno* 12 two alternate journeys thus intersect: the one highlighted by the repetition of "ruina," as put forth by Singleton, and the one highlighted by the repetition of "vo' che sappi" and "color," presented in this chapter.

It is primarily in *Inferno* 12 and later in *Inferno* 21 that the journeying pilgrim and the reader see the actual result of the earthquake which took place 1266 years before and which happened just before Christ's descent into Limbo. In *Inferno* 21, when Virgil and Dante flee from the devils of the fifth *bolgia*, they will discover that all the bridges are down which had connected it with the sixth *bolgia*. This is something Virgil would not have known, since he journeyed this way before the earthquake, before Christ's descent to Limbo. There is also the barest mention of damage done to Hell by the earthquake in *Inferno* 5.34, with mention of the "ruina."

7 The "or" plus the formula has two functions. Appearing as it does in the first and the third instance of the formula, it frames the route of these three signposts. As well, immediately following these are the two instances when Virgil refers to himself: in the first instance as soul-resident of Limbo and in the last as one who already journeyed through Hell.

8 For analysis of the *descensus Christi* within the context of this episode see Amilcare A. Iannucci, "Dottrina e allegoria in *Inferno* VIII, 67–IX, 105."

9 Amilcare Iannucci, "Virgil's Erichthean Descent and the Crisis of Intertextuality" 23, points out the parallel in the *Aeneid* 6.562–5 where the Sibyl discloses to Aeneas that she journeyed throughout the underworld with the arch-witch Hecate as her guide.

10 The formula "altra fïata," with the denotation of *one* other time, is unique to *Inferno* 9. 22 and *Inferno* 12. 34. Furthermore they both refer to the same event: Virgil's prior journey to the bottom of Hell. "L'una e l'altra fïata"

(*Inf.* 10. 50) and "una e altra fïata" (*Inf.* 30. 3) are the only other two references in the *Commedia* which contain "altra fïata"; however, with the "una e" preceding the "altra fïata," they denote more than one time.

11 No doubt a reason why Beatrice journeyed down to Limbo and requested that Virgil aid Dante was because she was aware that Virgil knew the way, having embarked on that journey before. One could say therefore that Virgil's first journey was part of the Providential plan.

12 See Amilcare A. Iannucci, "Beatrice in Limbo: A Metaphoric Harrowing of Hell," who points out the link between Beatrice's descent into Limbo, which Virgil describes in *Inferno* 2, and Christ's descent into Limbo, which Virgil describes in *Inferno* 4 and *Inferno* 8 and 9, and where "it is Dante, and hence everyman, who is 'harrowed' from hell. Actually, the divine messenger intervenes to make it possible for the pilgrim to descend into lower hell, into the mosqued City of Dis, as he must do if he is to ascend Mount Purgatory and rise into Paradise" (31).

CHAPTER 4

1 The rhyme word configuration "offense"/"pense"/"spense" also appears in *Paradiso* 4.104–8, but without the formula of repetition "disse: 'Che pense?' " fixed within it.

2 It is not my claim that this is the first reference to links between these two episodes. There are so few female characters in the *Commedia*, and even fewer who were courtly ladies, that Francesca and Beatrice beg to be scrutinized and contrasted. As far as I know, however, this study is the first that analyses these two episodes within the context of the repeated formula (the question that requires an answer), within the wider configuration of rhyme words. In Singleton, *Purgatory* 762, "piacer" is highlighted in both *Inferno* 5 and *Purgatorio* 31. In Diskin Clay, "Dante's Broken Faith: The Sin of the Second Circle" 100–2, the relationship between the Francesca episode and Beatrice's reprimand forms part of wider-ranging discussion of Dante's broken faith.

3 Teodolinda Barolini, *The Undivine Comedy* 44–5, discusses fainting as a vehicle for transition from the action of one canto to the next between *Inferno* 3 and 4 and between *Inferno* 5 and 6.

4 There are only three instances in the *Commedia* when "cadere" is adopted in the first person singular past remote, with Dante as subject: first when Dante "fell" in 1.3.136 ("… e caddi come l'uom cui sonno piglia" ["… and I fell like one who is seized by sleep"]), the last line of the canto, before Dante and Virgil crossed the Acheron in Caron's bark; second when Dante "fell" in 1.5.142 ("e caddi come corpo morto cade"), again the last line of the canto, after Francesca spoke her last words to Dante; and third when the contrite Dante "fell" before Beatrice in 2.31.89 ("… ch'io caddi

vinto" ["… that I fell overcome"]). In Clay, "Dante's Broken Faith" 100, this repetition of the "caddi" is noted: "His collapse, first at the inner threshold of the second circle of Hell, and then on the Mount of Purgatory, defines the progress of the major statement of the most important of the confessional themes of the *Commedia* – that of Dante's broken faith" (100).

5 In Lanfranco Caretti, *Il Canto V dell'Inferno* 5, it is noted that the words "quasi smarrito" appear at the exact midway point through *Inferno* 5.

6 Caretti 22.

7 According to Mark Musa, "Behold Francesca Who Speaks So Well (*Inferno* v)," unbeknownst to Dante, behind Francesca's courtly veneer of graciousness and generosity towards Dante and Virgil and the initial nod she gives to Paolo, she is self-centred, unwilling to allow the others to speak, and apparently willing to "exploit her own scandal" (313).

8 In Musa 315, it is pointed out that these words have nothing to do with Guinizzelli and courtly love: what Paolo desired was Francesca's "beautiful body," making this a sensual love on both their parts, since she responded with equal desire, and this paved the way for their sin and their fall. The fact that Dante the pilgrim does not discern this point, that he does not comprehend the difference between love in an idealized courtly sense and sensual, physical love, for the moment's pleasure, would be a further indication of how lost Dante has become since Beatrice's death.

9 See Di Salvo, *Inferno* 89, for discussion of Francesca's aristocratic demeanour, which is reflected in the language she uses, despite being buffeted by the infernal winds of the second circle. For Di Salvo, Francesca is to be viewed as an aristocratic heroine, not a romantic one: "Questa radice squisitamente letteraria dell'episodio di Francesca è in antitesi con l'interpretazione romantica che vedeva in Francesca l'eroina sfortunata della passione travolgente. Francesca è, invece, un'aristocratica, cresciuta in corte tra libri e in una società che dava molta importanza alla raffinatezza, al controllo razionale, al decoro" ["This exquisitely literary source of the episode of Francesca is the antithesis of the romantic interpretation that saw in Francesca the ill-starred heroine of overwhelming passion. Francesca is instead an aristocrat, raised at court with books and in a society that gave much importance to refinement, to rational control, to dignity"].

10 Scholars agree that Dante the pilgrim's reference to "dubbiosi disiri" does not reflect a negative judgment on his part towards Paolo and Francesca. "Dubbiosi disiri" refer to the love between the two of them which up to that point they had not recognized or communicated.

11 For similar use of the adjective "dolce," see 1.10.69, when Guido Cavalcanti's father, Cavalcante, misinterprets Dante's response to him and fears that his son is dead, that his son's eyes no longer see the "sweet light," the "dolce lume." For an Epicurean like Cavalcante there is no afterlife, only

the life when the "sweet light" struck his son's eyes before death. Dante the pilgrim's reference to the "dolci sospiri," the "sweet sighs" enjoyed by the courtly Francesca when she was still alive, also suggests a time now past for the damned Francesca, back when the sweet light still struck her eyes.

12 For a contrary opinion see Antonino Pagliaro, "… e 'l modo ancor m'offende," who suggests that it was not the "manner" of Francesca's death which still offends her, but the intensity of Paolo's passion for her, a passion she cannot escape. Disagreement among Dante scholars continues. Singleton, *Inferno* 90, disagrees with Pagliaro's interpretation, as do others including myself, arguing that it is precisely the "manner" of Francesca's death which still offends her. Singleton maintains that if one analyses the passage "e 'l modo ancor m'offende" within the context of all Francesca's other words, Pagliaro's interpretation is "farfetched," "despite the apparent correspondence of 'ancor m'offende' (vs. 102) and 'ancor non m'abbandona' (vs. 105) cited in support of it."

13 In Ruggero Stefanini, "Canto xxx" 455, the anger of Beatrice towards Dante is compared to "the inflexible disdain Guinivere shows to the stupefied Lancelot who has finally managed to reach her." Stefanini suggests that Dante would have seen himself in the "cotanto amante" ["so great a lover"] (1.5.134), Lancelot of the *Galeotto*. The first one to see himself in the "cotanto amante" is of course Paolo, seduced by the story of the *Galeotto*, who falls to death and damnation, much as Dante is seduced by Francesca's story and falls as a dead weight falls.

14 See Di Salvo, *Purgatorio* 552, who points out that Beatrice's demand that Dante confess openly reflects the law in Dante's day that the guilty parties admit their guilt in public. Since their crime had been public, a crime against society, so too then must their confession be public.

15 I agree with Mario Marti, *Realismo dantesco ed altri studi* 31, who maintains that Dante's backsliding is due to no specific sin, but a combination of sins understood in hindsight by the poet: "Il traviamento di Dante non è solo amoroso, né solo religioso, o intellettuale o morale o stilistico, e sarà stato magari tutte queste cose insieme senza essere specificamente nessuna di esse. Il traviamento più che una precisa cronaca biograficamente rintracciabile, è il giudizio a posteriori che Dante emette sulla propria vita, su tutta la propria attività negli anni che precedettero immediatamente l'esilio e che egli considera divergenti dalla via che Beatrice stilnovistica gli aveva indicata. La confessione di Dante è chiara" ["Dante's backsliding is not just amorous, nor just religious, or intellectual or moral or stylistic, and it was perhaps all these things together without being specifically any one of these. More than any precise, traceable biographical account, the backsliding is the judgment Dante pronounces on his life after the fact, on all his activities in the years that immediately preceded his exile and

which he considers divergent from the way that Beatrice of the *stilnovo* had indicated to him. Dante's confession is clear"]. For further discussion in this study on sins that led to Dante's backsliding in the years just before his exile, see chapters 7 (politics) and 9 (philosophy).

16 "Fossi" and "catene" would be familiar terms to Dante's contemporary readers and suggest military strategies for blocking the enemy's entrance into a besieged city.

17 Michele Barbi, *Problemi di critica dantesca: prima serie* 284.

18 Two obvious examples of Dante wasting time during his journey come to mind, obvious because the pilgrim is scolded for his bad behaviour: in *Inferno* 30 with Dante's attention fixed on the trivial fray between Master Adam and Sinon, Virgil takes him to task: "Or pur mira, / che per poco che teco non mi risso!" ["Now just you keep on looking a little more and I will quarrel with you!"] (1.30.131–2); similarly in *Purgatorio* 2 Dante and Virgil and the other pilgrims are fixed on Casella's song, until Cato comes and scolds: "Che è ciò, spiriti lenti? / Qual negligenza, quale stare è questo?" ["What is this, you laggard spirits? What negligence, what stay is this?"] (2.2.120–1), the departure for the signposted journey under scrutiny in chapter 9.

19 See Singleton, *Purgatorio* 762, who maintains that this ambiguous use of "piacer" appears in three episodes: *Inferno* 5. 104; *Purgatorio* 18.21 and 27; *Purgatorio* 31.35.

20 While it is unclear whether the fire which divides the seventh terrace of the lustful in Purgatory from Earthly Paradise is one solely for the penitent lustful or whether all penitent souls must endure it, Dante the pilgrim, who will one day no doubt spend some time himself among those of the seventh terrace, must pass through the fire before he can reach Beatrice in Earthly Paradise; indeed, the pain he feels is so extreme that he would have thrown himself into molten glass to cool off (see chapter 6).

21 Singleton sees this reference to "piacer" as meaning predominantly "beauty"; however, I believe it can be argued that, because of the way Beatrice's "piacer" affected Dante, here too "piacer" can be read ambiguously.

22 See Dante Alighieri, *Rime*, ed. Gianfranco Contini, 113. Contini points out, as have other commentators before and since, that the "pargoletta" reference is made necessarily vague in the *Commedia* ("nell'uso di *pargoletta* sarà da scorgere una semplice preferenza lessicale"). Barolini, "Dante and Cavalcanti (On Making Distinctions in Matters of Love)" 46, identifies the presence of "non m'abbandona" in both *Inferno* 5.105 and *Io son venuto* of the *rime petrose*, maintaining that this repetition is a confirmation of the link between this episode and the *petrose*.

23 Herman Gmelin, *Kommentar II* 304; see Robert Hollander, "*Purgatorio* xix: Dante's Siren/Harpy" 79, who also has no doubt that the lady is Beatrice:

"And surely we also wish to understand the identity of the *donna ... santa e presta* [lady ... holy and alert] who opposes the *serena*. In my opinion the second task presents little difficulty: Beatrice is the presence who informs the actions of the dream's holy lady. Dante's dream should be seen as recreating the offstage encounter of Virgil and Beatrice as this was narrated by his *autore* in *Inferno* II, carefully incorporating Virgil's charge, as this was enunciated by Beatrice."

24 Amilcare A. Iannucci, "Forbidden Love: Metaphor and History (*Inferno* 5)" 107: "In the *Vita Nuova* the young Dante had read the book of his memory and had identified Beatrice, metaphorically, with love. In the *Commedia*, as he reads from the book of the universe (*Par.* 33.85–93), he rediscovers and reaffirms that analogy. Dante has found an interpretation of history which will lead to the reign of charity. His *poema sacro* celebrates not *fole amor* but *caritas*, not Francesca but Beatrice."

CHAPTER 5

1 See Eugenio Ragni, "Ciacco," *ED* 982–6, who along with the recent commentators of the *Commedia* (e.g. Bosco-Reggio and Chiavacci Leonardi) cites the early lines of the Marchiano Manuscript IX 179, known as the *Chiose Selmi*. These lines have been edited by Avalle to indicate that Ciacco knew Dante before he died, at which time Dante was fourteen.

2 See John A. Scott, "Inferno X: Farinata as 'Magnanimo' " 404 (repr. in his *Dante Magnanimo Studi sulla "Commedia"* 28), who distinguishes between "Dante the pilgrim" and "Dante the author" and argues that when Dante the pilgrim inquires after Farinata, Tegghiaio, Iacopo Rusticucci, Arrigo, and Mosca, "he is speaking as the sinner who has not yet accomplished the journey necessary for his salvation and illumination ... Dante the pilgrim had judged *sub specie mundi* (or, as Boccaccio writes, as one of those who 'secondo l'apparenza delle cose esteriori giudicano, senza guardare quello onde si muovono o che importino'), and he is here given a quick rebuttal to his illusions – not, it may be pointed out, by Ciacco, a character in the *Inferno*, but by Dante himself, the poet." I would submit that Dante the pilgrim already has more understanding than Scott suggests above. The fact that he asks the question at all implies that Dante has no illusions about the fate of their Christian souls. And in his question to Ciacco, Dante allows equally for the possibility that they may be in Hell: "se 'l ciel li addolcia o lo 'nferno li attosca" (v. 84).

3 Arrigo, named fifth on the list of the six "degni," is the only one whom Dante does not encounter on his journey down through Hell, even though Dante includes him in his question to Ciacco, and Ciacco refers to him in his response as one of those "tra l'anime più nere" and advises Dante that if he gets that far "là i potrai vedere." Not only does Dante not meet any

Florentine "degno" named Arrigo, but scholars over the centuries have admittedly never arrived at the name of a solid, viable candidate. See P. Santini, "Sui fiorentini 'che fur sì degni' " 40–4, who glosses the various attempts by commentators to supply names, which include Odarrigo Fifanti, Odarrigo Giandonati (possibly the same person), Arriguccio Compagni, or (as Santini suggests himself) Arrigo di Cascia, all the while admitting that he also is problematical. For further names suggested and rejected over time, see Vincenzo Presta, "Arrigo," *ED* 391–2.

4 The marriage pact between Guido Cavalcanti and Beatrice degli Uberti was signed in 1267, three years after the death of Beatrice's father, Farinata. It was hoped that by this marriage a leading Guelf family, the Cavalcanti, could then make peace with a leading Ghibelline family, the Uberti. These hopes were soon dashed as the late 1260s saw partisan politics at its most extreme during and immediately after the rule of Catalano and Loderingo. With regard to the Uberti, this was the time of the destruction of their houses and their permanent exile from Florence.

5 Dante does not mince words in the *Convivio* ii, viii 8 when it comes to Epicureans and their rejection of the afterlife: "Dico che intra tutte le bestialitadi quella è stoltissima, vilissima e dannosissima, chi crede dopo questa vita non essere altra vita; però che, se noi rivolgiamo tutte le scritture sì de' filosofi come de li altri savi scrittori, tutti concordano in questo, che in noi sia parte alcuna perpetuale" ["I declare that of all brutish opinions none is more stupid, more base or more pernicious than the belief that there is no other life after this. For if we go through the whole corpus of writings produced either by philosophers or by others endowed with wisdom, we find that all agree on this: there is in us something that endures for ever"]. The fact that Dante the pilgrim does not address this issue with Farinata at some point in their long conversation is, I believe, worthy of more critical consideration, but the matter is outside the concern of this study.

6 In the *Vita Nuova* xxx Dante declares that he is dedicating the work to Guido Cavalcanti: "E simile intenzione so ch'ebbe questo mio primo amico a cui io ciò scrivo, cioè ch'io li scrivessi solamente volgare" ["I am well aware, too, that my closest friend, for whom I write this work, also desired that I should write it entirely in the vernacular"]. Earlier in chapter iii Dante describes the genesis of his friendship with Guido Cavalcanti, the one he calls his "primo amico": "A questo sonetto fue risposto da molti e di diverse sentenzie; tra li quali fue risponditore quelli cui io chiamo primo de li miei amici, e disse allora uno sonetto, lo quale comincia: *Vedeste, al mio parere, onne valore*. E questo fue quasi lo principio de l'amistà tra lui e me, quando elli seppe che io era quelli che li avea ciò mandato" ["This sonnet drew replies from many, who all had different opinions as to its meaning. Among those who replied was someone

whom I call my closest friend; he wrote a sonnet beginning: *In my opinion you beheld all virtue.* Our friendship dated from the time he learned that it was I who had sent him the sonnet"].

7 With the exception of a few scholars such as Robert Davidsohn, *Storia di Firenze* III 156 (translation of the original *Geschichte von Florenz*), it is the general view that Guido Cavalcanti was exiled to Sarzana while Dante was prior, that is after 15 June 1300, not before in May as Davidsohn believes. See, for example, Singleton, *Inferno* 152: "There were continued hostilities between the two factions, and on June 24, 1300, the priors of Florence decided to put an end to these disturbances. The leading *Neri* were banished to Castel della Pieve in Perugia, and the leading *Bianchi*, including Guido, were exiled to Sarzana in Lunigiana. Among those who approved this decision were Dante in his capacity as prior (June–August) and Dino Compagni, who, as he informs us in his *Cronica* (see I, 21), also belonged to the council: '… e io Dino fui uno di quelli' ['… and I Dino was one of them']." If Compagni was already prior, as his term coincides with that of Dante, then the vote for exile must have taken place in late June. For an in depth discussion on the chronology of events during Dante's time as prior, see Arsenio Frugoni, *Il Canto X dell'Inferno* 22, who very convincingly disputes Davidsohn's view.

8 Villani cites the death of Guido Cavalcanti, caused by an illness he contracted while in exile, shortly after he and the other *Bianchi* are allowed to return to Florence: "Questa parte vi stette meno a' confini, che furono revocati per lo infermo luogo, e tornonne malato Guido Cavalcanti, onde morìo, e di lui fu grande dammaggio perocchè era come filosofo, virtudioso uomo in più cose, se non ch'era troppo tenero e stizzoso" ["This faction remained in exile a shorter time, for when the location proved to be unhealthy they were recalled. Guido Cavalcanti was ill when he returned, and died soon afterward. It was a great pity, for he was a philosopher and an able man in many respects, though, to be sure, much too sensitive and irritable"] (*Cronica* VIII 42). In Singleton, *Inferno* 152, the death of Cavalcanti is cited as occurring on 29 August 1300, according to the *Registro* of Santa Reparata. Frugoni, 22, refers to a letter written by Dante, now lost but known to Bruni, in which Dante felt obliged to explain that he was no longer prior when the others were called back: "e la ritornata loro fu per l'infermità e morte di Guido Cavalanti, il quale ammalò per l'aere cattiva e poco appresso morì" ["and their return was on account of the illness and death of Guido Cavalcanti, who had taken ill due to the bad air and soon after he died"].

9 Fifty months would take us from April of 1300 to June of 1304, when hope was lost that the exiled *Bianchi* could return to Florence. See Singleton, *Inferno* 155, who refers to the failed attempt of Pope Benedict XI to negotiate the return of Dante and his fellow exiles.

10 Villani describes Farinata's stand against his fellow Ghibellines: "Nel detto parlamento tutte le città vicine ... e tutti i baroni d'intorno propsono e furono in concordia per lo miglior di parte ghibellina, di disfare al tutto la città di Firenze, e di recarla a borgora, acciochè mai di suo stato non fosse rinomo, fama, nè podere. Alla quale proposta si levò e contradisse il valente e savio cavaliere messer Farinata degli Uberti ... dicendo ... com'era follia di ciò parlare, e come gran pericolo e danno ne potea avvenire, e s'altri ch'egli non fosse, mentre ch'egli avesse vita in corpo, colla spada in mano la difenderebbe" ["At this meeting all the nearby cities ... and all the barons of the surrounding area proposed and agreed that, for the good of the Ghibelline faction, the city of Florence be completely destroyed, and reduced to the status of a village. No trace of the fame, reputation, and power of the former state was to survive. When this proposal was made, the valiant and wise knight, Farinata degli Uberti, arose and opposed it ... saying ... that such talk was madness, and might well bring about great danger and harm. So long as there was life in his body, he said, he would defend the city with sword in hand, even if he had to do it alone"] (*Cronica* VI 81).

11 As Santini and Davidsohn have pointed out, Farinata was on the political stage in Florence over a period of some twenty years (1241–63). Reference is made in Santini, "Sui fiorentini 'che fur sì degni'" 30–1 to Farinata's contribution to Florence during periods of Ghibelline rule long before 1260: "Durante tali periodi di ghibellinismo i Sangeminianesi mandarono frequenti ambasciate a Firenze per aver consigli ed aiuti da Farinata. Questa amicizia strettissima fra il capo ghibellino e S. Gimignano ridondò a vantaggio dei Fiorentini, i quali per mezzo di Farinata e dei suoi esercitarono, anche nei periodi di prevalenza imperiale, la loro autorità sopra quella terra ... e ciò costituì al certo un titolo di benemerenza dell'Uberti verso la sua città" ["During such periods of Ghibellinism, the Sangeminianesi sent frequent embassies to Florence for advice and aid from Farinata. This close friendship between the head of the Ghibellines and San Gimignano resulted in an advantage for the Florentines, who by means of Farinata and his family exercised, even in periods of imperial predominance, their authority over that territory ... and that certainly constituted a meritorious deed on the part of Farinata towards his city"].

12 See Scott, *Dante Magnanimo* 71, who links Dante's delayed sense of being "lost" in reaction to Farinata's prediction of his exile to Farinata's wounded state, after the interruption of Cavalcante, in reaction to Dante's statement that Farinata's descendants have not been allowed to return to Florence.

13 See Umberto Bosco, "Canto XV dell' *Inferno*" 500, who draws the link between Dante's "ben fare," cited here by Brunetto, and a bygone world that was once inhabited by the likes of Tegghiaio, Iacopo Rusticucci, and

Brunetto himself. Bosco quotes a passage from Brunetto's *Tesoretto*, which, as he explains, contains the expression "ben fare" in precisely the same context: di pace e di *ben fare* ["of peace and of good deeds"]: "... non è senza interesse notare che in una fondamentale posizione politica, quale è la deplorazione della 'città partita,' la concordanza tra Brunetto e Dante è così piena da riflettersi persino sul lessico" ["... it is not without interest to note that on a fundamental political position like deploring the state of the 'divided city' the agreement between Brunetto and Dante is so full as to be reflected even with regard to vocabulary"].

14 Sapegno, *Inferno* 171.

15 While Guido Guerra is not listed among the "degni" in *Inferno* 6, he certainly could have been. See Santini, "Sui fiorentini 'che fur sì degni' " 28, who details Guido's contributions to Guelf Florence in the 1250s and 1260s, despite the fact that his clan, the Guidi, were Ghibelline: "Pertanto il Poeta rappresenta in Guido il simbolo del cittadino maggiore, che pone al disopra degli interessi della stirpe quelli dello Stato; del cittadino che vuole essere della fazione, la cui buona sorte si identifica con la prosperità e con la grandezza di Firenze, ma nell'istesso tempo desidera e promuove, quando la crede possibile, la pacificazione degli animi tra le parti, per il supremo interesse della sua città natale e per il benessere generale" ["For that reason the poet represents in Guido the symbol of the greatest citizen, who puts above the interests of his family the interests of the state; of the citizen who wants to be of that faction whose good fate identifies itself with the prosperity and greatness of Florence, but at the same time desires and promotes, when he thinks it possible, the reconciliation of the minds of the factions, for the supreme interest of his native city and for its general well-being"].

16 Some relatively recent scholarship including that of Silvio Pasquazi, *Il Canto XVI dell'Inferno*, Paolo Brezzi, *Il Canto XVI dell'Inferno* 401–20, and Joan M. Ferrante, *The Political Vision of the Divine Comedy* 165, disputes the centuries-old view that the sin of Guido Guerra, Tegghiaio Aldobrandi, and Iacopo Rusticucci is a separate issue from their role as "degni" politicians. The poet is clearly sending a message which is much more complex than that of the pilgrim who has such admiration for these three politicians that he would have jumped down to embrace them.

17 Santini, "Sui fiorentini 'che fur sì degni' " 40.

18 See Santini, "Sui fiorentini 'che fur sì degni' " 31–40, who goes into considerable detail in describing the services Tegghiaio Aldobrandi and Iacopo Rusticucci provided for Florence "quasi sempre l'uno accanto all'altro" ["almost always the one alongside the other"] (32).

19 To gain insight into the perception of Dante's contemporaries of the 1250 to 1260 period, when Florence was ruled by the *Primo Popolo*, as the "buon tempo antico," see Charles Davis, *Dante's Italy and Other Essays* 71–93, who refers (78) to the following words of Villani, reminiscent of those used by

Cacciaguida to describe Florence in his day: "E nota che al tempo del detto popolo, e in prima, e poi a gran tempo, i cittadini di Firenze viveano sobrii … e di grossi drappi vestíeno loro e le loro donne, e molti portavano le pelli scoperte sanza panno, e colle berrette in capo, e tutti con gli usatti in piede, e le donne fiorentine co'calzari sanza ornamenti …" ["And note that in the time of the said people, and before, and then for a long time, the citizens of Florence lived soberly … and they dressed with coarse cloth as did their women, and many wore skins without cloth, and with caps on their heads, and everyone with boots on their feet, and the Florentine women with boots without ornamentation …"] (*Cronica* VI 70).

20 Dante reveals himself to the two hypocrites, whose identity he has not yet learned, as follows: "I' fui nato e cresciuto / sovra 'l bel fiume d'Arno a la gran villa" ["I was born and grew up on the fair stream of Arno, at the great town"] (vv. 94–5). As Dante's birth took place in 1265, one year before their arrival in the "gran villa" on the Arno, could this reference be a not so subtle reminder to the reader of the irony that Dante, a Guelf, was born at the time of Ghibelline rule in a city which still existed thanks to Farinata who saved it, but whose descendants along with the Uberti houses were to be lost with the return of the Guelfs, starting with the hypocritical rule of Catalano and Loderingo?

21 Singleton, *Inferno* 401.

22 See Bosco-Reggio, *Inferno* 344, who relate that when Catalano and Loderingo first arrived in Florence their intentions were honourable: they tried to mediate between the two factions, as they had done previously in Bologna. Bosco-Reggio cite G. Salvemini (*Magnati e Popolani in Firenze dal 1280 al 1295* 292–5) as having demonstrated that the accusation that Catalano and Loderingo were hypocrites was in fact false: they had no choice but to obey their pope: "… costretti a diventare strumenti del papa, anche se finirono con lo scontentare i partiti e il papa stesso" ["… forced to become instruments of the Pope, even if they ended up disappointing the factions and the Pope himself"].

23 Santini, "Sui fiorentini che 'fur sì degni' " 29: "Nel 1202 Mosca, insieme con il padre suo Lamberto, e con molti altri cittadini, che avevano cooperato a sottrarre la terra di Montepulciano al dominio dei senesi, fu presente al giuramento di sottomissione dei Montepulcianesi ai Fiorentini" ["In 1202 Mosca, alongside his father Lamberto, and with many other citizens, who had cooperated to take away the land of Montepulciano from the control of the Sienese, was present at the oath of submission of the people of Montepulciano to the Florentines"].

24 See Bosco-Reggio, *Inferno* 412, who discuss the legitimacy of the "vendetta privata" in Dante's day and the death of Geri Alighieri figlio di Bello, Dante's father's cousin, at the hands of one of the Sacchetti family, followed by the Alighieri murder of one of the Sacchetti in revenge some thirty years later in 1310 (when this *cantica* is being written).

25 In Joan M. Ferrante, *The Political Vision of the Divine Comedy* 142–3, the repetition of "dimmi" within the canto is detailed: "The gluttons lose the
   power to act or to communicate with others. Dante finds it very difficult
   to get anything out of them; he has to keep coaxing "tell me, tell me": "Ma
   dimmi chi tu sei" ["But tell me who you are"] 6.46, "ma dimmi, se tu sai"
   ["But tell me, if you know"] 6.60, "e dimmi la cagione" ["But tell me
   why"] 6.62, "dimmi ove sono" ["tell me where they are"] 6.82.
26 "Unimportant," that is, because these words are without thematic significance, in no way suggestive of the identity or the current state of these
   politicians whom Dante encounters in his journey. They function solely as
   linguistic signals.
27 See Lloyd Howard, "The Episodes of the 'tre ombre' and the 'frati godenti': Linguistic and Structural Parallels."
28 Part 2 essentially reproduces Lloyd Howard and Elena Rossi, "Textual
   Mapping of Dante's Journey Back to Political Original Sin in Florence,"
   which follows the nine formulas of repetition first announced in Lloyd
   Howard, "Linguistic Patterns and Internal Structure in Five *canti* of the
   Inferno."
29 See Charles S. Singleton, *Dante Studies* 2: *Journey to Beatrice* 283, who concludes his extraordinary study as follows: "The pattern of the original for-
   mation of man is thus seen to repeat itself in the re-formation of a man
   named Dante, who attains first to a condition of justice with Virgil, within
   the proportion of his nature and under the natural light, and then, in a
   second moment attains to Eden proper, crossing the river to a kind of justice with Beatrice that is truly beyond all human measure." As well in
   Dante's concurrent journey, after fathoming the depths of political sin in
   Florence, with Virgil ever at his side, Dante now with Beatrice will ultimately reach Cacciaguida and attain with Cacciaguida an understanding
   of the "viver lieto" that existed in Florence once, before the fall that came
   with discord, following the murder of Buondelmonte.

CHAPTER 6

1 As in chapter 5, the episode of the three politicians surfaces as a key stop
   along the way of a signposted journey. For an examination of *Inferno* 16
   within the wider context of the *Commedia*, see Baranski, "The 'Marvellous'" 72–95, previously noted in the Introduction, where he identifies *Inferno* xvi as the first canto the reader encounters in the *Commedia* which
   "demands to be read as part of a broader ideological and formal framework" and that "Dante scatters textual markers to this effect" (73). The
   formulas of repetition highlighted both in the previous chapter and in the
   present one further substantiate Baranski's premise.
2 Two synonyms for "gittare" found elsewhere in the *Commedia* are
   "lanciare" and "buttare," with Dante adopting the reflexive "lanciarsi"

instead of "gittarsi" in 1.25.50. In both 1.16.47 and 2.27.50 Dante selects "gittarsi" over "lanciarsi" when repeating the image that "he would have thrown himself."

3 With the exception of two dissenting studies recognized as informative and provocative, it has always been accepted that these souls are sodomites. The two dissenting studies are André Pézard, *Dante sous la Pluie de Feu*, and Richard Kay, *Dante's Swift and Strong: Essays on Inferno XV.*

4 When the Angel of God proclaims: "Più non si va, se pria non morde, / anime sante, il foco: intrate in esso, / e al cantar di là non siate sorde" ["No farther may you go, holy souls, if first the fire sting not; enter into it, and to the singing beyond be not deaf"] (2.27.10–12), the reference to the "anime sante" suggests that all penitent souls must pass through this fire that purges the lustful of their sin. Commentators agree that this fire serves a dual purpose: not only is it for the penitent lustful of the seventh terrace but also for all blessed souls on their ascent to salvation. See for example Sapegno, *Purgatorio* 301, who describes this wall of fire as encircling all of Earthly Paradise; therefore, it is not a purifying fire alone for the penitent lustful, but for all "anime sante" released from Purgatory. Bosco-Reggio, *Purgatorio* 453, 458 refer to the medieval tradition which saw Eden as completely surrounded by a barrier of fire, based on an interpretation of Genesis 3:24. If the flames circle the entire summit of the mountain, it would be impossible for souls desirous of attaining the top to do so without eventually making this rite of passage through the flames.

5 Steven Botterill, "Canto xxvii" 399, details the "plausible psychological situation" of Virgil's "gentle persuasion," much like that between a father and a son, when the son refuses to do as the father asks, until the father finally comes up with his "trump card": "Or vedi, figlio: / tra Beatrice e te è questo muro" ["Now see, son, between Beatrice and you is this wall"] (35–6).

6 Until the 1960s commentators normally regarded Guido Guerra, Tegghiaio Aldobrandi, and Iacopo Rusticucci as worthy politicians who endeavoured to keep peace where possible and to aid in the advance of the Guelf cause when peace between Guelf and Ghibelline could not be preserved. Their private lives as unrepentant sodomites were not known to the populace at large, to the extent that Dante the pilgrim, in the Ciacco episode, was unaware of Tegghiaio and Iacopo's fate. If their sin was unknown to most, scholars inferred that it did not adversely affect their own political judgment and therefore did not merit examination in the political context. See Pietro Santini, "Sui fiorentini 'che fur sì degni'"; Aleardo Sacchetto, "Il canto dei tre fiorentini," *Dieci letture dantesche*; and Aldo Vallone, "Il canto xvi dell'Inferno," for this traditional view, which dates back to Filippo Villani, Giovanni Villani, and Giovanni Boccaccio. More recent scholarship has tended to argue against a separation of the three politi-

cians' private lives as sodomites from their public lives as leaders of Florence, suggesting that a careful reading of the text, along with an awareness of what they and their families actually did in the thirteenth century, will unmask the corruption which lurks beneath. See Silvio Pasquazi, *Il Canto XVI dell'Inferno*; Paolo Brezzi, *Il Canto XVI dell'Inferno*; Joan M. Ferrante, *The Political Vision of the Divine Comedy* 165, for this opposing view.

7 Politicians who put their "ingegno" to "ben far," like those Dante refers to in 1.6.81 and like Dante himself according to Brunetto Latini in 1.15.64, are those who placed the welfare of Florence above factional dissension (see chapter 5).

8 See Eva Cantarella, *Bisexuality in the Ancient World* 141, who describes the love between Corydon and Alexis as "a romantic love with all the trimmings, which the critics have sometimes interpreted as an account of a personal experience of the poet." While it is anyone's guess what Dante's reaction would have been to the second *Eclogue*, or for that matter the love between Euryalus and Nisus in the *Aeneid*, I believe it is reasonable to conclude that Dante's awareness of Virgil was such that references in Virgil's poetry to male love could partially explain Dante the pilgrim's reasoning that Virgil would have allowed him to jump down and embrace Iacopo, Tegghiaio, and Guido.

9 For an overview of the commentary of Albertus Magnus and St Thomas Aquinas, which regards homosexuality as a sin against nature, and the standing in general of homosexuals in Christian Europe in the Middle Ages, see John Boswell, *Christianity, Social Tolerance and Homosexuality* 316–32, who details the rise in intolerance during the thirteenth and fourteenth centuries that culminates in the passage of laws in Italy in the late thirteenth and early fourteenth centuries calling for the death sentence for homosexuals (291–3); for specific reference to the secular law in Italy, see Michael Goodich, "Sodomy in Medieval Secular Law."

10 The image of the broad flakes of fire which rain down upon these sinners recalls the rain of fire that also fell upon Sodom and Gomorrah: "Dominus pluit super Sodomam et Gomorrham sulphur et ignem a Domino de caelo" ["The Lord poured down on Sodom and Gomorrah brimstone and fire from the Lord out of heaven"] (Genesis 19:24).

11 See John A. Scott, *Dante's Political Purgatory* 3–35, for an outstanding gloss of Dante's political career between 1295 and 1301.

12 See 2.13.136–8, where Dante tells Sapia that he will have to spend time among the proud of the first terrace.

13 In Hell the lustful heterosexuals inhabit the second circle, separate from the lustful homosexuals of the seventh circle, unlike Purgatory where all the penitent lustful share the seventh terrace. Therefore, were Dante to be condemned to Hell and not to be saved, he would have felt the pain from the heat of the second circle, not the fire of seventh circle.

14 In this sonnet of praise, one of Cavalcanti's few which views the lady Giovanna positively, he tells of this most beautiful creature whose essence surpasses the most splendid sight mortal man can possibly imagine. It is in the first two *quadernari* that Cavalcanti enumerates the beautiful images. The words "e bianca neve scender senza venti" are found in verse 6. They exude complete tranquillity and silence and are borrowed not only by Dante but also by Petrarch in his *Trionfo della Morte* (1.67): "Che senza venti in un bel colle fiocchi" ["That without winds on a beautiful hill snow falls"].

15 Dante's words here are normally recalled by commentators to point out that the "chi" refers to Dante. These words appear problematical particularly here on the first terrace of the penitent proud where the poet should not show pride in his future fame. For discussion on Guido Cavalcanti's fame as the one who holds supreme the "gloria de la lingua" in the year 1300, see Gianfranco Contini, "Cavalcanti in Dante" 434.

16 I base my view that Guido Cavalcanti was a heretic, an Averroist to be more precise, on Bruno Nardi's reading of Cavalcanti's philosophical *canzone*, "Donna me prega," and on Cavalcanti's relationship with the philosopher Iacopo da Pistoia, who dedicated his Averroistic work to his friend Guido Cavalcanti. See Bruno Nardi, "L'averroismo del 'primo' amico di Dante"; "Di un nuovo commento alla Canzone del Cavalcanti sull'amore"; "Noterella polemica sull'averroismo di Guido Cavalcanti"; and Paul O. Kristeller, "A Philosophical Treatise from Bologna Dedicated to Guido Cavalcanti: Magister Jacobus de pistorio and his 'Quaestio de felicitate.'" See Lloyd Howard, "Giovanna as John the Baptist and the 'disdegno' of Guido," for an analysis of the role Guido's heresy played in his rejection of Giovanna and Beatrice in the *Vita Nuova* xxiv and Guido's rejection of a journey to salvation and Beatrice in *Inferno* 10.

17 There is a third adoption of the word "lembo" in 2.7.72, but in that instance "lembo" does not refer to the "edge" of Dante's clothing, but to the "edge" of a path.

18 Words other than "panni" used in the *Commedia* include "abito" and "veste." Indeed in 1.16.8 Iacopo Rusticucci recognizes by Dante's "abito" that he is Florentine.

19 Commentators see this angel as similar to those at the exit of the previous terraces: Sapegno, *Purgatorio* 300 refers to the angel as the custodian of the seventh terrace; Singleton, *Purgatorio* 650 similarly describes this angel as at the exit of this terrace, like those at the exits of the previous terraces. But as is indicated in Bosco-Reggio, *Purgatorio* 458, this angel does not invite Dante to ascend to the next terrace, but invites all "anime sante" to enter the fire as a rite of passage.

20 See Zygmunt G. Baranski, "Structural Retrospection in Dante's *Comedy*: The Case of *Purgatorio* xxvii" 18, who relates Dante's rejection of Virgil's

request that he step into the fire to earlier moments in the journey when Virgil kept Dante safe from the fire, including the *girone* of the sodomites "across the burning sands onto which, Virgil had stressed, he must not step" (*Inf.* 16. 16–18).

21 See Bosco-Reggio, *Purgatorio* 433, who cite the version of the hymn that appears in the commentary of Iacopo della Lana, a version somewhat different from the one read today. However, the third stanza in both versions refers to the sin of lust.

22 See Botterill, "*Purgatorio* xxvii" 398–410, who perceptively comments on "the range of readerly possibilities" (409) of this canto very much at the crossroads; Baranski, "Structural Restrospection in Dante's *Comedy*," who maintains that there has been too much emphasis on the part of scholars who restrict their interpretation of this canto purely "prospectively," that is in the direction of Earthly Paradise and beyond, and argues for an interpretation of the canto based on the text that preceded it, a series of signposts which point to *Purgatorio* 27: "In *Purgatorio* xxvii's first forty-five lines, therefore, Dante skilfully weaves a complex web of structural repetitions whose constituent elements interconnect over sixty-one cantos, spinning backwards from the narratively crucial vantage-point – an obvious Singletonian 'goal' or 'pivot' – of a major moment of arrival and transition" (6).

23 While Dante does not employ the word "padre" with Brunetto, as is the case with Guinizzelli, he does refer to "la cara e buona imagine paterna" ["the dear, kind, paternal image"] (1.15.83) of Brunetto, and on two occasions Brunetto refers to Dante as "figliuol": "O figliuol mio" (1.15.31); "O figliuol" (1.15.37).

CHAPTER 7

1 See Zygmunt Baranski, "Canto vi," who notes signposts in the canto which reflect that "Dante's description of Sordello is nowhere near as flattering as has normally been assumed" (88). Perhaps these signposts to which Baranski refers will guide the reader to question other assumptions and to look for other signposts.

2 See *Inferno* 25.92/94/96 and *Purgatorio* 25.17/19/21, where "la bocca" appears in a configuration with "tocca" and "scocca" but not "de la bocca." The latter case, situated between the two occurrences of the formula of repetition under study, requires some further scrutiny. When Virgil says to Dante to let loose the bow of his speech ("Scocca / l'arco del dir, che 'nfino al ferro hai tratto" ["Discharge the bow of your speech which you have drawn to the iron"] *Purg.* 25.17–18) and Dante quickly lets his words fly ("Allor sicuramente apri' la bocca / e cominciai: 'Come …'" ["Then I opened my mouth confidently and began, 'How …'"] *Purg.* 25.19–20),

this reference to Dante's successful "arco del dir" foreshadows the break-down of his "arco" and his inability to respond audibly to Beatrice some six cantos later in *Purgatorio* 31.

3 Baranski, *Purgatorio* VI 84 notes the important role of repetitions within the canto which "bind the whole canto together or at least large sections of it." If repetition is key within *Purgatorio* 6, then it should not be surprising that repetition likewise links this canto and another. Barolini, *Dante's Poets* 170 sees the episode as a point of convergence of several politcal themes, going back to *Inferno* 6, with the reference to the "degni," *Inferno* 10, with Farinata's love of *patria*, and Inferno 28, where Bertran, a political poet like Sordello, is condemned.

4 Earlier in *Purgatorio* 6 Virgil states that Dante will be seeing Beatrice in Earthly Paradise, and embedded in the text is a signal that points to *Purgatorio* 30 and 31: "Non so se 'ntendi: io dico di Beatrice; / tu la vedrai di sopra, in su la vetta / di questo monte, ridere e felice" ["I know not if you understand: I speak of Beatrice. You will see her above, smiling and happy, on the summit of this mountain"] (2.6.46–8).

5 See John A. Scott, *Dante's Political Purgatory* 17, 217, who refers to a letter written by Dante and chronicled by Leonardo Bruni in which Dante reveals that his problems in life go back to when he served as prior: "Tutti li mali e l'inconvenienti miei dalli infausti comizi del mio priorato ebbono cagione e principio" ["All my ills and troubles were caused and began with the inauspicious meetings of my priorate"] (*Le vite di Dante, Petrarca e Boccaccio*, ed. A. Solerti [Milano, 1904], 100).

6 Chiavacci Leonardi, *Purgatorio* 192.

7 See Singleton, *Purgatorio* 135; Di Salvo, *Purgatorio* 106; and Chiavacci Leonardi, *Purgatorio* 192.

8 Bosco-Reggio, *Purgatorio* 108.

9 See Sapegno, *Purgatorio* 70, who cites the archery reference in 1.8.13; 1.17.136; 2.31.16–17; and especially in 2.25.17–18.

10 See Isidoro Del Lungo, *Dante ne' tempi di Dante* 159, who was the first to point out the connection between Dante's reference to the months of October and November and the last Priorato of the White Guelfs in 1301, who had been elected for their two-month term 15 October 1301, but had been forced to resign 7 November 1301 before the now more powerful Black Guelfs.

11 Singleton, *Purgatorio* 756.

12 See Bosco-Reggio 529, who detail the two interpretations held by commentators: "come la balestra (*balestro*) quando lascia partire il colpo (*scocca*) da un'eccessiva tensione (*tesa*), spezza (*frange*) la sua corda e l'arco, e quindi, a causa di ciò, la freccia (*asta*) raggiunge il bersaglio (*il segno*) con minore impeto (*foga*) … La struttura sintattica della similitudine è un po' contorta, così che, oltre all'interpretazione che si è data, ne è

stata proposta una seconda in cui: *frange* è inteso come intransitivo
(=*si frange*) e si fa *corda* e *arco* non oggetto di *frange*, bensì soggetto di *scocca*
(col verbo al singolare non ostante i due soggetti, cosa già ripetutamente
vista). In tal caso, si sopprime la virgola dopo *tesa* e il senso della terzina
sarebbe: come la balestra si spezza, quando la sua corda e l'arco scoccano
da una eccessiva tensione e la freccia raggiunge ecc." ["as the crossbow
(*balestro*) when it lets its shot (*scocca*) fly, from excess tension (*tesa*) it
breaks (*frange*) its cord and bow, and then, in consequence, the arrow
(*freccia*) reaches its target (*il segno*) with less force (*foga*) … the syntactic
structure of the simile is a bit contorted, so that, beyond the interpretation
which is given, there has been a second one proposed in which: *frange*, to
break, is understood as intransitive (=*si frange*, it breaks) which makes
corda, cord, and *arco*, bow, not the object of *frange*, but rather the subject of
scocca, let fly (with the verb in the singular despite the two subjects, such
as has already been repeatedly seen). In such a case the comma after *tesa* is
taken out and the sense of the tercet would be: 'as the crossbow breaks,
when its cord and bow let fly the shot from excessive tension and the arrow reaches etc.' "]. They argue that the latter reading is less likely, but in
any case would change little, as the result is the same: the arrow reaches
its target with less impetus. Recent commentators are divided on this
point. Di Salvo 553 and Singleton 759 are in agreement with Bosco and
Reggio that it is the bow and bowstring that break, while Sapegno 349 and
Chiavacci Leonardi 910–11 interpret the crossbow as breaking.

13 See 1.10.79, 1.15.61, 1.24.140, 2.8.133, 2.11.139, for those who had "parole
gravi" to say about Dante's future.

14 Marguerite Mills Chiarenza, "Time and Eternity in the Myths of *Paradiso*
XVII" 139–40, points to a reference in John of Salisbury's *Polycraticus*
"iacula quae previdentur feriunt minus" ("spears which are foreseen
inflict lighter wounds") as the source for Dante's adoption of a similar
image to relay the pilgrim's concern for his uncertain future.

15 As well, see 1.26.1–3, where Dante decries the fact that Hell is full of sinners from Florence: "Godi, Fiorenza, poi che se' sì grande / che per mare
e per terra bàtti l'ali, / e per lo 'nferno tuo nome si spande!" ["Rejoice,
O Florence, since you are so great that over sea and land you beat your
wings, and your name is spread through Hell!"].

16 Dante also makes reference to the dark wood as a valley in *Inferno* 1:
"quella valle / che m'avea di paura il cor compunto" vv. 14–15.

17 See Bosco-Reggio, *Paradiso* 288, who gloss 3.17.61–6 ("E quel che più ti
graverà le spalle, / sarà la compagnia malvagia e scempia / con la qual tu
cadrai in questa valle / …"). They refer to the testimony of the *Ottimo
Commento*, most likely Andrea Lancia, who was an acquaintance of
Dante's, that in all likelihood Dante attempted to dissuade his fellow
Whites from taking any ill-prepared, hasty action against Florence in

1304. Ill-conceived action was taken in the summer of 1304, but without Dante's involvement.

18 Dante was elected prior for the 15 June to August 15 1300 period. See also Michele Barbi, "L'ordinamento della repubblica fiorentina e la vita politica di Dante, *Problemi di critica dantesca, prima serie* Sansoni: 141–55, for a close examination of Dante's involvement in Florentine politics between 1295 and 1301.

19 See also chapters 5 and 6.

20 See John A. Scott, "Beatrice's Reproaches in Eden: Which 'School' Had Dante Followed?" 9, who ties Dante's self-confessed pride in 2.13.136–8 to a "pride and ambition in his soul" owing to his political career.

21 See Scott, "Beatrice's Reproaches in Eden" 1–23, who convincingly argues (despite the traditional view) that Beatrice's reference to the wrong "School" (2.33.85) Dante followed is the "scuola guelfa," which rejected the guidance of the Emperor to terrestrial happiness: "Dante in 1300, a citizen and soon to be elected Prior of a defiantly Guelph commune, had followed a path remote from that traced out by God for the well-being of humanity" (2–3). By the time of Henry VII's entry into Italy, Dante the poet rejected the school to which he once belonged. If Dante now condemns the "scuola guelfa" through Beatrice as his mouthpiece in *Purgatorio* 33, then arguments put forward in this chapter linking the unsatisfactory behaviour of Florentine politicians of *Purgatorio* 6 with Dante's confession before Beatrice in *Purgatorio* 31 by means of the linguistic configuration are more easily understood. Scott points out that the "presenti cose," which Dante confesses in 2.31.34, and which turned Dante away from Beatrice, may well have "included the mirages of political ambition and the internecine rivalries of petty political factions – especially, when we recall the bitter description of Dante's fellow White Guelphs as 'la compagnia malvagia e scempia' whose 'bestialitate' is angrily denounced in *Paradiso* XVII, 61–69, where the pilgrim boasts of being above all parties ('sì ch'a te fia bello / averti fatta parte per te stesso') ['so that it will be for your fair fame to have made you a party by yourself']. Or, to put it another way, the mature Dante of the *Comedy* had evidently come to regret the compromises and adjustments necessary in the realities of political life, a line of conduct far removed from the idealism that had inspired the *Vita Nuova* and what we know of Dante's youthful love for Beatrice" (6). In Guido Cavalcanti's sonnet of criticism to Dante, *I' vegno 'l giorno a te 'nfinite volte*, Guido scolds Dante for frequenting the "annoiosa gente," people who, according to Scott (6) and Mario Marti (in *Poeti del Dolce stil nuovo* 228–9), are Dante's political bedfellows.

22 Scott, "Beatrice's Reproaches in Eden" 1–23.

23 See Singleton, *Paradiso* 32, who glosses this "arco": "Beatrice's discourse is concerned with what is properly termed teleology. The term *telos*, in

Greek (often in Aristotle), means the end or purpose of an action and commonly suggests the metaphor which is now implicit in Beatrice's words, namely, archery, the aiming of an arrow at some target. This figure in the present context makes God, who governs the heavens and all things, an archer who aims (through the motive force of natural love) the creature at its own proper target or resting-place. The Archer is not named as such, but His bow, His instrument in the total movement of the universe, is this love, natural love."

CHAPTER 8

1 See Antonio Rossini, "La 'bella scola' ed il 'salutevol cenno': una ricerca semantica e stilistica," who traces the rhyme words "cenno – senno" through the *Commedia*, reflecting among other links a linguistic link between the Statius episode and Limbo.
2 Basing his argument on canto lengths, not lines of text within a given canto, Charles Singleton, in "The Poet's Number at the Center," shows how the reader's attention is drawn inside the seven framing cantos where new conclusions can be made once the frame is recognized.
3 See for example the commentaries of Sapegno and Singleton. It appears that commentators are more likely to note the repetition of formulas with thematic significance such as "ne l'etterno essilio," but not the more hidden repetition of words without thematic significance discussed in other chapters, or repeated rhyme words within a configuration.
4 In Kevin Brownlee, "Canto XXVI" 395, the repetition of the rhyme words "Virgilio"/"essilio"/"concilio" in each of the three *cantiche* is noted.
5 The particular damage caused in the sixth *bolgia*, the earthquake during the crucifixion, is a reminder both to those of the Council of the Pharisees who dwell here and to the reader of the tremendous consequences of the Council's actions.
6 See chapter 3 and the alternate journey highlighted by the formula "vo' che sappi," and with the references to Virgil's previous journey down to the ninth circle. There is also a linguistic link between the episodes in the *Inferno* linked by the "vo' che sappi" and the episode now under review in *Inferno* 23. "La ruina" appears twice in *Inferno* 12 (verses 4 and 32), referring to the damage done in Hell by the earthquake at the time of the crucifixion, and again here in *Inferno* 23.137 with "la ruina" referring to the same. See Matthew 27:51: "Terra mota est, et petrae scissae sunt" ["The earth quaked, and the rocks were rent"]. As well, the rhyme words "sospiri" and "martìri" appear both in the first episode of the "vo' che sappi" formula, in *Inferno* 4. 26 and 28 with reference to Limbo dwellers such as Virgil, and also here in *Inferno* 23. 113 and 117 with reference to the "martiri" of Christ and the "sospiri" of Caiaphas upon seeing Dante.

7 See John 11:45–52, and in particular Caiaphas's words: "Vos nescitis quidquam; nec cogitatis, quia expedit vobis ut unus moriatur homo pro populo, et non tota gens pereat" ["You know nothing at all; nor do you reflect that it is expedient for us that one man die for the people, instead of the whole nation perishing"].

8 The importance of the number three at this juncture should not be overlooked. Dante is explicit when he describes the "crucifixion" of Caiaphas: "in terra con tre pali" ["on the ground with three stakes"] (1.23.111). Caiaphas is not crucified on a cross but with three stakes, one through the feet and one through each of his hands.

9 See Matthew 27:25: "Et respondens universus populus dixit: Sanguis eius super nos, et super filios nostros" ["And all the people answered and said, 'His blood be on us and on our children'"].

10 See Singleton, *Inferno* 405, who cites I. Della Giovanna (*Lectura Dantis*, 25). Virgil's "marvelling" has been the subject of critical discussion. Bosco-Reggio, *Inferno* 336, 345, suggest that his marvelling underscores that Caiaphas's sin was the most grave of sins. In response to those who maintain that Virgil marvels because the last time he passed this way Caiaphas was not there, Bosco-Reggio rightly point out that everyone in Hell from the Christian Age is new to the place from Virgil's perspective and he does not marvel over all the others. If one considers Virgil's presence in this scene from the point of view of his name, "Virgilio," which forms part of the linguistic configuration under study, then his marvelling may only be understood once the reader completes the signposted journey to the other stops on the way, in *Purgatorio* 21 and *Paradiso* 26.

11 The role of Pontius Pilate and his personal responsibility in the crucifixion of Christ for handing him over to the people is here made evident by Dante when he refers to Philip the Fair as the new Pilate. See Villani's quotation of the Bishop of Ansiona, VIII 64, where, as in Dante, Philip is held responsible for the death of Boniface VIII and Philip and his descendants are to be condemned by God for Philip's actions.

12 See Matthew 27:31: "Et postquam illuserunt ei, exuerunt eum chlamyde, et induerunt eum vestimentis eius; et duxerunt eum ut crucifigerent" ["And when they had mocked him, they took the cloak off him and put his own garments on him, and led him away to crucify him"].

13 Di Salvo, *Purgatorio* 357, refers to an "anonimo medievale" who quotes Pope Benedict XI as saying: "non pianse tanto la sventura cui era stata sottoposta la sua persona: ma diceva che lo stesso Cristo era stato spogliato dai soldati del nuovo Pilato" ["he did not so much lament the misfortune to which his person was subjected: but he said that the same Christ had been stripped by the soldiers of the new Pilate"].

14 It is widely accepted by historians nowadays that the reason the Knights Templar were condemned was not because they were sodomites or here-

tics as Philip charged, but because they were wealthy. Dante, as a contemporary to the event, also recognizes that Philip persecuted them because he wanted to gain for himself the wealth of their order. See Malcolm Barber, *The New Knighthood: A History of the Order of the Temple*.

15 See *Purgatorio* 21.82–7, where Dante mistakenly assumes that Titus was already Emperor and speaks through Statius of Titus, who with divine assistance destroys Jerusalem to avenge Judas's betrayal of Christ. In the general destruction, the Temple of Herod the Great, which replaced Solomon's Temple, was destroyed: "Nel tempo che 'l buon Tito, con l'aiuto / del sommo rege, vendicò le fóra / ond'uscì 'l sangue per Giuda venduto ..." ["In the time when the good Titus, with help of the Highest King, avenged the wounds whence issued the blood sold by Judas ..."] (2.21.82–4). In this passage Dante does not refer specifically to the Jews, but he will later in *Paradiso* 7 when he returns to this theme.

16 Along with the "giusta vendetta" being meted out towards those who persecuted Christ will be the "vendetta" meted out towards those who will persecute Dante, the unjust who will unfairly accuse and exile him. Cacciaguida foretells this fate in *Paradiso* 17 along with the ultimate revenge against the perpetrators of Dante's exile: "La colpa seguirà la parte offensa / in grido, come suol; ma la *vendetta* / fia testimonio al ver che la dispensa" ["The blame, as always, will follow the injured party, in outcry; but vengeance shall bear witness to the truth which dispenses it"] (3.17.52–4).

17 While the formula "giusta vendetta" does not appear in *Paradiso* 6, "vendetta" surfaces three times in close succession, all relating to the crucifixion, starting with the third Caesar, Tiberius, who ruled at the time of the Redemption: "... ché la viva giustizia che mi spira, / li concedette, in mano a quel ch'i' dico, / gloria di far *vendetta* a la sua ira. / Or qui t'ammira in ciò ch'io ti replìco: / poscia con Tito a far *vendetta* corse / de la *vendetta* del peccato antico" ["... because the living Justice which inspires me granted to it, in his living hand of whom I speak, the glory of doing vengeance for Its own wrath. Now marvel here at what I unfold to you: afterwards it sped with Titus to do vengeance for the vengeance of the ancient sin"] (3.6.88–93).

18 Along with Matthew 27:51, see Mark 15:38 and Luke 23:45.

19 Statius explains later in *Purgatorio* 21 that this upper part of Purgatory never experiences terrestial earthquakes. The upper region of Purgatory trembles when a soul's time in Purgatory is over and the soul is freed: "Tremaci quando alcuna anima monda / sentesi, sì che surga o che si mova / per salir sù; e tal grido seconda" ["It trembles here when some soul feels itself pure so that it may rise or set out for the ascent, and that shout follows"] (2.21.58–60).

20 See Luke 24:13–16: "Ec ecce duo ex illis ibant ipsa die in castellum, quod erat in spatio stadiorum sexaginta ab Ierusalem, nomine Emmaus. Et ipsi

loquebantur ad invicem de his omnibus quae acciderant. Et factum est dum fabularentur et secum quaererent, et ipse Iesus appropinquans ibat cum illis. Oculi autem illorum tenebantur ne eum agnoscerent." ["And behold, two of them were going that very day to a village named Emmaus, which is sixty stadia from Jerusalem. And they were talking to each other about all these things that had happened. And it came to pass, while they were conversing and arguing together, that Jesus himself also drew near and went about with them; but their eyes were held, that they should not recognize him."]

21 Christ greets his disciples in a similar manner: "pax vobis" ["peace be with you"]. See Luke 24:36 and John 20:19/26.

22 See Kenelm Foster, *The Two Dantes* 174–89 for an analysis of Virgil's lack of faith in Christ to come, as opposed to the implicit faith in Christ to come on the part of the Old Testament worthies and some noble pagans such as Cato, Trajan, and Ripheus. See also Robert Hollander, *Il Virgilio dantesco: Tragedia nella Commedia*, for a comprehensive study of Dante's negative judgment of Virgil; and Cassell, *Lectura Dantis Americana: Inferno I* for a careful overview of Virgil's rebellion, including an exhaustive bibliography of those recent studies which have looked at Virgil's shortcomings in the *Commedia* (166).

23 An examination of both Justinian's complex discourse in *Paradiso* 6 and the *Monarchia* II xii 5 makes it clear that Tiberius and his procurator Pontius Pilate were doing what God willed that they do: avenging God's anger for original sin by sacrificing Christ. But this does not free them from responsibility, as they did not know that. Dante's only direct reference to Pontius Pilate occurs in *Purgatorio* 20 when he compares the hated Philip the Fair to Pilate: "Veggiolo un'altra volta esser deriso; / veggio rinovellar l'aceto e 'l fiele, / e tra vivi ladroni esser anciso. / Veggio il novo Pilato sì crudele ..." ["I see Him mocked a second time; and I see renewed the vinegar and the gall, and Him slain between living thieves. I see the new Pilate so cruel ..."] (2.20.88–91). Similarly, the Jews did God's will but without knowing it: "Però d'un atto uscir cose diverse: / ch'a Dio e a' Giudei piacque una morte; / per lei tremò la terra 'l ciel s'aperse" ["Therefore from one act issued things diverse, for one same death was pleasing to God and to the Jews; thereat the earth trembled and Heaven was opened"] (3.7.46–8).

24 The only reward for Virgil is that Beatrice will often praise him before the God he will never know: "Quando sarò dinanzi al segnor mio, / di te mi loderò sovente a lui" ["When I am before my Lord I will often praise you to Him"] (1.2.73–4).

25 Kevin Brownlee, "Canto xxvi" 395, notes this last reference to Virgil in the *Commedia*: "This is the last time that Virgil is explicitly named in the entire *Commedia*, rhyming – significantly – with the word 'exile' (*essilio*, v. 116)."

26 The only other time that "Virgilio" appears in *Paradiso*, in *Paradiso* 17.19, is when Dante asks his ancestor, Cacciaguida, to explain the meaning of the "parole gravi" that he heard with regard to his future life, while being guided by Virgil in the world below. Of course the "parole gravi" refer to Dante's forthcoming exile, an exile that Cacciaguida explains to him. Therefore, both times Virgil's name appears in the *Paradiso*, it is associated with exile: first Dante's exile in this life; second Adam's temporary eternal exile in Limbo. But by association, even this first reference to "Virgilio" in the *Paradiso*, and the penultimate of the total thirty-two "Virgilio" references in the *Commedia*, may be setting the stage for conclusions about Virgil's own exile in Limbo that can be drawn from the last reference to him by name in *Paradiso* 26.118.

27 See Randolph Starn, *Contrary Commonwealth* 45. He quotes a number of contemporary chroniclers who detail how widespread exile was for entire groups of people in Dante's day. While exile was widespread among the "gente tosca," Dante's fellow Florentines were not the only exiles. Starn takes figures from the *Chronica parva Ferrariense*, col. 485 and from Salvioli, *Annali bolognesi* III 300ff, and concludes: "If these figures can be trusted, they mean that anywhere from a third to a half of the population of Ferrara and Bologna was in exile at any one time."

28 Kevin Brownlee, "Canto XXVI" 395 notes this one other occurrence of the "concilio" / "essilio" rhyme in the *Paradiso*, but where Christ, the "figlio," is found in the place of "Virgilio."

29 In verse 121, fifteen lines before the "Filio" reference, the once only repetition of "fantolin ... la mamma," emerges. "Fantolin ... la mamma" previously appears in *Purgatorio* 30.44 when the frightened Dante turns to Virgil, like a child who seeks his mother, for not one "dramma" ["drop"] of blood runs through Dante's veins that does not tremble before the old "fiamma" ["flame"] of Beatrice. In *Paradiso* 23 Dante, still the "fantolin," turns to the true "mamma," the Virgin Mary, the "fiamma" ascending to the Empyrean. And the "dramma" of Dante's blood that trembles before the old love is here replaced by Dante's affection which "s'infiamma" ("glows forth") to the Queen of Paradise.

CHAPTER 9

1 In the Petrocchi text the noun in the rhyme position of verse 108 appears as "doglie." In the past the noun has appeared as "voglie," and Singleton more recently still argued for "voglie" over "doglie." While the replacement of "voglie" with "doglie" in the text obviously changes the meaning, whether it be Dante's "desires" or "pains" that require soothing, the fact remains that Dante the pilgrim, newly come from the depths of Hell, is hoping for some distraction after the rigours of his infernal journey.

2 See Bosco-Reggio, *Purgatorio* 39, who endorse the view held by most modern scholars that *Amor che ne la mente mi ragiona* was a *canzone* originally written by Dante most likely for the "Donna Gentile" of the *Vita Nuova* and only later allegorized and placed at the beginning of book III of the *Convivio*. If the *canzone* was originally sung by Casella as an "amoroso canto" then the problems raised by the Anonimo Fiorentino that *canzoni* with a moral or doctrinal message were not put to music would evaporate. Casella could not know that the *Convivio* confirms (see also I i 16) that the "Donna Gentile" is Lady Philosophy: "… la filosofia, che era donna di questi autori, di queste scienze e di questi libri, fosse somma cosa. E imaginava lei fatta come una donna gentile, e non la poteva imaginare in atto alcuno se non misercordioso …" ["… philosophy, who was the lady of these authors, these disciplines and these books, was something of supreme importance. I imagined it as having the form of a noble lady, and I could not imagine her with a bearing other than full of pity …"] (*Convivio* II xii 6–7).

3 "Antica" (*Purg.* 32.6) as an adjective modifies "rete," appears twice two cantos earlier in *Purgatorio* 30, in verse 39 where it modifies "amor" ("d'antico amor") and in verse 48 where as an adjective it modifies "fiamma" ("antica fiamma"). All three references to "antico" refer to early days in the *Vita Nuova* when as a boy Dante first laid eyes on Beatrice.

4 As previously mentioned in the Introduction, n. 19, Storey, "Canto XXXI" 470, has noted the repetition of the formula "fissi e attenti."

5 Robert Hollander, "Canto II" 28, looks at the context of the reunion between Dante and Casella, who both behave as if they were still living in their lives of the past, not their "hoped-for future life." With this in mind, the question Dante poses to Casella regarding whether any new law removes from Casella his ability to practise his old profession is proof of the degree to which Dante is "deflected from his ordained purpose." Dante should recall Cato's words from the previous canto that there is a new law, the law which was decreed with Christ's Harrowing of Hell, that removes those in Purgatory from their emotional attachments in the past, in Cato's case his past life with his wife Marcia still in Limbo: "Or che di là dal mal fiume dimora, / più muover non mi può, per quella legge / che fatta fu quando me n'usci' fora" ["Now that she dwells beyond the evil stream no more may she move me, by the law which was made when I came forth from there"] (2.1.88–90).

6 In John Freccero, "Casella's Song," the long-held view of most critics that the song Casella sings is merely a love song is challenged. Freccero argues convincingly that Casella's song must be seen with "its full philosophical force" (74), despite the implication of the Anonimo Fiorentino that if doctrinal songs were never sung *Amor che ne la mente mi ragiona* can be nothing more than a simple love song. He builds his case by showing the

parallels between Dante's Donna Gentile in the *Convivio* and Lady Philosophy in the *Consolation* of Boethius and points out that Casella sings of a
lady, the Donna Gentile who can offer a similar consolation which has
nothing to do with erotic love. In Robert Hollander, "*Purgatorio* II: Cato's
Rebuke and Dante's *scoglio*" (repr. in his *Studies in Dante* 91–105), the con-
ventional critical view is similarly challenged. Hollander establishes that
Casella's singing of the second ode of the *Convivio,* in contravention of the
New Law, is harmful in the extreme by tempting those who stop and listen much as the Golden Calf tempted the Israelites. The only other reference in the *Commedia* to an ode from the *Convivio* is similarly negative. It
appears in *Paradiso* 8.34–9, where the example of *Voi ch 'ntendendo il terzo
ciel movete* [*You who move the third heaven by intellection*] is raised to convey
the error in Dante's thinking when he composed it.

7 Giuseppe Mazzotta, *Dante Poet of the Desert* 54, refers to this space for the
moment of the song, not as the shore of Purgatory, but "as a fictive space
of gathering."

8 In Freccero, "Casella's Song" 74, the "Amore" of feminine beauty in
Francesca's tercets is contrasted with the "Amore" of Lady Philosophy in
Casella's *canzone*, marking Dante's way into a new realm of interest.

9 See Scott, "Beatrice's Reproaches in Eden" 4–5, who suggests that the
temptations in Dante's life to which Beatrice refers in *Purgatorio* 31 may
bring to mind the "Donna Gentile" episode of chapters xxxv, xxxvi, and
xxxvii of the *Vita Nuova* .

10 "E imaginava lei fatta come una donna gentile, e non la poteva imaginare
in atto alcuno se non misericordioso … E da questo imaginare cominciai
ad andare là dov'ella si dimostrava veracemente, cioè ne le scuole de li re-
ligiosi e a le disputazioni de li filosofanti. Sì che in picciol tempo, forse di
trenta mesi, cominciai tanto a sentire de la sua dolcezza, che lo suo amore
cacciava e distruggeva ogni altro pensiero" ["I imagined it as having the
form of a noble lady, and I could not imagine her with a bearing other
than full of pity … Drawn by this image, I began to go to where she truly
revealed herself, that is, to the schools of the religious and the disputa-
tions of the philosophers. And so in a short time, perhaps some thirty
months, I began to experience so profoundly the sweetness she brings
that love of her drove out and destroyed all thought of anything else"]
(*Conv.* II xii 6–8).

11 Hollander, "Canto II" 30.

12 Scott, *Dante's Political Purgatory* 208, rejects the notion that Dante turned
away from philosophy, using as examples Dante's *Epistle* xii iii 6, written
in 1315, and his placement of Siger of Brabant in Paradise. I agree that
Dante did not turn away from philosophy. What I believe he turned away
from was the embrace of philosophy for its own sake. The study of philosophy is a worthy pursuit of which Dante is proud, but he must be mindful

of the limits, as he himself makes clear at the start of *Inferno* 26. Dante is reminded of those limits in *Purgatorio* 25 when Statius, poised to explain to him the error of the wiser Averroes, commands Dante to be open to the truth before proceeding to deliver his explanation, which rejects Averroes' view that the possible intellect is separate from the soul. Dante the poet admires the pure philosophy of Averroes and refers to him as the one who wrote the "gran comento," but Averroes' inability to understand the limitations of his vision, like his fellow philosophers Aristotle and Plato, condemns him to the first circle of Hell.

13 I agree with the vast majority of modern scholars who accept the "cui" in 1.10.63 as a dative not an accusative, meaning that Beatrice, not Virgil, is held in disdain by Guido. Two studies that have done much to convince many Dantists are Siro A. Chimenz, "Il disdegno di Guido e i suoi interpreti," and Antonino Pagliaro, "Il disdegno di Guido."

14 See Lloyd Howard, "Giovanna as John the Baptist" 63–70. Dante's references in chapter XXIV of the *Vita Nuova* to Guido's estrangement from Giovanna suggest that he has turned instead to another lady, Lady Philosophy of his *canzone*: *Donna me prega*. But there is to be no reconciliation between Guido and Giovanna. Her call into the wilderness as John the Baptist will remain unheeded. Guido held in disdain the kind of journey to salvation that Dante has undertaken, and preferred to remain in the company of his Lady Philosophy in the wilderness, which will in all probability destine him to the sixth circle of Hell alongside his father.

15 See Giuseppe Mazzotta, *Dante's Vision and the Circle of Knowledge* 135–53, where Dante's dream of the Femmina Balba relates to "interactions between imagination, love, knowledge, and moral choices articulated in the two previous cantos (*Purgatorio* XVII and XVIII)" (136).

16 Hollander, *Studies in Dante* 101–2, suggests that Lady Philosophy appears to Dante as the Femmina Balba in his dream in *Purgatorio* 19 where she attempts to lure Dante as she claims to have lured Ulysses. Hollander submits that her words "Io volsi Ulisse del suo cammin vago / al canto mio" ["Ulysses, eager to journey on, I turned aside to my song"] support his argument "that the *Convivio* was Dante's Ulyssean embracing of false philosophy."

17 While the Femmina Balba claims as the sweet siren to have turned Ulysses from his way, we know from Homer's *Odyssey* that she did no such thing. As the readers of *Inferno* 26 recognize, this is not the first instance where Dante's rendering of Ulysses' voyage is at variance with Homer, and in both instances Dante's changes relate to Ulysses straying from his journey home. Bosco-Reggio suggest that Ulysses' surrender to the siren may have come from a medieval source unknown to us. They also point out that these words are placed in the mouth of the vain Femmina Balba. Is she necessarily to be believed?

18 See the reference in chapter 4 n. 23 to Hollander, "*Purgatorio* XIX: Dante's Siren/Harpy" 79–80, who supports Gmelin's interpretation: "that simple and best hypothesis may not yet be said to have achieved common acceptance, even if most commentators do take note of the obvious echo of this passage in Beatrice's reproach to Dante in *Purgatorio* XXXI.45 … especially when we remember that in *Purgatorio* XXX.134, Beatrice says that she has previously tried to call Dante back to herself 'in sogno.'"

19 Singleton, *Purgatorio* 777, interprets "fedele" in this context "as one whose sins of backsliding have been forgiven."

20 Mazzotta, *Dante's Vision* 147, draws to our attention Dante's oblique reference to the Narcissus myth in *Purgatorio* 30.76–8, and Narcissus's thirsting for his own image, which leads to his fall and death once "he knows himself." Dante's journey to self-knowledge will not mirror Narcissus's. His thirst will be quenched, but the object of this thirst, Beatrice, will also be the one to force him to self-confrontation, allowing for true self-knowledge.

21 The formula "levai li occhi" ["I raised my eyes"] also appears in chapter XIV, where Dante sees Beatrice, with all the accompanying effects of love sickness: "e temendo non altri si fosse accorto del mio tremare, *levai li occhi*, e mirando le donne, vidi tra loro la genilissima Beatrice" ["Afraid that other people might notice how I was trembling, I raised my eyes and as they rested on the women gathered there I saw among them the most gracious Beatrice"].

22 The other four references to Phaeton's flight of folly occur in 1.17.106–8, 2.4.72, 2.29.118–20, and 3.17.1–3.

23 Storey, "Canto XXXI" 475, points to the intensification of the "occhi fissi e attenti" in *Paradiso* 33.97–8.

24 Porena, *Paradiso* 325.

Bibliography

Ahern, John. "Singing the Book: Orality in the Reception of Dante's *Comedy*." In Amilcare A. Iannucci, ed., *Dante: Contemporary Perspectives*. Toronto: University of Toronto Press, 1997, 214–39.

Alighieri, Dante. *Rime*, ed. Gianfranco Contini. Torino: Einaudi, 1973.

Baranski, Zygmunt G. "Structural Retrospection in Dante's *Comedy*: The Case of *Purgatorio* XXVII." *Italian Studies* 41 (1986): 1–23.

– "The 'Marvellous' and the 'Comic': Toward a Reading of *Inferno* XVI." *Lectura Dantis* 7 (1990): 72–95.

– "Canto VI." In Tibor Wlassics, ed., *Dante's "Divine Comedy." Introductory Readings, II: "Purgatorio."* Charlottesville: University of Virginia Press, 1993, 88–97.

Barber, Malcolm. *The New Knighthood: A History of the Order of the Temple*. Cambridge: Cambridge University Press, 1994.

Barbi, Michele. *Problemi di critica dantesca: prima serie*. Firenze: Sansoni, 1934.

Barolini, Teodolinda. *Dante's Poets*. Princeton: Princeton University Press, 1984.

– "Casella's Song." In Harold Bloom, ed., *Modern Critical Interpretations: Dante's Divine Comedy*. New York: Chelsea House, 1987, 151–8.

– *The Undivine Comedy*. Princeton: Princeton University Press, 1992.

– "Dante and Cavalcanti (On Making Distinctions in Matters of Love): *Inferno* V in Its Lyric Content." *Dante Studies* 116 (1998): 31–63.

Bosco, Umberto. "La 'Follia' di Dante." *Lettere italiane* 10 (1958), 417–30.

– "Canto XV dell'*Inferno*. In *Lectura Dantis Scaligera*. Firenze: Le Monnier, 1971, 485–512.

Boswell, John. *Christianity, Social Tolerance and Homosexuality*. Chicago: University of Chicago Press, 1980.

Botterill, Steven. "Canto xxvii." In Tibor Wlassics, ed., *Dante's "Divine Comedy." Introductory Readings, II: "Purgatorio."* Charlottesville: University of Virginia Press, 1993, 398–410.

Brezzi, Paolo. *Il Canto XVI dell'Inferno.* Roma: Bonacci, 1974, 401–20.

Brownlee, Kevin. "Canto xxvi." In Tibor Wlassics, ed., *Dante's "Divine Comedy." Introductory Readings, III: "Paradiso."* Charlottesville: University of Virginia Press, 1995, 388–401.

Cantarella, Eva. *Bisexuality in the Ancient World.* New Haven: Yale University Press, 1992.

Caretti, Lanfranco. *Il Canto V dell'Inferno.* Firenze: Le Monnier, 1967.

Carruthers, Mary. *The Book of Memory.* Cambridge: Cambridge University Press, 1990.

Cassell, Anthony K. *Lectura Dantis Americana: Inferno I.* Philadelphia: University of Pennsylvania Press, 1989.

Chiarenza, Marguerite Mills. "Time and Eternity in the Myths of *Paradiso* xvii." In Aldo S. Bernardo and Anthony L. Pellegrini, eds., *Studies in the Italian Trecento in Honor of Charles S. Singleton.* Binghampton, NY: Medieval and Renaissance Texts and Studies, 1983, 133–50.

Chimenz, S.A. "Il disdegno di Guido e i suoi interpreti." *Orientamenti culturali* 1 (1945).

Clanchy, Michael. *From Memory to Written Record: England 1066–1307.* London: Arnold, 1993.

Clay, Diskin. "Dante's Broken Faith: The Sin of the Second Circle." *Quaderni d'italianistica* 10.1–2 (1989): 91–108.

Contini, Gianfranco. "Cavalcanti in Dante." In *Varianti e altra linguistica: Una raccolta di saggi.* Torino: Einaudi, 1970.

Davidsohn, Robert. *Storia di Firenze* iii. Firenze: Sansoni, 1973.

Davis, Charles. *Dante's Italy and Other Essays.* Philadelphia: University of Pennsylvania Press, 1984.

Del Lungo, Isidoro. *Dante ne' tempi di Dante.* Bologna, 1888.

Della Giovanna, Ildebrando. *Lectura Dantis: Il canto XXIII dell'Inferno letto da Ildebrando Della Giovanna nella Sala di Dante in Orsanmichele.* Firenze, 1901.

Ferrante, Joan M. *The Political Vision of the Divine Comedy.* Princeton: Princeton University Press, 1984.

Foster, Kenelm. *The Two Dantes.* London: Darton, Longman and Todd, 1977.

Freccero, John. "Dante's Firm Foot and the Journey without a Guide." *Harvard Theological Review* 52 (1959): 245–81.

– "The Prologue Scene." *Dante Studies* 84 (1966): 1–25.

– "Casella's Song." *Dante Studies* 91 (1973): 73–80.

– "The Significance of *Terza Rima*." In Aldo S. Bernardo and Anthony L. Pellegrini, eds., *Studies in the Italian Trecento in Honor of Charles S. Singleton.* Binghampton, NY: Medieval and Renaissance Texts and Studies, 1983, 3–17.

– *The Poetics of Conversion.* Cambridge: Harvard University Press, 1986.

Frugoni, Arsenio. *Il Canto X dell'Inferno.* Firenze: Le Monnier, 1967, 5–32.

Gmelin, Herman. *Kommentar II.* Stuttgart: Klett, 1955.

Goodich, Michael. "Sodomy in Medieval Secular Law." *Journal of Homosexuality* 1.3 (1976): 295–302.

Harrison, Robert Pogue. *The Body of Beatrice.* Baltimore: Johns Hopkins University Press, 1988.

Hollander, Robert. "*Purgatorio* 11: Cato's Rebuke and Dante's *scoglio.*" *Italica* 52 (1975): 348–63.

– *Studies in Dante.* Ravenna: Longo, 1980.

– "*Purgatorio* xix: Dante's Siren/Harpy." In Aldo S. Bernardo and Anthony L. Pellegrini, eds., *Studies in the Italian Trecento in Honor of Charles S. Singleton.* Binghampton, NY: Medieval and Renaissance Texts and Studies, 1983, 77–88.

– *Il Virgilio dantesco: Tragedia nella Commedia.* Firenze: Olschki, 1983.

– "Canto 11." In Tibor Wlassics, ed., *Dante's "Divine Comedy." Introductory Readings, II: "Purgatorio."* Charlottesville: University of Virginia Press, 1993, 17–34.

Howard, Lloyd. "Giovanna as John the Baptist and the 'disdegno' of Guido." *Quaderni d'italianistica* 2.1 (1981): 63–9.

– "Linguistic Configuration as a Clue to the Impossible Made Possible: *Inferno* I, *Purgatory* xi, *and Purgatory* xii." *Italian Quarterly* 114 (Fall 1988): 5–9.

– "The Episodes of the 'tre ombre' and the 'frati godenti': Linguistic and Structural Parallels." *Modern Language Notes* 104 (1989): 189–92.

– "Linguistic Patterns and Internal Structure in Five *canti* of the *Inferno.*" *Quaderni d'italianistica* 11.1 (1990): 85–90.

– "Decoding the Parallelism of Three Descents into Dante's Hell." *Quaderni d'italianistica* 14.1 (1993): 111–19.

Howard, Lloyd, and Elena Rossi. "Textual Mapping of Dante's Journey Back to Political Original Sin in Florence." *Modern Language Notes* 106 (1991): 184–8.

Iannucci, Amilcare A. "Beatrice in Limbo: A Metaphoric Harrowing of Hell." *Dante Studies* 97 (1979): 23–45.

– "Limbo: The Emptiness of Time." *Studi danteschi* 52 (1979–80): 69–128.

– *Forma ed evento nella Divina Commedia.* Roma: Bulzoni, 1984.

– "Autoesegesi dantesca: la tecnica dell''episodio parallelo' (*Inferno* xv–*Purgatorio* xi)." *Forma ed Evento nella Divina Commedia.* Rome: Bulzoni, 1985, 85–114.

– "Dottrina e allegoria in *Inferno* viii, 67–ix, 105." In Michelangelo Picone, ed., *Dante e le forme dell'allegoresi.* Ravenna: Longo, 1987, 99–124.

– "Dante's *Inferno*, Canto iv." In Mark Musa, ed., *Dante's Inferno: The Indiana Critical Edition.* Indianapolis: Indiana University Press, 1995, 299–309.

- "Canto xxxi." In Tibor Wlassics, ed., *Dante's "Divine Comedy." Introductory Readings III: "Paradiso."* Charlottesville: University of Virginia Press, 1995, 470–85.
- "Forbidden Love: Metaphor and History (*Inferno* 5)." In Amilcare A. Iannucci, ed., *Dante: Contemporary Perspectives.* Toronto: University of Toronto Press, 1997, 94–112.
- "The Mountainquake of *Purgatorio* and Virgil's Story." *Lectura Dantis* 20–1 (1997): 48–58.
- "Dante's Intertextual and Intratextual Strategies in the *Commedia*: The Limbo of the Children." In Franco Fido, Rena A. Syska-Lamparska, and Pamela D. Stewart, eds., *Studies for Dante: Essays in Honor of Dante Della Terza.* Florence: Edizioni Cadmo, 1998, 61–87.
- "Virgil's Erichthean Descent and the Crisis of Intertextuality." *Forum Italicum* 33.1 (1999): 13–26.
Kay, Richard. *Dante's Swift and Strong: Essays on Inferno XV.* Lawrence, Kansas: Regents Press of Kansas, 1978.
Kristeller, Paul O. "A Philosophical Treatise from Bologna Dedicated to Guido Cavalcanti: Magister Jacobus de pistorio and his 'Quaestio de felicitate'." In *Medioevo e Rinascimento* 1. Firenze: Sansoni, 1955, 425–63.
Lewis, Suzanne. *Reading Images: Narrative Discourse and Reception in the Thirteenth-Century Apocalypse.* Cambridge: Cambridge University Press, 1995.
Marti, Mario. *Realismo dantesco ed altri studi.* Milano-Napoli: Ricciardi, 1961.
- *Poeti del Dolce stil nuovo.* Firenze: Le Monnier, 1969.
Mazzotta, Giuseppe. *Dante Poet of the Desert.* Princeton: Princeton University Press, 1979.
- *Dante's Vision and the Circle of Knowledge.* Princeton: Princeton University Press, 1993.
Musa, Mark. "Behold Francesca Who Speaks So Well (*Inferno* v)." In Mark Musa, ed., *Dante's Inferno, The Indiana Critical Edition.* Indianapolis: Indiana University Press, 1995, 310–24.
Nardi, Bruno. "L'averroismo del 'primo' amico di Dante." *Studi danteschi* 25 (1940): 43–79.
- "Di un nuovo commento alla Canzone del Cavalcanti sull'amore." *Cultura neolatina* 6–7 (1946–7): 125–35.
- "Noterella polemica sull'averroismo di Guido Cavalcanti." *Rassegna di Filosofia* 3 (1954): 41–71.
Pagliaro, Antonino. "Il disdegno di Guido." *Letterature moderne* 1 (1950).
- "... e 'l modo ancor m'offende." *Saggi di critica semantica* (1953): 333–53.
- "... lo passo Che non lasciò già mai persona viva." In *Studi letterari: Miscellanea in onore di Emilio Santini.* Palermo: U. Manfredi, 1956.
Parry, Milman. *The Making of Homeric Verse.* Ed. Adam Parry. Oxford: Clarendon Press, 1971.

Pasquazi, Silvio. *Il Canto XVI dell'Inferno*. Firenze: Le Monnier, 1961, 514–49.

Pézard, André. *Dante sous la Pluie de Feu*. Paris: Librairie Philosophique J. Vrin, 1950.

Presta, Vincenzo. "Arrigo." *Enciclopedia Dantesca*. Roma: Istituto dell'Enciclopedia Italiana, 1970–8, 391–2.

Ragni, Eugenio. "Ciacco." *Enciclopedia Dantesca*. Roma: Istituto dell'Enciclopedia Italiana, 1970–8, 982–6.

Rosenberg, Bruce A. "Oral Literature in the Middle Ages." In John Miles Foley, ed., *Oral Traditional Literature: A Festschrift for Albert Bates Lord*. Columbus, Ohio: Slavica Publishers, 1981.

Rossini, Antonio. "La 'bella scola' ed il 'salutevol cenno': una ricerca semantica e stilistica." *Quaderni d'italianistica* 18.2 (1997): 163–82.

Sacchetto, Aleardo. "Il canto dei tre fiorentini." In *Dieci letture dantesche*. Firenze: Le Monnier, 1960, 27–56.

Saenger, Paul. "Silent Reading: Its Impact on Late Medieval Script and Society." *Viator* 13 (1982): 367–414.

Salvemini, G. *Magnati e Popolani in Firenze dal 1280 al 1295* [repr. Torino, 1960]. Firenze, 1899.

Santini, Pietro. "Sui fiorentini 'che fur sì degni.'" *Studi danteschi* 6 (1923): 25–44.

Scott, John A. "*Inferno* x: Farinata as 'Magnanimo.'" *Romance Philology* 15.4 (1962): 395–411.

– *Dante Magnanimo Studi sulla "Commedia."* Firenze: Olschki, 1977.

– "Beatrice's Reproaches in Eden: Which 'School' Had Dante Followed?" *Dante Studies* 109 (1991): 1–23.

– *Dante's Political Purgatory*. Philadelphia: University of Pennsylvania Press, 1996.

Singleton, Charles S. *Dante Studies 1: Commedia Elements of Structure*. Cambridge: Harvard University Press, 1954.

– *Dante Studies 2: Journey to Beatrice*. Cambridge: Harvard University Press, 1958.

– "The Poet's Number at the Center." *Modern Language Notes* 80.1 (1965): 1–10.

– "The Vistas in Retrospect." *Modern Language Notes* 81.1 (1966): 55–80.

– "In Exitu Israel de Aegypto." In John Freccero, ed., *Dante: A Collection of Critical Essays*. Englewood Cliffs, NJ: Prentice Hall, 1966, 102–21.

Solerti, Angelo, ed., *Le vite di Dante, Petrarca e Boccaccio*. Milano: Vallardi, 1904.

Starn, Randolph. *Contrary Commonwealth*. Berkeley: University of California Press, 1982.

Stefanini, Ruggero. "Canto xxx." In Tibor Wlassics, ed., *Dante's "Divine Comedy." Introductory Readings, II: "Purgatorio."* Charlottesville: University of Virginia Press, 1993, 448–62.

Storey, H. Wayne. "Canto xxxi." In Tibor Wlassics, ed., *Dante's "Divine Comedy." Introductory Readings, II: "Purgatorio."* Charlottesville: University of Virginia Press, 1993, 463–75.

Trovato, Mario. "Canto xvi." In Tibor Wlassics, ed., *Dante's "Divine Comedy."* *Introductory Readings, II: "Purgatorio."* Charlottesville: University of Virginia Press, 1993, 235–47.

Vallone, Aldo. "Il Canto xvi dell'Inferno." In *Studi su Dante medievale.* Firenze: Olschki, 1965, 179–205.

Villani, Giovanni. *Cronica.* Roma: Multigrafica, 1980.

Zumthor, Paul. *Oral Poetry: An Introduction.* Minneapolis: University of Minnesota Press, 1990.

Index